AMBEDKAR, DALITS AND SOCIAL CHANGE

AMBEDKAR, DALITS AND SOCIAL CHANGE

Nandu Ram

GYAN

Published by

Gyan Publishing House
5, Ansari Road
Daryaganj, New Delhi-110002
Phone: 011-47034999, 9811692060
E-mail: books@gyanbooks.com

Distribution Network
gyanbooks.com
India, USA, Canada, UK, Australia, France

ISBN: 978-81-2129-603-8

First Published, 2024

Printed at: Gyan Press, Delhi.

AMBEDKAR, DALITS AND SOCIAL CHANGE
Author: NANDU RAM

Contents

1.	Ambedkar on Exhumation of Society and Culture in Ancient India	7
2.	Gandhi, Ambedkar and the Dalits: Retrospects and Prospects	37
3.	Abstraction to Substantiation: Ambedkar's Thought on Justice and Socialequauty in Comparative Perspective	59
4.	Marginalised Groups and the State of Human Rights in India	83
5.	Genesis, Mechanism and Growth of Caste System in South India	105
6.	Studying Dalit Movements, Protests and Social Change: Some Theoretico-Methodological Issus	159
7.	Dalit Movements and Changes in the Caste System in India	171
8.	Migration and social Mobility in India: Some Theoretico-Methodological Issues	215
9.	Migration, Social Mobility and Town – Country Nexus in North India	225
10.	Values and Changes in an Industrial Metropolis: The Case of a Slum in Kanpur	247

11. Housing and the Urban Poor in India: A Hypothetical Refinement 267

12. The Growth of National Capital Region (Delhi): Some Critical Issues 277

1

Ambedkar on Exhumation of Society and Culture in Ancient India

Introduction

Texts are generally accepted as representative views of the people living at a given in point in time in any society, though the span of such time may not be abrupt but a prolonged one. These are also held as sermon to be revered and obeyed by the people. But in a democratic and secular society of the present time, textsusuallyincorporate in them and present the diverse moral, ethical and political customs and practices of the people, scientific and technological innovations, processes of social development and change, and so forth. All these ate organised in a text or texts with the view of instilling a holistic knowledge in the mind of the younger generation and even sensitizing the older ones about the complexities of a society in which they live. These also provide a new vista to reorient their mind and their society to co-up with the future challenges. Needless to say that both types of texts, the sacred or religious and the secular ones, are construed in a given time and space, and these may not completely be free from the socio-cultural, ideological, intellectual and temporal biases of their creators of compilers and interpreters.

Further, society receives lesson from these texts, both religious and secular, to reorganise itself in its temporal life and to reorient itself to fit-in the time to come. However, in both the anthropological and sociological literature, texts have been accepted as those religious book s or treatises which ought to govern, in principle, the moral code of conduct of a people, and which regulate their socio-cultural, behaviors, social relations and interaction in the society. Because these are revered and are attributed to divinity, besides their being moral code of conducts or even in a way, being instrumental to construct a new society and a new type of social relationship, these also act as an effective means of control of deviance, though these are often misused by the vested and dominant interests in a society. It is in this context when we look at the Hindu religious texts of the different varieties, we find that these have been written or complied with two sole manifest objectives of forcing the people to revere then and of regulating the code of conduct of the people, according to their (of the religious texts) dictates, both prescribed and proscribed therein. One more latent objective in writing or compiling these texts is of depicting the form(s) of organisationof the society of that period. Since these texts were written/ complied by a group of scholars (sages or their disciples) hailed from the privileged status or socio-economic and cultural background who also enjoyed the tremendous amount of patronage from the ruling classes and, in some cases, they themselves were rulers, they looked at society and culture of their time(and of future) from a different vantage point. While they bore the responsibility of guiding the society by writing/compiling the religious texts, they left sufficient scope for the privileges and the social maneuvering for their patrons, for themselves and for their own class of people.

Hence, looking at the Hindu religioustexts and their depiction (s) of the then existed society and culture or even of the one to be evolved in the time to come in India from the perspective from below the perspective of those masses and classes who happened to be (or are even today) at the receiving end, one finds altogether a different picture that existed or supposedly existed in the traditional time in the Indian history. Such perspective(s) was articulated during the late nineteenth and the early twentieth centuries; but the same has recently regained momentum wherein a few scholars, mostly

Dalits, have started re-articulating social reality, especially of the Hindu social system, in India (for instance, see Mencher 1974, Ram 1995)within that perspective. Most pioneers among those who had articulated earlier the views of the masses vis-à-vis the depictions and dictates of the Hindu religious texts were Periyar E.V.Ramaswamy Naiker in Madras the present day Tamil Nadu and parts of a few other adjoining sates in the south, Jyotirao Phule and Dr.B.RAmbedkar in Bombay (now Maharashtra, part of Madhya Pradesh, of Gujarat, and of Karnataka states)in the west, Swami Achchutanad and Mangoo Ram (see Juergensmeyer 1983) in the north, Guru Ghasidas and his son Balakdas (Dube 2001) in central, and Jogendranath Mandal In east India. Keeping aside their politics, In east India. Keeping aside their politics, prime motive in critiquing and attacking the Hindu religious texts was to arouse the sensitivity and sensibility, and to develop the critical faculty of the Dalits and the backward masses about the religious sanctity of these texts, about their depiction(s) of the Hindu society and culture, and about their (of texts) providing legitimacy to the status-quo. Also, they advocated and worked for the basic transformation in the society and the cultural practices of the people in India, and for ensuring a respectable place for the masses in that.

Amongst the pioneers mentioned above, Ambedkar was the most learned, intellectually well-equipped and academically articulate about not only critically reflecting on the Hindus, but also providing his own counter-thesis (ses) to that. Being trained in the Western tradition of the logic of social enquiry and having a full grasp over the grass-root reality of the Indian society and culture he very succinctly and religion-social issues, or the economic, political and international relational ones. Regarding his inter pretentions of the Hindu texts written in Sanskrit (he although had an earnest desire to study theSanskritlanhyage at his collage in bomby, but was not allowed to do so because of his untouchable caste background). But this may be true in the case of most of the scholars who had written on the subject or, for that matter, on the ancient Indian society and culture. This is also to be seen as delimiting the knowledge and understandings of the issues to a tiny group of scholars being well-versed with the Sanskritlanguage. This contravenes the methods of social enquiry and pursuit of knowledge as, “There are obviously different ways of working at the evidence with varying priorities and differing theories of cessation and explanation. What is required is a familiarity with the sources and reasonable level of logic and rationality in the explanation. What is required is a familiarity”(Thapar1995: vi) through whatsoever authentic sources there could be. The aforesaid charge against Ambedkar, then, can easily be dismissed. Nevertheless, while analyzing the Hindu society and culture, Ambedkar had relied heavily on English translations of the various Hindu religious texts, and got occasionally verified his understandings and interpretations by discussing about that with a few Sanskrit scholars.

It is evident from his writings and speeches that Ambedkar has a deep sense of historicity of the social phenomena which he had analysed at various points in time, though he was not a historian by training or profession but by his keen interests and temperament. As historical sociology views a social phenomenon by location it in a specific historical setting, Ambedkar hadanalysedthe contemporary social issues by delving into the ample evidences, drawn from the history, (written with the help of literary sources), even of the cross-cultural societies, with his own logical interpretations. This was essential, in his reckoning, for the proper and better understanding of a social phenomenon. But at the same time, he did not undermine the contemporaneity of such phenomenon profoundly lived with by the people and the attempts of the social scientists to theories that. Anyway, this is not our immediate concern in this paper. Instead, we are interested here to know how Ambedkar has viewed the traditional society and culture, mainly that of the Hindus in India, and in what way his interpretations are different from those given by a few Indologists and social scientists, especially the historians who are considered to be authority on the subject. It is obvious that our frame of reference here is to the interpretations of Ambedkarvis-à-vis that of other of the Hindu religious texts about the various aspects of the traditional Hindu society and culture in India which, of course, have undergone varieties of charges in the modern time.

Society and culture in ancient India: genesis and development

Not all is fully and authoritatively known about the traditional society and culture in India. This is so because the written history in India, in regard to studying the social facts, does not go too far in the past. Even the known history of the traditional society, culture and of the people in India is generally based on the conjectures and derivative interpretations of the literary accounts or the religious texts. It is also a conceded view that the literary accounts do not always portray the actual nature of a society and of the cultural practices of its people (Thapar 1995:80). Instead, they idealise the situations with the view that these would lead the society and could, in future, the socio-cultural practices of its to the expected or the normatmelevel. These idealized situations often to not go in consonance with some of the archaeological evidences, available from different parts of the country, whose interpretative objectivity and scientific precision may not necessarily be accepted without contestation.

Notwithstanding the efficacy of the aforesaid contestations, these accounts also set forth certain norms, values, ideals, etc. which the people ought to follow. Moreover, most of the Sanskrit texts and the other literary accounts about the ancient Indian society and culture or cultural practices are the compositions of oral characcteisation of the Vedic and post-Vedic society and culture; and these were actually written or compiled in the post-Vedic period. These and a few more texts, which exclusively depicted the nature of the society that supposedly existed during that period, either praised the war-heroes, including chiefs of the tribal clans, or these legitimsed the privileges of the Brahmins, and prescribed as well as proscribed the rules and restrictions for other. Therefore, these in actuality do not provide a real account of the society and the culture that existed or lived particularly with by the masses of the various racial stocks during both the Vedic and the post-Vedic periods.

Anyway, the available evidences suggest that both the society and culture or cultural practices of the people in the traditional India, before the Aryan's invasion (thus thesis is now contested by the same group of historians, for instance, Thapar 1995, who had formulated this thesis earlier; and also, by a few archaeologists like Sarma2000) sometimes around 2000 B.Cwas pluralistic in nature. Incidently, unlike Phule and Naiker, Ambedkar was silent on the issue of the Aryan's invasion, but he analysed extensively the society and culture of the Indo-Aryan or the indigenous and the Aryan people (Ambedkar 1946). But according to Sarma (2000:175)," Vedic Aryans had not migrated to India. They were autochthonous around the five major rivers (in Punjab) and more particularly early groups among them lived on the banks of Sarasvati-Dhrishadvati River valleys from time immemorial." It is not out of context to mention here that while indicating towards some archaeological evidences, Thapar (1995) has stated that both Aryans and non-Aryans or Dravidians were living side by side in their separate settlements, Same completely silent on these issues. But both rely on some scattered archaeological evidences available about the Harrapan of Indus Valley or Indus- Sarasvati-Cicilisation, and the latter has sated about its roots being traced sometimes in about 4500 B.C. Yet, the analysis of the available archaeological evidences is not uniform regarding the exact date(s) of the Harrapan civilization not about the Aryans being migrant to or indigenous people of India.

Even the Aryans were divided into a few groups of their own along with their clans and Varnas, and did not initially mix-up with the 'native'or the indigenous people. In the course of time, they confronted with the members of their own different clans and Varnas as well as with the native people and got the latter assimilated in their own social system, but with the considerable amount of physical and social distance practiced against them. Thus, they lived with their Indo-Aryan society (Ambedkar 1946, 1990), which got systematised at a later stage as the Hindu society, with its distinct system and culture. Then, there were societies of the Dravidians and other indigenous groups of the people whose values, customs, traditions, rituals, belief systems, etc. were entirely different form these of the Aryans. Evidences also suggest that the Dravidians in the farthest south, and relegated the other groups of the people into the remote forests and hills in the different regions (for details, see Thapar 1991). Yet, another thesis subscribes to the view that the numerous indigenous groups of people, with their own district traditions, social systems, cultures, etc. were already living in the southern peninsula, and they first came into contact with the Dravidians and later with the Aryans who in few numbers travelled there, especially through the passage of the east-coast, and mixed up with them (see Kosambi 1992, Jaiswal 1998)

The later accounts, however, suggest that there existed two majors, yet separate, societies of the Aryans and the non-Aryans or Dravidiand, besides the numerous distinct groups and sub-groups with their societies and culturesabout which not much systematically written accounts are available. These two major societies sometimes co-operated among themselves but most of the times they confronted with each other for preserving their specific values, customs, life-patterns, etc. and also for establishing the superiority of their own society and culture over that of others. But in such a complex society and culture in the traditional period, the different societies and cultural groups also confronted frequently with the dominant society and culture of the Aryans (though as stated above, the different groups or strata of the Aryans also fought several fierce battles among themselves for establishing their supremacy over others).Ultimately, the former got subjugated into the latter, though some indigenous societies and cultural group as those of most of the tribals of today have survived with their distinct systems and cultural characteristics.

Contrary to the view about the traditional Indo-Aryan or the Hindu society being sui generis, the commonly agreed viewis that it existed between the 1500 B.C.and the 10th or 11th century A.D. For justifying the suggested Hindu unity even during the colonial India, the Hindu nationalist like B.G. Tilak pushed back the history of Indian (Hindu) civilization "by dating the Vedic literature to 4000 B.C. or even earlier to that" (Thapar 1990:16). Even Kosambi (1992:72-95) has stated that the Rigveda, the oldest of all the four Vedas, was composed during the 1500-1200 B.C. If this is accepted valid, them the Aryans might have invaded India sometimes earlier to this, say, in 2000 or 2500 or utmost in 3500 B.C. They would have fought against the native people and got settled and, finally, their scholars might have then composed or compiled the literary texts. This would have certainly taken the sufficient tines to complete.

Then, there are sub-periodisationsof evolution of the traditional Aryan or Hindu society and culture. According to the non-materialistic or functional classification given by Ghurye (1979:43), the first period-the Vedic period-ended with 600 B.C. But he has not mentioned the specific time since when this period vis-à-vis society and culture of the Aryans come into being. He further says that the literary texts comprising of the Vedic Samhitas and Brahmanas, besides the four Vedas, were composed during this period. But according to another account, the Vedic period had and oral literary tradition and all the said texts or religious books were actually composed or compiled during the post-Vedic period, as mentioned above. The second period-the post-Vedic period, ranging for about 900 years, ended by 300 A.D. During this period, mostly two types of literary books were written or compiled. In the first type were the books comprising of the sacred laws, and the epics of the Ramayana and the Mahabharata. These provided the idealistic stand-point of the Aryan or the Hindu society, though Aryans had started calling themselves Hindus much after the 300 A.D. In the second type were the numerous Buddhist jatakas, which provided a 'natural' picture of some aspects of the caste or caste system, and also of the society and culture as such characterised by the rebellions against the earlier and the contemporary systems. The third period, ended with the 10thor11thcentury A.D.wasknownas the period of the Dharma Shastras. A number of the smritis (memoirs) and the brahmanas (the books eulogizing the Brahmins), puranas (the stories of the heroes and heroines mostly the kings and their queens-projecting them as ideal gods and goddesses, and also man and women protecting and preserving the idealistic image of society and 'moral'cultural practices of the traditional society in India) were written compiled during this period, enthroning the Brahmins and kings or the rulers by prescribing all kinds if privileges to them and making more stringent ruled, though in varying degrees, for other.

Ambedkar on the exhumation of society and culture ancient India

As mentioned above, Ambedkar had a deep sense of history. In his own words, "Much of the ancient history of India is no history at all. Not that ancient India has no history. It has plenty of it. But it has lost its character. It has been made mythology to amuse women and children. This seems to have been done deliberately by the Brahminical writers" (Ambedkar 1987a:151). Without going into his substantiation of such argument wherein he has given numerous examples of how the history was converted into mythology, it may simply be said here that he relied on the literary vis-à-vis, primarily the Buddhist canonical literature, in exhumating the nature of society and culture in the ancient India. In his opinion, "Fortunately with the help of the Buddhist literature, Ancient Indian History can be dug out of the debris which the Brahmin writers have heaped upon in a fit of madness" (Ibid: 152)

A somewhat similar explanation has also been given by Thapar who has stated that, "Thus, much of the early history of ancient India was reconstructed almost entirely from Sanskritvis-à-vis, i.e., from material preserved in the ancient classical language (Sanskrit)." Many of these works were religious in nature and this naturally coloured the interpretation of the past. Even somewhat more secular literature such as the Dharmashastras (Law Books) has Brahman authors and commentators was therefore biased in favour of those in authority and generally adhered to the Brahmanical interpretation of past, irrespective of its historical validity" (Thapar 2001: 18).

Unlike the professional historians, Ambedkar was not much concerned either with the archaeological evidences (this may be so even due to the fact that not much archaeological evidences were available when he wrote about the nature of society and culture in traditional India) or with the explicit periodisation(periodicities) or evolutionary development of the traditional Indian society and culture, though he had obviously recognised the dynamic or changing aspect of it which fitted very well in his consistently pursued thesis not only about the traditional but even the contemporary society in India. More so, Ambedkar was much interested in analyzing the nature and social organizations, along with the social relationships of its members with it as well as among themselves. In his opinion, the entire Vedic literature, including those written during the post-Vedic and even later periods, do not provide the true picture of the real society and culture in India. Instead, the earlier Sanskritic texts were written by the Aryan or the Brahmin scholars in the praise of their war-heroes and clan chiefs. These were also intended for preserving and safeguarding the rank or status, and according proportionately more privileges to the Brahmins themselves (Ambedkar has called them the supermen), against less or almost no privilege to others. They also crafted the imposition of the maximum possible degree of the numerous types of socio-religious ignominies and restrictions on the non-Brahmins, as stated earlier.

It is then pertinent to examine briefly here the type of society and culture existed in the traditional or ancient India and the explicit reflection by Ambedkar on that. But before doing that, it also necessary to look at Ambedkar's understanding of society and culture, both as a system and a process. It is not out a context to mention here that his understanding of society and culture, both as a system and a process, is derived from the essential principles and features of an open society, with the help of which he has reflected retrospectively on the ancient society and culture in India. Anyway, according to him, any society, whether traditional or modern, is based on certain essential principles and it possesses some essential features. These essential principles, in Ambedkar's opinion, are the relationships of the individual or individual member with the society, and the relationship among the individuals in the society. In a free society or social order, the individual and not the society is an end in himself or herself, and "the aim and object of society is the growth of the individual and the development of his personality.

Society is not above the individual and if the individual has to subordinate himself (herself) to society, it is because such subordination is for his/her betterment and only to the extend necessary" (Ambedkar 1987: 95). Similarly, the relationship among the individuals in a free society, in his view, is based on equality, liberty and fraternity. Keeping such perspective in mind, Ambedkar has stated that both the essential principles and features of a free society have completely been absent in the Hindu social order, since its inception, making the order a closed one. In other words, it neither recognizes the individual as an end in himself/herself nor it emphasises the growth of his/her personality. The unit of the Hindu society, in Ambedkar's view, is nor an individual Brahmin, or Kshatriya, or Vaishya, or Shudra. Even family is not the unit, except in the matter of marriage and inheritance. What is the unit of the individual and his privileges or deprivations are attributed to that of his varna or caste (Ambedkar 1987a:99-100). Ambedkar has considered this the first essential principle of the Hindu society or social order. Such view has also been endorsed by Dumont (1972:43-46) who says that an individual in the Hindu society is a part of collectivity or holism, unlike that in the West where he/she has his/her own free existence with the minimal societal control.

Further, in case of the second essential principle, Ambedkar is of the view that the traditional Hindu social order (though he speaks of the Hindu social order as such and not of the traditional or of the present time) is a ladder of the varnas, vertically placed one above the other. It imbibes in it the graded-inequality (as each varna is graded unequal to the other in the deseeding order) evolving the graded-inequality of the whole system, though the principled or the idealized Hindu view is that the each varna is equal to one another. It does not provide fraternity between the members of the varnas, besides a limited degree of fraternity existing among the members of a particular varna against the other. "This is so especially in event of antagonistic relations between the two varnas or castes. But such fraternity cannot be characterized as fraternity of the system or social order in which an individual belonging to a class or varna or caste "(Ram 1995:52). Coupled with equality and fraternity is the liberty of thought and action. In the Hindu social order, each varna or caste for that matter, is traditionally assigned the specific type of role or occupation and behavior pattern which its members ought to follow. Thus, there is fixity of occupations for each varna and their continuance by heredity. Ambedkar has accepted it the second essential principle of the Hindu social order.

The third and final principle of the Hindu social order, in Ambedkar 's view, is fixation of individuals into the four varnas, and the non-Hindu societies including that of the Panchamas (untouchables), the varnashankaras (progenies of members of the tow different varnas), etc. have not been taken note of the four varnas are the fixed and the rigid social categories (contrary to the general impression of their being open) in which there is a complete restriction on free social intercourse, commensality and intermarriages which have largely been highlighted in many studies on caste system (and on the varna system) in India" (Ram 1955:52). The member of one varna cannot change his/ her membership to that of another varna. Related to these three essential principles are the three essential features of the Hindu social order. In Ambedkar's opinion, these are: worship of the Brahmin (superman)-the Brahmin Devata, the representative of the God, the divine origin of the social order, and a complete ban on the dissents or rebellions against such social order (for details, see his 1987a, Ram 1995: 50-60).

Without going into further details of the Hindu social order, consisting both of the varna system as well as the caste system and their moral as well as existential order, it may be said here that Ambedkar's views on this subject are based on his scientific reading and his contextual interpretations of the Hindu religious texts, which have conventionally been accepted by the Hindus in the tradition of divinity. To come from the first draft thus, his readings and interpretations of these texts testify the highest degree of scientific analysis and precision of a social phenomenon. One agrees or not with his approach is to be taken in view of the existential cogency of the well-established dominant thesis with a bigger intellectual clout and of the one with a wider yet tamed mass base. This is also to be taken in terms of the perceptual and interpretational variability in social sciences.

Brahmin and the priesthood

Of the four varnas, the Brahmin the upper most has been portrayed to be associated, in principles, with the learning, teaching and the priesthood. Contrary to the modern usage of the term profession, these 'profession' religious in nature were in accordance with the 'principled orientation' of the then existed society and were also monopolized by the single class or varna of the Brahmins. Accepting the difference between principle or theory (in loose sense) and practice, the Brahmins as a whole could not be associated with such professions because all the theory (in loose sense) and practice, the Brahmins as a whole could not be associated with such professions because all the three were supposedly specialized professions or occupations. More specifically, learning and teaching of the Vedas and the other religious texts in the later period could be undertaken by one group of the Brahmins and the performance of the priesthood by the other. Not only that but the learning and teaching of the Vedas, samhitas and other religious texts was confined exclusively to the people of the Brahmin varna or caste, though in a few cases the pupils were also from the nobility or the princely class who necessarily did not belong to the Kshatriya varna or caste of the Vedic or even of the post Vedic society. Nonetheless during the Vedic and the early post-Vedic periods, the priesthood had become a very lucrative profession or avocation, and in many cases, the Brahmin priests could prove to be quite prosperous and attain nobility.

Origin of the Shudras

Keeping apart the controversy over the origin of the varnas (classes or castes as composite categories), or the varna vyaastha (system) for that matter, there exists a near unanimity among the scholars about the numbers of varnas initially prevalent during the Vedic period. The Vedas make reference of only three varnas of Brahman (Brahmin), Rajan or Rajanya (Ksharta or Kshatriya or king) and vis (Vaishya). The mention of the Shudra the fourth Varna is only once in the Rigveda (the oldest amongst all the four Vedas), which is said to be a later interpolation. The basis of this is that the term Shudra or its synonym did not find any occurrence in the entire Rigveda, except in the Tenth Order of the Mandal-Part (DashamSkandha of the PurushShukta) in which the mystical or divine origin of the four varnas has been described. But the metric style of the hymn referring to it is totally different from the style used in rest of the hymns in the Rigveda. This was done perhaps with the vested interest for not only to establish the superior ranks especially of the Brahmin and the Kshatriya varnas, but to denigrade the Shudras through their origin from the feet of the Purush or the Brahma.

Ambedkar (1946, 1990) has formulated a novel thesis about the origin of the Shudra varna on the basis of his logical interpretations of the literary accounts of the traditional society written and/ or compiled by the Brahminic scholars. Endorsing the thesis of the three varnas of the initial period, he has argued that the first two varnas namely the Brahmin and Kshatriya always fought, against each other, over the right of the purohiti (priesthood) or performing the sacrifices ad the rituals and rites which was regarded to be associated not only with the superior most status in the society but also fetched the handsome remunerations. Since the Brahmins traditionally had upper hand in the matter, they were always opposed and fought against by the Shudra clan of the Khatriyas. Yet, in the long run, they succeeded in retaining their privileges and status-superiority. The status of the religious status (of the Brahmin) was accepted, forever, as superior to the power-both economic and political power-of the Kshatriyas and other (for the detailed sociological interpretations and criticism see Dumont 1970; and a number of articles published in the *Symposium on Contributions to Indian Sociology 1971)*. But both always considered the Vaishyas, the third Varna, as servile and subordinate to them. They extracted the material goods and the various kinds of services from them in different ways. Since both the Brahmins and the Kshatriyas, alongwith their different clans or sub groups, fought several fierce battles against each other, one of the groups of the Kshatriyas-known as the Shudra clan got badly defeated by the Brahmins. As a consequence, the Shudra clan lost their rights of undergoing through the UpanayanSanskara (putting on the scared thread through performing certain religious rituals) and performing the rituals, rites and sacrifices. In the place of their being treated as prisoners of war, they were kept like helots (slave-servants) without having any human rights with all kinds of social and religious disabilities imposed on them, they were pushed down to the fourth Shudra Varna (for details, see Ambedkar 's Who were the Shudra (1946, 1990).

Ambedkar's thesis seems to be valid on three grounds. One, the Vedic texts speak only of three varnas and the Shudra Varna is frequently mentioned in the post-Vedic literature. Two, the frequent fights between the Brahmins and Kshatriyas, both in the Vedic and post-Vedic periods, are well known. Even the Rigveda mentions of the Das RajnyaYudha (war of the ten kings) the war among then kings divided into two groups, each led by Vasishta -a Brahmin priest and Vishwamitra- a Kshatriya kind who also wanted to establish his claim over the purohiti (priesthood). Vishwamitra was aided by Sudas and other kings of the Shudra clan of the Kshatryas. Since he lost the battle, Sudas and other were condemned and degraded to the fourth varna. Referring to Ambedkar's thesis, Sharma (1990) refutes it on the ground that the kshatriya varna is not mentioned in the Rig Veda. But he simply undermines the fact that it does faid the mention is the PurushShukta of the Dasham Mandal (Tenth order or part) of the Rig Veda, though the same is said to be extrapolated in it Anyway, the Shudra castes generally known as the backward castes or classes invariably claim today their origin from the Kshatriya varna, which may not be easily dismissed in the name of their undergoing the process of more sanskritisation (for detailed analysis of sanskritisation, see Srinivas 1966).Any claim of morethan fifty percent of India's population, divided into thousands of castes and sub-castes and scattered all over the country, cannot be sustained for hundreds of years or so, without sufficient valid ground, besides that of only a cultural process of Sanskritisaition. It also may not provide the style of economic and political dominance to them merely on the basis of their emulation of the Sanskritic style of the upper varnas or castes. Moreover, any social or cultural process, operating at such a massive level, has never been found anywhere in the world.

But a point is to be made clear here that Ambedkar's thesis is about the origin and status of the Shudras of the Indo-Aryan society who were different from the Shudras of the Hindu social order. This raises two specific questions one, what happened to the Shudras of the Indo-Aryan society when it got transformed into the Hindu society? Two, why have the Sudras of the Hindu society been called Shudras? Way not with different nomenclature, if they do not have any relation with the Shudras of the Indo-Aryansociety? A categorical answer to these questions is that Ambedkar's thesis exclusively speaks of the Shudras of the Indo-Aryansociety and does not cover the Shudras of the Hindu society, as stated above.

Anyway, the traditional Indo-Aryan society has been characterised as the one based on the for-fold division of its people identified as Barhmin, Kshatriya, Vaishya and Shudra. The native Dravidians and the numerous indigenous groups of the people, including tribals, who were ideologically accommodated in the Hindu fold much later (see Bose 1975,1994; Ghurye1979) did not find any place in the Varna scheme. Since they did not believe in the hero-worship and were strongly opposed to the indigenous groups, found during the Vedic period and mentioned even in the Rigveda, were of Chandals, Nishadas, Asuras, Rakshas, etc. (for Nishads, see jha 1977). A few scholars and ideologues of Hinduism have tried erroneously to put them into one class of group and called them Panchama or the ati-Shudra, the fifth varna. This may be regarded another case of interpolation of the 'alien' or the native people into the varna scheme. But the terms like savarnas (with varna or within the varna-fold) and avarna (without varna or outside the varna-fold), which have occurred in the Sanskritic texts as well as remained in the usage,scuttle such attempts. Even the post-Vedic literature, especially the *Manu smriti*, has clearly mentioned that there were four and only four varnas of the Indo-Aryan society (for details, see Ghury 1979, Kosambi 1992,Thapar 1975, Ruben 1977).

Besides, Ambedkar has also reflected extensively on the origin of the Vedas-written compiled by man or God, their infallibility, their moral and spiritual contents if they have had any; the Brahmins' treatments to the Hindu Gods and Goddesses; the Dharama and the Ashraamas (See, his Riddlesin Hinduism 1987a). He has also written authoritatively on the Philosophy of Hinduism, the Hindu Social Order, the Revolution and Counter-Revolution in ancient

India, a host of other important aspects of the Indo-Aryan society, and the Hindu society and culture that existed in the ancient or in the post-Vedic period in India (seehis vol.3, 1987 b). It is neither possible nor necessary to reflect on all these here. We shall, however refer below to his thesis of the origin of the Untouchables and the institution of untouchability practiced against them since the early time. A brief discussion on Ambedkar's thesis on this issue is pertinent here on the ground that there is a sufficient amount of controversy over the historical origin of the Untouchables and their untouchability. Whether the Untouchables and their untouchability were part of the Varna system of the initial Indo-Aryan society or of the later Hindu social order? Why were they called Untouchables forever? Whether today's Untouchables are different from those of the earlier time? These are the questions whose answers we would like to tracethrough the writings and speeches of Ambedkar.

The untouchables and untouchability

The untouchables had undoubtedly been placed at the bottom in the hierarchies of both the Indo-Aryan society and of the Hindu social order or the Varna system and the caste system respectively, if we accept, for the time being, that they were also a part of the former system.Those who argue in favour of the untouchables being part of the Varna system rely on the usage of the terms like Sat andAsat or clean and unclean Shudras mentioned in the Hindu religious texts and they conclude that the latter has been used for the Untouchables. In their understanding, the untouchables were placed at the lowest order in the Varna hierarchy and constituted the Panchama Varna or the fifth Varna. Then by implication, the Untouchables were to be considered the savarna, like other varnas, and the varna system was to be stretched to the five, instead of the four-fold division of the people. But this thesis has neither been endorsed by the ideologues and the scholars nor the practioners of the varna system. Even the humanly gesture and the moral persuasion of M.K.Gandhi would not change the mind on the ideologues and the practitioners to accept the extended varna division due to their entrenched faith in the Manu's dictate of being four and only four varnas in the varna system.

Contrarily, those who consider the Untouchables being outside the pale of the *varna* system emphasise the terms savarna and avarna, and they trat them as people of the litter category consisting, besides them, of the Dasas, Dasyus, Rakshhasas, Asuras and Panis (indigenous traders) of the Vedic period. Even tribals of the present time may be included in that. The available references suggest that the indigenous groups of people of the Vedic period were not only pre-settlers and superior in many respects to the Aryans, but were also hostile to them. However, it cannot be concluded that all to then constituted the group of Untouchables even if they got defeated by or voluntarily co- operated with the Aryans at some later age, because it was not possible for such a vast population to completely assuage and remain relegated to the most down-graded status of the Untouchables.

Then, who are the Untouchables and how and when did they got co-opted in the Hindu social system? Before examining the more convincing thesis of Ambedkar about the origin of the Untouchables and untouchability practiced against them, it is necessary to pause for a moment and like more closely if they were also ground in the Rigvedic or Vedic and post-Vedic societies. We have made above the reference of the Panchama. The exact words occurred frequently in the Rigveda and other Vedas are pancha(five), Panchajana, Panchajati, etc, which are controversial and create confusions rather than solving the problem. These cannot three specific meanings and are said to have been used for different purposes. For instance, during or before the 7thcountry A.D., the pancha stood "for the four varnas and a group of people known as Nisada which was regarded as the fifth member of the four-varna structured society" (e.f. Mukherjee 1988:26). This does not seem to be tenable as how there could be a fifth member in the four-varna structured society, "especially when a carna-a category of people is taken identical to a person or to the people and when Manu categorically stated at a later age (around second century A.D.) that there could be four and only four varnas (and not five varnas) in the society, as mentioned above. Alternatively, the term pancha also denoted the five families of the Aryans namely, Yadu, Turvasu, Druhyu, Anu and Puru who entered the land of Punjab simultaneously (Ibid). But this does not explain their varna identity or status (rank or order) of that.

The term Panchajana represented five persons or groups namely Pitra, Gandharva, Deva Asura. And Rakshasa. The term Panchamanv-the five persons-was also in the usage. Similarly, Panchahati denoted five groups or categories or classes of people. This means, that the Asuras and Rakshasas were subjugated and absorbed in the Indo-Aryan society when this term came into vogue. But the descriptions in the Rigveda do not confirm the usage of these terms for Nishadas, Asuras, add Raksjasas who were put in regaled caps opposed to the Vedic Yajna (Sacrifice) and other religious practices of the Aryans. Moreover, Nishadas did not find any reference in the Rigveda, yet they appeared to be co-opted in the system much later. In spite of that, the Vedic literature suggest that the Aryans were very friendly to the Nishadas who were indispensable to them for the political and military purposes (for detail, see Jha 1977:67-84). In the then given situation, why the Nishadas were relegated even at a later age to the status of untouchables if the latter represented the Panchama category of the Indo-Aryan people. Though we are not concern here with this question, this needs to be answered by the scholars.

The Chandalas, another category of avarnas, whom Ambedkar considered as the old name for or progenitors of the Untouchables (see his 1948, 1990 and also 1987b), found mentions in the Vedic and post-Vedic literature and more frequent mentions in the later Brahminic law texts. In fact, in the earlier literature they were treated a separategroup but were not subjected to social and religious condemnation. Yet, according to another account, they were equated with fowls and animals. "The Chandals lived outsidethe town (and villages) in a hamlet of their own, and it seems that the other low castes, mentioned together with them, like Pukkasa, Rathakara, Nishadas, did likewise" (e.f.Ghurye 1979:81) The religious literature have also mentioned both the Nishadas and the Chandalas as the progeny of illegal sexual intercourse between a Shudra male and a Brahmin female respectively. Hence, they were condemned to the sub-human condition.

This raise three questions: one, whether all Nishadas and Chandalas constituting large group of avarnas were born of such illegal sexual intercourse? If so, then were not the Brahmin and Kshatriya females "sluts and whores" and the Sudra males adulterous and completely abandoned? Such a wild allegation may be attributed to Manu who called both the Nishadas and Chandalas the progenies of miscegenation two. What happened to those who committed adulteries the real "culprits"? Whether they were also condemned to the sluts of the Nishadas and Chandals?If no, then why their progenies were punished because of no faults of their own? Third, apart from the four major castes or varnas the numerous castes and their sub-castes are said to be originated from pratiloma (hypergamous) marriages or the unlawful sexual inter-mincing of people of the four major castes (varnas). Then, why the similar course of action was not adopted in the cased of such inter-mixing of other and why the offenders were not condemned to the status of Nishadas and Chandalas or the Untouchables? Besides, both the Nishadas and Chandalas are presently small segments of hundreds of the Untouchable castes and sub-castes, constituting more than 16 per cent of the total population in the country and are found in a few regions in north India. How could they produce such a large chunk of Untouchable castes and sub-castes over a period of time? in any case, we do not wish to find answer to this question which are not of the immediate concern here.

It is necessary, at this stage, to have a close likeareAmbedkar's thesis of origin of the Untouchables and Untouchability. He has presented his thesis in his book-The Untouchables: Who were They and why They became Untouchables?(1948), which he wrote as a sequel to his earlier book who were the Shudras? Published in 1946. In his own words, "The thesis on the origin of Untouchability advanced in the book is an altogether novel thesis. It comprises the following propositions: (1) There is no racial difference between the Hindus and Untouchables, (2) The distinction between the Hindusand Untouchables in its original form, before the advent of Untouchability, was the distinction between Tribesmen (the settled ones) and (reconciled with the settled alien tribes and) subsequently came to be treated as Untouchables; (3) Just as Untouchability has no racial basis so also has it no occupational basis; (4) There are two roots from which Untouchability has sprung: (a) Contempt and hatred of the Broken Men as of Buddhists by Brahmins (b) Continuation of beef-eating by the Broken Men after it had been given up other (5) In searching for the origin of Untouchability care must be taken to distinguish the Untouchables. This is an error. Untouchable are distinct from the impure(6) While the Impure as a class came into existence at the time of the Dharma Sutras, the Untouchables came into being much later than 400 A.D. "(Ambedkar 1990 preface 242). He has formulated his thesis. After verifying these propositions, with the help of the historical data a scientific method followed in the contemporary social science researches. In the following pages, we shall examine the validity of his thesis.

Before putting forth his thesis about the origin of the Untouchables and untouchability, Ambedkar has made a comparative survey of untouchability prevalent among Hindus and non-Hindus. He has said that the untouchability in terms of notion of defilement, pollution and contamination existed even in the primitive and ancient societies. It got reflected more in the body of rites and rituals, and in the performance of natural functions like eating, drinking, etc. rather than in the routine social and material transactions of the people. More precisely, the untouchability or defilement was associated with certain events like birth, initiation, puberty, marriage, cohabitation and death. For Ambedkar, both sacred (religious or ritual) and profane (material) were separate in which the former was observed in the caseof natural functions, objects and even human beings (1987 6; 251-53). Such distinction between sacred and profane has extensively been analysed in sociological writings also (for instance, see 19 durmast 1972).

As mentioned above, untouchability or defilement in terms of polluting even temporarily to the sacred, according to Ambedkar, was practiced in almost all primitive and ancient societies in the World, though a person or group was not treated Untouchable or permanently condemned to untouchability. The primitive society had also developed certain purificatory methods and ceremonies for dispelling impurity or pollutionor Defilement or untouchability. These were sprinkling water and blood on the defiled one, changing clothes, cutting hair and nail, taking bath, fumigation, etc. The nature of pollution or untouchability in the ancient society was similar to that in the primitive society but its sources and purificatory ceremonies were different. The sources of defilement were bloodshed, presence of ghost, contact with dead body, sexual intercourse, child birth, eating prohibited foods, intrusion of unauthorized persons, etc. The purificatory ceremonies were related to eating the prescribed foods, using eustral water, sacrificing animals and so forth.

Contrary to this, untouchability among the Hindus was considered both physical and notional defilement during the second century A.D., according to Ambedkar, and was caused mainly by birth, death and menstruation. The purificatory agents were water, cow's urine and dungs, kusa grass, fire, ashes, milk and milk produces, blood and animal sacrifice, etc. in course of time, the individual defilement or impurity got extended to community and territory with more emphasis on animal sacrifices for purification. But in the case of certain communities, the defilement or impurity became hereditary. But in the case of certain communities, the defilement or impurity became hereditary. Hence, untouchability got permanently associated with certain castes and communities, and the purification became inevitable of the defiled or polluted being and not of polluter one. In the present time, "They (Untouchables) are born impure, they are impure while they live, they die the death of the impure, and they give birth to children who are born with the stigma of untouchability affixed to them. It is a case of permanent hereditary stain which nothing can cleanse" (Ambedkar 1990:266). Further, the fundamental feature of untouchability practiced by Hindus is that Untouchables are required to live in separate settlement, physically located at a distance from the main village. "It is not a case of social separation (as both Bougle 1971 and Dumont 1972 also would say), a mere stoppage of social intercourse for a temporary period. It is a case of territorial segregation and of a cordon sanitaire putting the impure people inside a barbed wire into a sort of cage. Every Hindu village has a ghetto. The Hindus live in the village and the Untouchables in the ghetto" (Ibid).Answering the self-posed question of why the Untouchables live outside the main settlement, Ambedkar interprets the terms like *antya, Antyaja*and *Antyavasin*used for those who live outside the village. He refutes their conventional interpretation for those born last on the ground that, according to the Hindu theory of the order of creation, "it is the shudra who is born last. The Untouchable is outside the scheme of creation. The *Shudra* is *Sayarna.* As against him the Untouchable is *ayarna,*i.e., outside the *Varnasystem*. The Hindu theory of priority in creation (that is, Brahmin was born first, then Kshatriya, then Vaishya, and lastly shudra, but, for some, Untouchables were born in the end) done not and cannot apply to the Untouchable" (1990:279) In his opinion, had the *Antyajas* born last, they would have been regarded *Sayarana*and had lived inside the main village, In that case it would have been completely impossible to throw them out of their village and live in separate hamlets. Hence, in Ambedkar's opinion, since the very beginning they lived outside the main village and the untouchability fell on them much later (somewhere around 4th century A.D.), resulting into their being knows as Untouchables.

Based on this, he has formulated his theory of origin of the Untouchables from the Broken Men or the unsettled people (wanderers) of the defeated alien tribes. Corroborating his argument for the Untouchables living outside the main village, he refers to the three stage of the societal evolution the natural process of transformation of the primitive society to the modern society through the ancient one. He has said that the former (the primitive society) was different from the latter (modern society) in two respects: "Primitive society consisted of the nomadic communities while Modern Society consists of settled communities. Secondly, Primitive Society consisted of tribal communities based on blood relationship. Modern Society consists of local communities based on territorial affiliation" (Ibid: 273). Thus, the transformation took place from primitive society (society of nomadic tribes) to the modern society (settled community) of the civilized people through the ancient society of the technologically backward communities.

Raising then two specific questions of what make the primitive society to give up its nomadic life the what happened in its transition from nomadic to settled form, Ambedkar traced the origin of the Untouchables from his answer to the second question. In the first case, the nomadic tribes of the primitive society, according to him, got settled as they found another valuable wealth of land and learnt the art of farming and cultivating, besides their earlier most valued wealth of cattle or cattle breeding. But not all the nomadic tribes of the primitive society got the settled plate at one and the sometime. In fact, some got settled earlier at the later stage. In the second case-The transition from nomadic to settled life, the settled ones confronted the problem of their defence against or (from) the nomadic tribes, and the broken men unsettled men of the nomadic tribes confronted the problems of their protection and shatter. In other words, some of the defeated nomadic tribes compromised with the earlier settled communities and got absorbed in their social organizations, while the remaining stray individuals or broken men of the floating people of these tribes confronted the problems of their protection and shelter (Ibid: 274). After their getting fed up from the continuous fights against the settled communities, they compromised, at a later stage, with the settled community (ies) and had to do the work of watch and word "against the raiders belonging to (the remaining) nomadic tribes". That means, the broken men consisted of the defeated nomadic tribes and were facing "the problem of finding patrons who would give them food and shelter" (Ibid: 276). Again, the same process of settlement of one after the other worked but, this time, it was qualitatively different as the broken men of the defeated nomadic tribes were made to settle nearby yet outside the settlements of the earlier settled (nomadic) tribes.

Three points are quite clear from the above. One, the broken men, who became Untouchables much later, were part of the primitive society existed say as early as in 2000 B. C. in India. Two, they lived outside the village or the settlement of settled tribes or tribal communities with no bar on social intercourse between their members. And three, they were neither regarded Untouchables nor Untouchability was practiced against them in the beginning till they were engaged in the work of watch and ward of the village. Untouchability started getting practiced against them and they were called Untouchables during decline of the Buddhism somewhere between fourth and 3rd century B.C.

Ambedkar has reported the old theories of racial and occupational differences, causing the origin of untouchability of the ground that these could have produced in permanent phenomenon of untouchability and a class of Untouchables all over the world. Then, he has supplemented his theory of Broken Men the Untouchables of the later period by adding two more elements of the Hindus' contempt for the Buddhists (the Broken Men) and the Buddhists' continued beef-eating (eating flesh of dead animals) as roots of untouchability. Though he has called these two as new theories of untouchability, these are integral parts of his theory of the origin of the Broken Men and of the resultant untouchability. Then, he has proceeded with the hypothesis that the Broken Men were Buddhists, he has extrapolated the Brahmins' hatred and abhorrence against Buddhists to the Broken Men who, like their co-religionists, were beef-eaters and, hence, impure. The hatred and abhorrence were reciprocal as the Buddhists vis-à-vis Broken Men also hated the Brahmins and treated them morally and spiritually or intellectually inferior. Further, in course of time others, except the Broken men, left beef-eating (the Brahmins had left much early and the Buddhists left later). The continued beef-eating by the Broken men earned them the stigma of untouchability and a status of their being regarded untouchables. This thesis gains its strength from two sources. One, since they were Broken Men, they were servile and dependent on the settled communities for their food and shelter. Two, they continued to remain Buddhists (against the wishes of the Hindus and Brahmins) and beef-eaters. Hence, they easily became susceptible to the folly of the social-religious disabilities and ignominies of untouchability.

Not going into Ambedkar's answers to other important questions like whether the Hindus ever ate beef, why did they give it up, why did beef-eating give rise to untouchability, etc., we would look at his dating the origin of untouchability and of the Untouchables.

Fixing the upper limit of the period (the earliest time) for the origin of Untouchables and untouchability, Ambedkar has referred to the use of the term *Antyajas* in the Rigveda and other *Dharma Sutras*. With help of these and other religious texts, he has concluded that the term denoted temporary impurity and not the permanent defilement. Even during the lowest percentile of this upper limit, i.e., during the period of Manu in the second century A.D. there is no clear mention in *Manusmriti*about the untouchability and the Untouchable class. All that Manu did was that he declared that there was no fifth varna. Why had Manu to make such declaration? Is it that some people from outside the Varna system were trying to be included in it, or some people from within the varna system, particularly the Chandals, Nishadas, etc. who were called the Varna Shankaras, wanted to form another varna over and above the four varnas? Why Manu was so obsessed to have only four and why not five or six or even more varnas? Anyway, this is not the subject of our enquiry here. Instead, as mentioned earlier, the Shudras were stigmatized by Manu, in this *Manusmriti* with numerous types of social and religious ignominies, and were equated even with the lowly ranked animals and birds. They were also subjected to various types of social and physical punishments, if they violated their Dharma of being servile. But in no case, were they addressed as Untouchables neither the Untouchables nor their untouchability existed during that period.

Then, Ambedkar had fixed the lower limit of the period, for tracing the birth of untouchability, i.e., 400 A.D. when the Chinese traveler Fah-Hian visited India and made reference, in his observations, of presence of the Chandalas who were named as 'evil men', lived separately and were discriminated by others. Ambedkar has also made reference on prevalence of the Chandalas during the 600 A. D. as described in the Bana Bhatt's Kadambari, a book in Sanskrit literature. Raising the doubt about capability of the Chandalas in spreading untouchability and creating numerous untouchable castes all over the country, Ambedkar has referred to Yuan Chwang, another Chinese traveler, who visited India in 629 A.D. and mentioned, in his observations, about creating other castes like butchers, fishermen, executioners, scavengers, etc. who were treated untouchables by that time. Then going back to his earlier thesis of the Brahmins' contempt against Buddhists and their ban on killing cows and eating beef, Ambedkar has concluded that since all these came into being during the fourth century A.D., this may be regarded the approximate date of period for the origin of Untouchables and untouchability.

Ambedkar has so scientifically formulated, logically argued and neatly presented his thesis of the Untouchables and the untouchability that it hardly needs any comments here. He has used the anthropo-sociological approach, has interpreted the Hindu lexicons and the historical evidences in the most scientific manner and arrived at the logical conclusion. This is a very novel thesis or even theory, contrary, contrary to the conventional racial and occupational but value-loaded Hindu theory (ies) of the origin of Untouchables and untouchability which hardly testifies the scientific verification and precision. It may, however, be said that when Ambedkar cited the case of the Mahars living, even today, in the separate hamlets in the moral Maharashtra, in support of his hypothesis of the Broken Men settled outside to main village, he was not relying on the induction method of locating present in to the past or analyzing the social reality existed in the past with the help of that found in the present time. Instead, he cited the example merely to remind the readers that the similar situation existed in the past. Such situations existed in the past and exist even today in all parts of the country (for the general features of untouchability and the pitiable socio-economic conditions of the Untouchables and atrocities committed on them see Ambedkar 1989).

REFERENCES

Ambedkar, B.R., 1987a Resolution and Centaury-Revolution in Ancient India, in Dr. Babasaheb Ambedkar: Writings and Speeches (Complied by Vasant Moon) 3 Government of Maharashtra, Bombay.

________ 1987b Riddles in Hinduism, in Dr.Babasaheb Ambedkar: Writings and Speeches, Vol.4. Government of Maharashtra, Bombay.

_______ 1989 Untouchables or the children of India's Ghetto and other Essays on Untouchable and Untouchable onehabilit, Socio-Political-Religious, in Dr.Babasaheb Ambedkar: Writings and Speeches, Vol.5. Government of Maharashtra, Bombay.

_______ 1990 who are the Scholars? How they came to be the Fourth Varna in the Indo-Aryan Society? (First published in 1946) in Dr. BabasahebAmbedkar Writings and Speeches Vol .7. Government of Maharashtra, Bombay.

Bose, N.K., 1994 the Stricture of Hindu Society. OrientLongman, New Delhi. (First published 1975).

Bougle, Celestin 1971 Essays on the Caste System. Cambridge University press, Cambridge.

Dube,Saurabh 2001 Untouchable Part: Religion. Identity and Power among a Control Indian Community, 1780-1950. Vistar Publications, New Delhi.

Dumont, Louis 1972 Homo-Hirarechicus: The caste system and its Implications, Vikas Publishing House, New Delhi (the same was published by Paladin, London, 1970).

Ghurye,G.S. 1979 Caste and Race in India. Popular Prakashan, Bombay.

Jha, Vivekanand 1977 "From Trible to Untouchable: The case of Nishads"In R.S Sharma and Vivekanand Jha (eds.),Indian Society: Historical Probing People's Publishing House, New Delhi, PP.67-84.

Jaiswal, Suvira 1998 Caste: origin, Function and Dimensions of change. ManoharPublishers andDistributers, New Delhi.

Juirgensmerer, Mark 1983 Religion as social Vision. University of California Press, Berkeley.

Kame, P.V.1941 History of Dharmashastras, Vol.II. Bhandarkar Oriental Research Institute, Pooria.

________ 1953 History of Dharmashastras, Vol IV. Bhandarkar Oriental Research Institute, Pooria.

Kosambi, D.D1992 The Culture and Civilization of Ancient India in Historical Outline. Vikas Publishing House, New Delhi.

Marrioth, Me Kim 1976 "Hindu Transactions: directly without dualism". In BruceKapfener (ed.) Transaction and Meaning: Directions in Anthropology of Exchange and Simboth Beavers Iotitnta for the study of Human Ishnes, Philadelphia.

Menchar, Joan P. 1974 "The caste System upsidedown: The Untouchables in India. Motilal Banarandas, Delhi.

Menchar, Joan P. Muller, Friedric Max 1883 India: What can it teach us. Longmans Green, London.

Ram Nandu 2009 Beyond Ambedkar: Essays on Dalits in India Har-Anand Publications, New Delhi (first published in 1995). R.S. Sharma and Vivekanand (eds), Indian.

Ruben Walter 1977 "outline of the Structure of Ancient Indian Society" In Society: Historical Proving. People's Publishing House, Delhi.

Sarma, I.K 2000 Roots of Indian Civilisation. Sundeep Publications, New Delhi.

Sharma, R.S. 1990 Sudras in Ancient India: A social History of the lower order down to circa AD 600. Motilal Banarsidas Publisher Pvt.Ltd., Delhi.

Srinivas, M.N.1966 Social Change in Modern India. Allied Publisher, Bombay.

Symposium 1971 Symposium on Louis Dumont's Homo-Hierarchicus, Contributions to Indian Sociology, Vol V.

Thapar, Romila 1975 Ancient India Social History. Orient Longman New Delhi.

Thapar, Romila 1990 Past and Prejudice. National Book Trust, New Delhi.

Thapar, Romila 1995 recent Perspectives of Early Indian History (ed.). Popular Prakashan, Bombay.

Thapar, Romila 2001 Weber, Max 1967 The Religion of India. Glencoe.

2

Gandhi, Ambedkar and the Dalits: Retrospects and Prospects

Amidst their coveted concerns and commitments to the cause of uplift and empowerments of the Untouchables or Dalits both Mahatma and Babasaheb Dr Ambedkar, the two great leaders and visionaries of the twentieth century, have now conventionally been regarded arch rivals and proponents of political articulations of caste Hindus and of the Dalits respectively. One may also take cognisance of the recent controversy over Gandhi being inimical to the politio-social empowerment of the Dalits and Ambedkar wishing longevity to the British rule in India. While some may dismay over such expositions, the said controversy and articulations need to be substantiated by viewing the socio-historical locations and cultural mooring of both Gandhi and Ambedkar, and the wider endorsement of these by them even at their formative stage which later got exemplified in their political usage during the era of struggle for political Independence of the country.

However, our intention here is neither to endorse the Dalits' eulogizing Ambedkar nor to affirm their condemning Gandhi's commitments and efforts to the cause of their welfare and uplift. The purpose is also not critique caste Hindus' attempts of political co-option of Ambedkar in the lexicon of their religious heroes and legendary along with their desperate strives to encash his name for collecting the Dalits' votes *inlock*. Rather, our main purpose in this paper is to erase some misgivings of both caste Hindus and the Dalits about Gandhi and Ambedkar by emphasising priority agenda of the two which they had chosen and pursued differently during the pre-Independence period. By extension, our concern is also to put in right perspective the wild and baseless charges or general misgivings of the case Hindu intelligentsia and ideologies about Ambedkar's wishing longevity to the British rule in India and thereby jeopardising the present need and efforts of the contemporary caste Hindu leadership achieving political Independence or transfer of power at an early date, besides his alleged hobnobbing with the Muslim League and thus 'extending' his tacit support partition of India or creation of Pakistan.

Since the nineteen thirties to date, Dalits as collectivity have systematically acclimatized themselves to assert for their rights of social respect, dignified social identity and equality of status besides for social, economic and political justice to be accorded to them. Being inspired fromAmbedkar's life-time struggle for preparing them for the purpose and also being guided by the main spirit of the Indian Constitution, their assertion has all along been spearheaded through a number of movements organised by them in different parts of the country. As such, all these have been accelerated and/or hindered by two favourable and unfavourable strategies adopted by the Government specially after Independence – the policy of reservation or of protective discrimination and the recent economic reforms (though the latter one has also been visualised as favourable to them both by Government and the privileged section of the people). It may be said here that whereas the former coupled with a number of allied measures has facilitated the process of empowerment of Dalits, the latter leaves lurching fear and uncertainty for their future. Towards this end, the paper intends to enquire into relevance of strategies of both Gandhi and Ambedkar to fulfilling general aspirations of the Dalits and their status enhancement along with political empowerment in particular. It finally probes into the possibility of convergence of the strategies propagated and pursued by both Gandhi and Ambedkar in fulfilling the ever-growing aspirations and expectations of Dalits in the present-day Indian society.

The Dalit Pespective

The perspective or framework in which the arguments have been presented in this paper is based neither on Ambedkar's direct critique of Gandhi's position nor Gandhi's both indirect and direct rejection of Ambedkar's propositions. Instead, it is based on the current perceptions and articulations of Dalits about the concerns and roles of both Gandhi and Ambedkar for their welfare and development or empowerment. This is, however, not to construe that all Dalits in the country now condemn Gandhi or his concerns for them and embrace that of Ambedkar. This was also not the case even during their life time specially in event of long continued concerns of Gandhi vis-à-visthe Indian National Congress whose leadership came to him in 1920. Rather, being timid due to their century-old subjugation, subordination and exploitation, a sizeable section of the Untouchables and their leadership looked, during the pre-Independence period, for some political concessions under initiatives of the Indian National Congress. Their such leadership largely played the 'politics of surrender' instead of assertion. The then Harijans or Untouchables also got attracted from the simplicity and enthusiasm of Gandhi for their uplift.While this was, to a great extent, continuation of the tradition of social reform which was on decline during the 1920's, majority of the Untouchables could not afford to adopt an assertive posture atleastupto 1920 due to their traditional mind-set resulted from their subjugation and the inhuman treatment meted to them in the past.

On the other hand, Ambedkar appeared actively on the political scene sometimes in 1923 to organise the Untouchables first in his own region and state, and later at the all-India level. It is a fact that by the early 1930's he had succeeded in having a large following of the Untouchables or Depressed Classes, including their leaders, throughout the country.This happened precisely due to his most successful roles played in mobilising public opinion particularly of the colonial rulers in favour of the Depressed Classes through his brilliant articulate testimonies before a number of imperial Committees and Commissions, and though his active participation in the Round Table Conferences held in London during 1930-31.

This followed signing of the Poona Pact in 1932 which provided political reservation and other concessions to the Untouchables or Depressed Classes. Through this he also proved himself to be the sole champion of articulating interest of the Depressed Classes in India. His such crucial roles and the quality important ones played later specially in the Viceroy's Council (as incharge of Labour) and in framing the Indian Constitution not only made him the national leader and the undisputed crusader of the Dalits' cause but, even after his death, sensitised and prepared them to assert their rights.

Though it is absolutely difficult to ascertain retrospectively the exact or even approximate number of Untouchables- Harijans or Depressed Classes who had shown allegiance to their Gandhi's persuasion or Ambedkar's assertion during the pre-Independence period. Nor is it easy to make a census of their followings among Dalits even in the present times. However, fact of the matter is that Ambedkar has become more powerful symbol of the Dalits' assertions throughout the country, and Gandhi, in perception of Dalits, is placed lower in the esteem due to his strategy of persuasion and gradualism or change of heart of the people specially of the caste Hindus towards them. Their such assessment of Gandhi is also drawn from his affirming and vindicating faith in Hinduism specially the Varna System and his sitting on fast unto death in September 1932 for opposing the separate electorate awarded to them. Moreover, Gandhi has been made redundant in view of the new priority agenda set by the contemporary political leadership itself in the country. This has obviously percolated to the mental frame of the Dalits and helped them pursue their current strategy of assertion for their self-liberation.

Socio-Political anchorage

With such perspective in offing, it is necessary to briefly look at the socio-politicalanchorage of both Gandhi and Ambedkar before delving into their roles and commitments for uplift and empowerment of the Dalits. Both Gandhi and Ambedkar had hailed from two different caste backgrounds and were born as Hindu though the latter embraced Buddhism and attained his *nirvana* (death) in December 1956. Being born (nearly twenty-two years earlier to Ambedkar) in a traditional Modh Bania caste- a sub-caste of Bania or merchant caste- at Porbander in Kathiawad of Sourashtra peninsula (now a part of Gujarat state), Gandhi as a childwas brought up in the conservative Hindu tradition. In spite of three generations of his fore-fathers serving as prime ministers in several princely states rather than practising their traditional caste occupation of trade and petty-merchandise, his family could not overlook the main tenets of "an essentially conservative region in its adherence to traditional patterns of social relations" (Zelliot 1996:152). In fact, his family was deeply entrenched in the neo-Vedantic religious faith of the late 19th century and in the devotional path of the *Bhakti* tradition of the medieval period which also helped Gandhi (like Lord Rama of the TulsiRamcharitmanasa) to imbibe 'compassion for the humble and care for the poor' (Rudolph and Rudolph 1987:18). It is this tradition which enabled him proceed later in politics "with implicit social criticism of the (caste) hierarchy, social distance (between rich and poor or between high caste and low caste) and exclusively of Brahminic Hinduism" (ibid).

However, with his traditional socio-cultural moorings and an introvert bent of mind Gandhi had completed is matriculation in 1887 and gone to England in the subsequent year to pursue the legal study for LLB degree. Though during his stay in England, he interacted with people specially of his peer group students drawn from diverse socio-cultural backgrounds, he largely retained with him the values and cultural traditions that he had inherited since his childhood. Anyway, Gandhi became Barrister in June 1891-nearly two months after the birth of Ambedkar on April 14 in the same year.

Then after dwindling with his unsuccessful career in legal profession and carrying social reform of some kinds in his own region, Gandhi went to South Africa for pursuing a legal suit and stayed there at first instance for three years, i.e.,upto 1900 where he glimpsed the racial discrimination and apartheids of Whites against the Blacks. After returning to India, he participated in the annual conference of the Indian National Congress held at Calcutta in 1901 in which he left his presence felt by the Congress leaders.

He again went back to South Africa and began his political action there in 1906. But he ultimately took charge of the Indian nationalist movement in 1920 and devoted the rest twenty-seven full years of his life in launching *Satyagrahas*, non-violence, mass-mobilisation and fast unto death. In other words, he participated in active politics against two enemies – the colonial regime and the civil practices specially untouchability of Hinduism. Finally, he was assassinated on January 30, 1948 and thus disappeared for ever from the Indian political scene after becoming the Mahatma or Bapu and Father of Nation.

Two points need to be mentioned here about Gandhi's childhood experiences and his entry into politics of the Indian National Congress. The first is related to his knowledge about untouchability and the temporal social boycott. The latter being milder than the former one could easily be removed after the required purification and fulfilling the caste or community obligations. As a child, he touched an Untouchable (sweeper) boy who had accompanied his parent- a domestic servant appointed to clean the latrine in his house. He had also touched another Untouchable boy while playing with him. On both the occasions, he was rebuked and punished by his mother and other members of the family and was asked to undergo the purificatory process. Secondly, he entered into the politics and joined the Indian National Congress at a time when it was almost thirty years old and had established itself as a strong political organization in spearheading its crusade against the British imperial regime and carrying out some activities for removal of social disabilities under the rubrics of social reform. Gandhi, on his part, tried in vain to mobilize the Indian National Congress for the cause of removal of untouchability. Yet, the Indian National Congress leadership was already divided into two schools of thoughts-the radicals and moderates or liberals on both the issues. After taking over reigns of the Congress, Gandhi succeeded in establishing supremacy of the moderates over the radicals who ultimately led to political Independence of the country in 1947.

On the contrary, Ambedkar had emerged from a very modest family background of an Untouchable (Mahar) caste of Maharashtra.

Born at MHOW (Military House of the War)- a small military town now in Madhya Pradesh where his father served as a teacher in the British army and retired as a Subedar Major, Ambedkar was brought up in Satara (Maharashtra) as his rather had settled there after retirement. He then with his father moved to Bombay and lived in two small rooms in a chawl at Parel from where Ambedkar completed his Matriculation in 1907 and B.A in 1912. He served barely for fifteen days in January 1913 as a lieutenant in the Baroda State Forces under the bond of agreement which he had signed for a scholarship granted to him by the Maharaja of Baroda for pursuing his graduation study.

In July 1913 Ambedkar, a young boy of 20 years and perhaps the first Indian Untouchable, went to Columbia University, New York (USA) on a scholarship from the same Maharaja of Baroda to pursue his higher study. He obtained his M.A. and Ph.D. degree from this University in 1915 and 1916 respectively. He also earned his MSc and DSc degrees frim London School of Economics in 1921 and 1923. In addition, he obtained his Bar-at-Law from the Grays-Inn, London in 1922. A point may be mentioned here that when Gandhi finally entered into the Indian politics in 1920, Ambedkar left again for London on a scholarship from the Maharaja of Kolhapur to complete the academic requirements for his M.Sc. and D.Sc. degrees and also for his law degree which he could not complete before termination of his earlier scholarship in 1917. Thus, there cannot be any parallel between Gandhi and Ambedkar not only in terms of their academic credentials but even in theoretico-empirical articulations as the latter had much superior intellectual acumen than the former one.

Ambedkar was born in a family which, like Gandhi's family, was also religious but had deep faith in the saintly tradition (specially of the lower caste saints) of the *Bhakti* period as the proponents of this tradition had condemned the caste system and rejected its rigidity. Ambedkar too continued with his faith in such tradition till the end of life but had accepted it as a revolt against the Brahamanic or orthodox Hindu tradition. On his own part, he not only revolted against any form of Hinduism but completely rejected it and embraced Buddhism, barely two months before his death, on the ground of its reverence to equal against unequal social order, its compassion for all creatures and *maitree* (fraternity) among the human-beings.

In spite of his father being educated, a sports man, a soldier in the army and having deep religious faith in Hinduism, Ambedkar and his family members, like his castemen, could not escape from the various of untouchability practised by the caste Hindus. As a school boy both in Satara and Bombay, he faced untouchability and other forms of discrimination on many occasions including those in the class rooms. As stated earlier, even as a young graduate and a lieutenant in the Baroda State Forces, he was discriminated against by his peon and colleagues. This also continued with his professorship in a college in Bombay in 1918 which he had accepted, for a brief period, after obtaining his Ph.D.degree. Besides, these incidents, there were numerous occasions on which untouchability and other forms of discrimination were practised against him. Some of these included throwing him down as a boy from a caste Hindu owned bullock cart, taking away their tiffin boxes by the school-mates in the class room to prevent pollution from his touch and not allowing him to drink water from the same tap or pitcher, and throwing him out of the rented room in Baroda (while serving in the State Forces)even in mid-night after knowing his caste.A vivid account of all this has been given by Dhananjay Keer – his biographer (see, Keer 1971). Ambedkar was also well aware of the horror of untouchability practised day and night against his castemen and other Untouchable's castes in Maharashtra and other states in the country.

Like Gandhi, Ambedkar also took up the leadership of Untouchables at a time when in Maharashtra and elsewhere in the country they had already formed a number of organisations and raised agitations for their socio-religious uplift and political rights. Without going into details of their organisational structures, objectives and major activities carried by them, it can simply be stated here that these organisations firstly were localised by covering a region or state for their area of activities and thus lacked networking and inter-organisational linkages at all India level. Secondly, the issues around which these had agitated were mostly local though these had resembled across the regions and states. Hence, their articulation at an all-India level was largely absent. And finally, though the leadership of most of these organisations was to some extent assertive, it did not have its autonomous political or ideological standpoints. In other words, many of these organisations were supported either by the Indian National Congress and a few other political parties or by the caste Hindu organisations.These lacked independent articulations and strong assertions in getting rights and justice to be granted to the Untouchables.

It is at this juncture in the socio-political history of the Untouchables or Depressed Classes as they were known at that time, Ambedkar took up their leadership in the early 1920's and in less than ten years' time became undisputed champion of their assertions for social uplift and political rights. With his high academic credentials, and much superior intellectual and rational argumentations, he creditably succeeded not only in getting the Indian Untouchables accepted as a distinct and separate political minority but also their right of political representations accorded first in the separate and later in the joint electorate systems. He also played crucial instrumental role in getting the special provisions enshrined in the Indian Constitution and enacting policy of reservation in favour of the Scheduled Castes and Scheduled Tribes.

Removal of untouchabality or annihilation of caste

With a knowledge of such frame of socio-political anchorage or location of both Gandhi and Ambedkar, it is necessary to briefly look here at their views on untouchability and caste or caste system and examine their strategies adopted for removal or eradication of these two.Sociologically speaking, caste is a traditional institution deeply entrenched in Indian society specially in the Hindu social system which has organically divided the entire Hindu population into thousands of castes and sub-castes vertically arranged with their superior and inferior ranks or statuses in a well-knit hierarchy. Each caste with a number of its sub-castes in the caste system practices and maintains its own hierarchy and social inequality making the entire system highly complex and unequal. That is why, Ambedkar has called it a system of graded order or inequality based on division of labourers (Ambedkar1979:47, 72) and not of labour – a thesis pursued by the caste Hindu social scientists and others including those from abroad. On the other hand, untouchability originated from the wombs of Hinduism imposed numerous forms of social and religious ignominies on the Ati-Shudras or Broken Men or Untouchables who were originally followers of Buddhism (Ambedkar 1990:239-382). It grew as a custom or inevitable practice and became an institution in itself. Since it put millions of low caste Hindus as a whole, it drew major concerns of both Gandhi and Ambedkar.

Notwithstanding the legal abolition of untouchability under the Constitutional dispensation in 1950, Gandhi had witnessed the act of untouchability in his early childhood with a rebuke from his family members as stated in the earlier section. There might have been couple of other occasions when he could have witnessed similar situation by touching consciously or unconsciously the Untouchables boys in his neighbourhood, playground, school etc. and tried to realize the pains and agonies of the one being born and treated as Untouchables. Nothing more is authentically known even from his autobiography (which actually covers his life events only upto 1921) whether he witnessed similar experiences before he went to England for his higher study or during the period of his unsuccessful legal practice in his hometown except his encounter with racial segregation and apartheid against the Blacks in South Africa, as stated earlier. But one thing is widely known that after he first returned from England, he had to face the social boycott from his castemen (on account of his travelling across the sea and eating and mixing up with the *mlechechas*– the White people) though that could not have been as severe as of an Untouchable's experience. In other words, this could have no bearing of 'the same damaging stigmatous effects (on him) as the cruelty (of untouchability) that inhered in calling some (in fact millions) men, women and children of humankind as Untouchable" (Anonymous, Nov.6.1997).

Yet, his limited experiences with untouchability and racial discrimination deeply touched his heart and sensitised his social and moral conscience to take up a vow to remove the evil of untouchability from this land. Between 1920 and 1932 he continuously wrote articles and issued statements in his journals – *Harijans* and *Young India* accepting untouchability in 1920 as a moral sin to God, humanity and Hinduism (though treating it not as a part of Hinduism), wishing in 1921 to be born as an Untouchable (a sweeper) in his next birth if it ;had to come at all, treating untouchability in 1926 as a hydra-headed monster and accepting it again in 1927 as a shame of Hinduism, calling Untouchables in 1931 as a real Harijan – a man of God and the God the caste Hindus as a Durjan or men or evil, treating himself in 1932 as an 'untouchable by choice' and undertaking in near future his program me (fast unto death) which he never undertook) for removal of untouchability if there was a call from the God (for details, see Pyarelal 1984). This may simply mean that a call or calls from the millions of the Untouchables perhaps would not have forced him to go on fast unto death for the purpose. He also rejected the need for tracing roots of untouchability but concentrated his attention on its removal by suggesting three specific modes or strategic for the purpose: the inter-caste drinking and dining, throwing open Hindu temples for the Untouchables, and finally, in 1946, the inter-caste marriages specially between the Untouchables and caste Hindus. But all these Gandhi left to the persuasion and gradualism or change of heart of the caste Hindus "to render of their motion, not as a matter of patronage but as a matter of duty" (referred in Pyarelal 1984:294).

This raises four sets of pertinent questions: one, if untouchability was not part of Hinduism, then how was it a sin or blot or shame of it? Why should Hindus at all have been concerned with removal of untouchability when it was not a part of their religion (Hinduism) or even of a system of cultural practices in which they have had deep and blind faith? Two, if untouchability did not find place in Hinduism of which caste system happens to be inherent and necessary social structural basis then why did Gandhi emphasise towards the end of his life that 'caste must go' especially when he had earlier vindicated caste and eulogized the *varna* and *varna* system? Also, why did he not suggest any concrete method or strategy to abolish the caste system if it was so bad in his late realisation? Three, if the root-cause of untouchability was not known, how scientific and effective was it to remove it through the aforesaid strategies suggested by him? Were then not all the three modes or strategies suggested by Gandhi mere preventive rather than curative of the practice of untouchability – a disease of Hinduism? Or, was Gandhi not bent upon to keep the untouchables within the Hindu-fold and make them loyal to the Indian National Congress? And finally, why did Gandhi suggest the inter-caste marriage as his strategy for removal of untouchability barely one and half years before his murder and why not earlier specially when he had taken a vow in 1932 to remove untouchabiity and had undertaken a nation-wide tour during 1933-34 for the purpose?Was he not convinced though lately by this strategy advocated strongly by Ambedkar as early as in 1936 for annihilation of caste? These questions raised from the Dalit perspective demand immediate answers from Gandhi or from his ideas compiled and published at the government expenses or from the Gandhians. Such questions need to be addressed seriously withadequate replies, else in absence of these the whole concerns and strategies of Gandhi may appear to be a mere political rhetoric as presently termed by Dalits in the country.

Contrary to Gandhi's treatment of untouchability, Ambedkar's analysis of its origin and eradication is more rational and scientific. Ambedkar had traced the root of untouchability in the caste system which is an off-shoot of the *varna* system and of an elaborate system ofl the *Varnashram Dharma*. There may not be absolute unanimity whether the caste system was an extended version of the varna system by incorporating birth in place of the *guna*(worth) as a criterion for status determination of a person in the post-Vedic period. A few scholars have also subscribed to the thesis that the *varna* system itself was an idealised system or scheme in which the four varnas were only notional categories and the actual categories of people were castes. Without going into details of it at this stage, we simply wish to state that by verifying a self-conceived hypothesis of Broken Men (members of a wanderer tribe) who were followers of Buddhism, Ambedkar formulated his theory of the origin of Untouchables and their untouchability which dated around 400 A.D. More precisely, Broken Men or the wanderer Buddhists were beef-eaters or used to eat the carrion and hence had befallen to the status of Untouchables due to contempt of the Brahmins who had left eating the flesh of cows, bulls, etc. by that time. Consequent upon that untouchability and various other social and religious ignominies were imposed on them once they accepted the Brabnanic version of Hinduism and became part of the caste system (Ambedkar 1990:235-382).

Caste system, for Ambedkar, enjoys religious sanction of the Hindu Dharmashashtras. In this respect, it not much different from the varna system which, in Ambedkar's opinion, was not divine in its origin but was legal and penal. It was a system of an artificial chopping-off the population divided earlier into numerous segments and sub-segments or castes and sub-castes (Ambedkar 1990:1-227). Since untouchability happens to be inherent part of the caste system, it has also enjoyed the religious sanction and thereby approval of the Hindu Shashtras. Therefore, Ambedkar advocated for annihilation of caste or the caste system by denouncing the religious sanctity of the Hindu Shashtras or Dharmashashtras and going for the inter-caste marriages (Ambedkar 1979:23-96). He perhaps thought that by annihilating the caste untouchability would automatically be eradicated. But when he did not foresee any future of annihilation of caste, he strived for empowerment of the Untouchables or Dalits as discussed below and finally got their untouchability legally abolished under Article 17 of the Indian Constitution.

A point of caution needs to be mentioned here that neither Gandhi's approach of moral persuasion nor Ambedkar's approach of legal injunction has succeeded in fully abolishing untouchability and not even a bit of the caste system. A simple reason for it may be stated here that the real denomination of Hindu is that of his caste with which he lives both his private and public life. So long he is a Hindu, he is a caste-man and so long he is a caste-man, he has to practise untouchability and social distance against another caste-man. A caste-man is either touchable or Untouchable, like Dumon's thesis of binary opposition of a Hindu either being twice born or once born, or being either pure or impure (Dumont, 1970). Therefore, to annihilate caste or caste system and thereby abolish untouchability is suicidal to a Hindu or Hinduism though numerous efforts have been made, though the ages, towards this end. This is not to suggest that both untouchability and caste system are desirable. Contrary to this, both have brought tremendous harms to the progress of the people in India. Perhaps what is desirable at this juncture is to have a convergence of approaches of both Gandhi and Ambedkar wherein the legal abolition of untouchability is to be taken to the logical end by arousing social and moral conscience of the people through a vigorous campaign and reform measures within a stipulated time-fame. Similarly, caste as an institution needs to be legally abolished, and the people's social moral conscience aroused for accepting it as an evil practice.

Empowerment of the Dalits

In the post-independent India specially since the last two decades or so a considerable *degree*of emphasis has been given on empowerment of certain vulnerable sections of people in India like Scheduled Castes or Dalits, Scheduled Tribes and the women. The empowerment of Dalits and tribals is facilitated through giving them representation in education, government services and in political participation or decision-making process. The political empowerment of women is in the way of reserving seats for them in the Assembles and Parliament. Their empowerment being ongoing process may take time to get fully ascertained. It is not our intention here to make any wild guess as to how much time would lit take and what would be its final shape. Instead, we simply wish to state here that the present urge for empowerment either of Dalits and tribals or of women is much assertive in its tone rather than patronising in nature. This is well demonstrated through a number of agitations and protest movements oganised by these sections of population in the recent past. This is also evident from their new leadership which is more offensive than defensive in its approach towards their empowerment. Nonetheless, instead of going into further details of strategies currently adopted for empowerment especially of the Dalits we shall try below to know if 'if has any root or roots in the perspective or frameworks adopted by Gandhi and Ambedkar for their welfare and uplift.

Gandhi never talked about empowerment exclusively of the Harijans in any sense of the terms though he emphasised on the *Ramrajya, Swadeshi* and self-sufficient village India. In the case of the Untouchables or his Harijans,he always showed his concerns for their welfare and uplift both in the Hindu social system and in Indian society as a whole. Since he spoke of the moral and spiritual development of the humanity, it can be stated that by extension it also applied to his Harijans. Making distinction between religion (conscience of heart) and *Dharma* (the duty, he asked all Hindus including Untouchables to strict to their traditional duties or caste cailings by eulogising the occupation of scavenging. He stated, "The law of Varna (system) prescribes that a person should, for his living, follow the lawful occupation of his forefathers.... A scavenger has the same (occupational) status as a Brahmin" (*Young India*, November 17, 1927). This he mentioned believing in traditional ordering of the Hindu society for preserving the social harmony and growth of the soul, and also by accepting all traditional caste callings or occupations equally honourable in the socialesteem (Zelliot 1996: 154). But a question is often asked from the Dalit perspective that why the forefathers of Gandhi, including Gandhi himself, did not strict to their traditional caste occupation of petty-business. This question still remains unanswered. Nonetheless, Gandhi strongly advocated fir admitting the Untouchable children in the same schools attended to by caste Hindu children.

Disagreeing completely with the Government's aids for economic and political empowerment of the Untouchables, Gandhi presented his own scheme for their uplift. On economic fronts, he appealed the rich- the industrialists and landlords to trust for the *Antyodyas (*welfare and uplift of the *Daridranarayans*or the Untouchables). Similarly, for their political representation he insisted and even got accepted through his fast unto death the joint electorate system. More specifically, he mentioned that out of their moral and spiritual concerns the rich should become trustee of their wealth and spend it judiciously for uplift of the Untouchables and other poor. He also asked the people to go for self-reliance by earning through *Khadi* and village industries and not become slave of the machine. But Gandhi's such schemes of economic and political uplift of the Untouchables or Dalits proved to be impractical soon after Independence.Even his insistence for Untouchables' political representation through the joint electorate system has led the Dalits to practically remain powerless in the wake of subordination of the contemporary Dalit leadership to their caste Hindu political bosses and voters of the reserved constituencies. Politics today has become a practical affair, rather, a power game in which Gandhi's moral appeal to caste Hindus has virtually failed.

Ambedkar, on his part, fought throughout his life for socio-economic and political empowerments of the Dalits. His main dictates to his men were to educate, take up white collar employment and achieve power through the democratic means or the parliamentary democracy. Looking at the economic vulnerability of Dalits and political ploy and patronizing tendency of the caste Hindu leaders and reformers, Ambedkar relied largely on the State's resources for their progress and empowerment. At the same time, he also tried to instill in both Dalit men and women the self-confidence and strong personal conviction for their uprising and competing with others. Besides encouraging them to have their own strong social organisations, he himself established a number of colleges and set up; hostels for educational advancement of Dalit boys and girls both in Bombay and Aurangabad in Maharashtra. Needless to say, that since his entry into the active politics in the nineteen twenties upto the dawn of lthe Independence, Ambedkar relentlessly fought and succeeded in getting formally incorporated in the Indian Constitution a number of socio-economic and political concessions in favour of the Dalits, as stated earlier. Even he suggested immediately after Independence (see, his *States and Minorties* 1947 in his Vol.I) for nationalisation of industry and collectivisation of agriculture, with the adequate financial support from the State. This he felt necessary for the rapid industrialisation and economic growth in the country and for economic uplift and betterment of the Dalits and the poor. It is a different matter that he could not effectively influence the planning process in Independent India as he remained in the Government at the Centre only for a brief period (1947-51) and had almost his lone voice. But it is a fact that the present assertions of Dalits for their empowerment have strong roots in the thoughts and actions of Ambedkar and not in that of Gandhi.

Dalits' assertion and shift in the development paradigms

We have mentioned elsewhere (Ram 1995,1998a,1998b) that, since the 1970's onwards, Dalits have started asserting for their rights of achieving self-respect, dignified social identity, status equality and social justice. For the purpose, they have also organised numerous agitations and even protest movements in different parts of the country. They now insist to be treated as 'subject' rather than an object-to be left on the mercy of other-be they Government and its various agencies or caste Hindu organisations. In the case of their insistence to be treated as subject, they assert for registration or recognition oftheir contributions made, throughout the history, for betterment of others even at the cost of their destitution. In other words, their contributions made for prosperity and development of lthe country, in their reckoning, need to be recognised now.

We shall briefly see here whether their such assertion has been shaped by the concerns and roles played by both Gandhi and Ambedkar for their uplift and empowerment. We shall also examine the compatibility between their self and social assertions in view of the contemporary shift in the paradigms for socio-economic development of the country. Going by the mental make-up of Gandhi and his strategy of non-violence and moral persuasion which was derived from his deep faith in the *Bhakti* or the non-vedantic tradition as stated earlier and which has also been termed as the **Brahmin- Bania-Kayastha strategy** or framework by Rudolph and Rudolph (1987) in the modern metaphor, it is quite clear that he was totally opposed to any kind of assertion or protest of the Dalits for achieving their rights and self-respect. Gandhi himself said, "By way of protest against Hinduism, the Panchamas(Untouchables) can certainly stop all contacts and connection with the other Hindus so long as the special grievances are maintained. But this means organized intelligent effort. And so far as I can see there is no leader among the Panchamas today who can lead them to victory through non-cooperation" (*Young India*, October 27, 1920; also referred in Pyarelal 1984: 294-95). Gandhi had expressed his view before Ambedkar came on the political scene and articulated interest of the Dalits. Also, one wonders why he dissuaded the Dalits from the use if non-violence for achieving their rights while he himself had applied it against the apartheids in South Africa and the British rule in India for achieving the country's political independence.

Contrary to this, protest remained the nuclei of Ambedkar's frame of thought and action which has greatly shaped the present-day assertion and agitative sensibility of the Dalits as stated earlier. That is why, Gore (1993) has accepted protest or protest movement as the core of Ambedkar's ideology which was in effect his strategy for achieving just rights and dignity for the Dalits. In the core of his ideology in actuality were equality, liberty and fraternity within the guiding principle of social justice (Ra, 1995:34-37) on the basis of which he had visioned for a just social order to be evolved especially in the Indian society. Ambedkar had asked the Dalits not only to educate themselves but also to agitate against any form of injustices inflicted on them and to get these resolved unitedly, i.e. through the democratic means. However, a point may be mentioned here that the nature and degree of their assertions and protests varies from issues and it depends largely upon the nature and extent of their unity. It is also true that all these are not found uniformly among the Dalits through the length and breadth of the country.

In any case, India has come a long way since the time of both Gandhi and Ambedkar. The rulers and planners have now fully rejected the strategies of both Gandhi and Ambedkar in pursuing their planning for the socio-economic development of the country in general and of Dalits in particular. The legal or constitutional strategy of Ambedkar has, to some extent, satisfactorily worked through all these decades though it could not deliver the desired results in favour of Dalits and the other neglected segments of population due to sluggish implementation of various programmes and schemes. But since 1990 the country has adopted, in a big way, the path of economic libealisation to become part of the global economy. It has also submitted to the international demand of structural adjustment or making adjustment of its earlier existed structure of the mixed economy to the structure of the liberal economy by relaxing its various relatively stricter policies. More specifically, globalisation in the country has two facets: one, on the economic front, the government has invited the multi-national corporations of including those of the Non-Resident Indians to invest their capital in certain key-industries whose products may help the country not only in gaining respectable place in the international market but also contributing significantly in its economic growth and technical know-how. Without going into details, what is important to mention here is that the desired benefits of the two-fold globalisation have not reached to the masses. Instead, it has widened the earlier existed void between the privileged and the under-privileged, and is in the way of evolving a culture which would definitely uproot ideal values of the Indian tradition and coronate the ugly face of modernisation. Then, the pertinent questions to be asked in this regard are: what kinds of adjustment would globalisation bring to the existing social structure and cultural practices of the people in the country?How would it accommodate the ongoing assertions and protests of the Dalits for their rights of equality, social respect and justice? To venture in the thoughts and philosophy of both Gandhi and Ambedkar retrospectively for the present purpose is only a matter of conjecture which perhaps may not provide any satisfactory answer at this stage.

In nutshell, Gandhi had taken a conservative or traditional standpoint on the issue of Dalit's uplift and their empowerment. Being located primarily in the moral and spiritual tradition of the *Bhakti* period and also perhaps due to the overall mood and resistance of the caste Hindus in general and their leadership in particular against empowerment of the Dalits, he had intermarried both mortality or spiritualism and politics to the maximum possible abstraction level. It was and is even today almost difficult or impossible for an ordinary human being to translate his such abstraction into a practical proposition. Such difficulty has clearly been seen among both the Dalits and non-Dalits in India and among others elsewhere. Moreover, the case of Dalits has always been a case of deprivation which cannot be met through the moral or spiritual preaching. Instead, it demands a practical political solution but not the one suggested by Gandhi which appears to be redundant atleast for the time being in the caste of Dalits.

The legal or constitutional strategy and the assertive or agitative sensibility of Ambedkar are in congruence with the present-day mind-set of a large majority of the Indian Dalits. In fact, Ambedkar's ideas and strategies have become more powerful among Dalits even after his death due to the simple reason that their sufferings and exploitations of various sorts have greater resemblances with those of Ambedkar. He is also regarded as a symbol of revolt against subordination and patronage besides his being modern in his outlook and approach to any problem and its resolution. For Dalits, Gandhi was and also is not only traditional but even conservative on the accord of their socio-economic and political rights. Dalits' present-day assertions, however, are not to be seen in isolation but in an overall scenario with full of all-round unrest and self-assertion. Ambedkar then fulfills their emotional and material needs but not Gandhi whose preachings of morality and peaceful co-existence may appeal to them only when Indian society becomes a just social order which was the core of Ambedkar's vision of a new society in India.

REFERENCES

Ambedkar, B.R. 1979, *Caste in India, Annihilation o Caste and States and Minorities. In Dr. Babasaheb Ambedkar: Writings and Speeches*, Vol. I. Bombay, Government of Maharashtra

________1990, *Who were the shudras* and *The Untouchables. In Dr.Babasaheb Ambedkar: Writings and Speeches*, Vol.7

Anonymous, 1997, Raising the lot of Untouchables. In *Mahatma Gandhi:The last 200 Days. The Hindu*(daily), Nov 6.

Dumont, Louis, 1970, Homo-hiearchicus: Caste systems and its implications in India; see also the symposium on it in Contributions to Indian sociology (N.S.), Vol.V,1971.

Gandhi, M.K., 1994, An Autobiography or My Experiment with Truth (first published in 1927). Ahemdabad, Navjivan Publishing House.

Gore, M.S., 1993, The Social Context of Ideology: Ambedkar's Social and Political thought. New Delhi, The Sage.

Keer, Dhananjay, 1971, Dr. Ambedkar: Life and Mission. Bombay, Popular Prakashan.

Pyarelal, 1984, The Epic Fast. Ahemdabad, Navjivan Publishing House.

Ram, Nandu1995Beyond Ambedkar: Essays on Dalits in India. New Delhi, Har-Anand Publications.

________, 1998a, Dalit Movements in India-A perspective from the below. Indian Journal of Social Work, Vol.59, Issue 1 (special Issue- Part I), pp. 99-123

________, 1998b, Dalit Movements in India- a macro-sociological perspective. In Anand Kumar (ed.). Nation-Buliding in India. New Delhi, Radiant Publications, pp. 232-257.

Rudolph L.I & S. Rudolph, 1987, Gandhi. Delhi, Orient Longman.

Zelliot, E., 1996, From Untouchables to Dalit. New Delhi, Manohar Publications.

3

Abstraction To Substantiation: Ambedkar's Thought on Justice and Socialequauty in Comparative Perspective

It may perhaps appear to be an overstatement to attributeto Dr. B.R. Ambedkar alone the present-day articulation andsubsequent discourse on justice and equality in Indian society.He is, however, to be accorded individual credit for his havingsuccessfully brought, through his intellectual exhumation, thenotions of justice, equality, liberty and fraternity on theforefront of socio-political scene, and thereby sensitizing thepeople especially the Dalits in the contemporary period in India.He conceived and shaped, from both the Western and Indiansources, his own characteristic yunderstanding of justice andequality or social equality, which he later incorporatedz hisstruggle or movement for the benefit of the people, particularlythe Dalits and other deprived sections of society, and for theestablishment of a just and equalitarian social order in India.In his frame of thought, both justice and equality were,however, not to be taken as isolatory units either at the levelof individual cognition or at the level of social reality; rather,these were to be complemented by liberty and fraternity. Thistrio of equality, liberty and fraternity within the overall frameof justice or social justice constituted the core of his ideologyor philosophy of life, centered on the individual, the Stateand the society at large.

We shall critically review here his conception of justice,equality, liberty and fraternity, and examine their viablepracticability for the Indian society. In doing this, we shallrely mainly on the primary source material, his own writingsand speeches, and make some passing references to othersources, as and when necessary, in clarifying and alsocomparing the arguments given by him. In the process, weshall also cursorily look at the possibility of extension of hisconception of equality, liberty, fraternity and justice speciallyin the social situations which have both qualitatively andquantitatively changed in the present-day Indian society.

The Analytic-frame of Social Equality

A free society or an open social order, according toAmbedkar, is based on two essential principles of freerelationship of individual with society and free relationshipamong individuals within it (Ambedkar 1987a:95-129). On aclose scrutiny, it is clear that Ambedkar finds both these typesof relationships completely suppressed and undermined inthe Hindu social order which emphasizes solely collectivity or holism as stated by Dumont (1974), and which Ambedkarterms caste system. Regarding relationship among individualsin the Hindu society, Ambedkar notes that it has always beenguided by the individual's structural placement in thehierarchy of the Varna system or caste system. Such socialorder or system is not only unjust but is inevitably governedby the graded-inequality operative at both the levels ofphilosophical justification and actual operation.With immediate reference to Ambedkar's conception ofjustice and equality, we find that he elaborately explains thetrio of liberty, equality and fraternity, and very sparselytouches upon the notion of justice or social justice. Moreover,he discusses these not in any sequentiality or sequentialordering though he appears to be particular about that whenhe explains their interrelationship. We shall come to. this alittle later. Here, it is necessary to note the specific contexts inwhich he reflected on these and also humbly admitted hisinadequacy in handling these quite comfortably at theepistemological level. It is so because he was more concernedwith the implicational or operative part of these than theirtheoretical or analytical explanations.

Anyway, he organized and systematically put forwardhis views relating to equality, liberty, fraternity, that is socialjustice, during 1927-56. His first reflection on liberty, equality,fraternity, in a word, social justice appeared in the late 1920swhen he was in his mid-thirties and was fully equipped withhis doctoral and post-doctoral research training from the twopremier universities in the most modernized and developedcountries like the USA and UK. In 1927, he addressed a massivegathering of the Dalits, mostly Mahars, at the Chavdar Tankin the Mahad taluka of Maharashtra, in his capacity asChairman of the Satyagraha Committee of the Dalit movement,organized for wrestling the right of having drinking waterfrom the tank which was traditionally denied to them. Thisincident is important because of two reasons: one, he wasarticulating equality, liberty and fraternity as an optimistHindu and was exploring the possibility of adoption of equalityin the Hindu society. He was also perhaps hopeful about thesocial structural relocation of the Dalits on an equal footingwithin it. Two, he was greatly fascinated by the socialtransformation that had taken place in Europe, particularly inFrance, in the wake of the French National Assemblyproclamations of 1789 for political, social and religiousreorganization of the French society. More precisely, he washighly impressed by a particular proclamation which read: "All human beings are equal by birth, and they shall remainequal till death. They may be distinguished in status only inthe public interest. Otherwise, their equal status must bemaintained" (cf. Ambedkar 1994:58).

With such a perspective in mind, in 1927, he was stronglyin favour of social and religious reorganization of the Hindusociety leaving the political reorganization to be pursued at alater stage. In his own words, "... the road that all progressednations (of the West) have followed, ought to be road adoptedfor the,development of the Hindu society by this meeting (ofthe Dalits held on December 25, 1927 at Mahad). We need topull away the nails which had the framework of caste-boundHindu society together, such as those of the prohibition onintermarriage down to the prohibition of social intercourse sothat the Hindu society becomes all of one caste. Otherwise,untouchability cannot be removed nor can equality beestablished" (Ibid). Interestingly, he assigned to the Dalits theresponsibility of flouting the ban on intermarriage andcommensality, that is, social intercourse, and thereby ofestablishing social equality among them at first because, in hisopinion, the Dalits would not have any interest in maintainingthe status quo. This may be taken in the same spirit in whichKarl Marx had asked the proletarians to break off the chain oftheir slavery by fighting against the bourgeoisie or the exploitingclass (Marx 1948). The Brahmins, said Ambedkar, were notconcerned with any principle but with fulfilling and legitimizingtheir "self-interest" only. The class of Hindus below them(today's Kshatriyas or Rajputs, Vaishyas or Baniyas- thetraditionally trading castes and the Other Backward Classes orCastes-OBCs) could not afford to show any generosity to theBrahmins who were above them. And this aforesaid class II doesnot develop the attachment to principles that develop in theclass below them (the Untouchables or the Dalits). This is whythis class is seen to be concerned not so much about attainingequality with the Brahmins as about maintaining its statusabove the untouchables" (Ambedkar 1994:60).

Two facts may, however, be mentioned here, First, sincethe 1930s till date, a few economically and politically dominantcastes such as Yadav, kurmi and Jat in U.P. and Haryana;Yadav, Kurmi and Koeri in Bihar; Maratha and Kanbi inMaharashtra; Kamma and Reddy in Andhra Pradesh and therest who are located in the middle echelons of the caste hierarchy and have been termed the socially and educationallybackward classes of citizens (cf. Article 16 of the IndianConstitution) and are properly known as the Other BackwardClasses or Castes (OBCs) have, after consolidating theireconomic and political positions, been claiming the status ofthe Kshatriya. Similarly, other castes like Lohar (blacksmith)and Kumhar (potter) who are below them but above theUntouchables or the Dalit castes have claimed the status ofBrahmin. This has been termed the process of Sanskritization by Srinivas (1986: 1-45). Although they themselves resent theirsubordination to the upper classes, these dominant castes arestrongly opposed to this process on the ground that havingaccess to the Sanskritic values and thereby going upward inthe caste-hierarchy is everyone's equal right irrespective ofstructural location in the caste system (for more details, seeRao 1987). Ambedkar's observation is, thus, partially true inthe present time as inthe idiom of social mobility the upwardlymobile middle level groups of castes keep maximum socialdistance with their immediate inferior castes (the Untouchablesor the Dalit castes) but they do not subordinate themselves totheir superior castes (Kshatriya and. Brahmin castes). In fact,the middle level dominant castes today try to climb up in thesocio-economic hierarchy and reach the level of the uppercastes not through Sanskritization (subordination) but throughconfrontation with them and intimidation of the lowest orthe untouchable castes (Ram 1995: 288). It is altogether adifferent matter that a few scholars (see for instance, *llaiah*1996) call these castes as Shudras or Bahujans and putting boththe Dalits and the Shudras together, as Dalit-Bahujans on thebasis of their imagined· unity or homo-equalis.

Secondly, it is interesting to note here that being fully aware of the political nuances and the rhetoricof the conceptof equality prevailing throughout the world in general andIndia in particular, Ambedkar conceived in 1927 the notion ofequality or social equality as an absolute term and began toarticulate its principles from a vantage point where ever itwas most needed for the Dalits - the worst victims ofthecaste inequality and other kinds of inequalities as well. In theprocess, he was also perhaps responding to the liberal'sarticulation of equality wherein it was conceived at thenotional level and was based on the worth of a person. Thatis why he stated, "If the principle of equality means thatprivilege should depend, not on birth, wealth, or anythingelse, but solely on the merits of each man, then how can it bedemanded that a man without merit, and who is dirty andvicious, should be treated on a level with a man who has meritand is clean and virtuous? Such is a counter-question sometimes posed. It is essential to define equality as giving equalprivileges to men of equal merit" (Ambedkar 1994:61).

One may be tempted to view here Ambedkar'sunderstanding of equality in relation to Alexis de Tocqueville'sand John Stuart Mill's notion of 'equality of conditions' whichmust be created by teaching the community that "wealth, fame,and power are the rewards of labour, that great success standsat the utmost range of long desires, and that nothing lastingis obtained except by toil" (de Tocqueville 1974: 80-81). Such'equality of conditions", in Mill's view, may produce both equalfreedom and servitude besides producing a populargovernment (Mill 1994: IX). But without referring to both deTocqueville and Mill in his writings, Ambedkar went a stepfurther and said, "But before people have had an opportunityto develop their inherent qualities and to merit privileges, itis just to treat them all equally'(Ambedkar 1994: 61). Thismeans, he was also conceiving, at this stage, of equality to beevolved in the Indian society which could stick to a singleprinciple of equality among the people irrespective of birth orlineage and then to provide equal opportunity to eachindividual to acquire merit and privileges.

One thing is clear that he conceived, by this time, the notionof equality in reference to caste system and, as stated above,he pleaded for sticking to one caste and one principle ofequality only. In other words, there should be only one castebased on a single principle (and not on many principles) oftreating all men (and women) equally before their inhering ofworth or quality or varying nature and degree. This, in a way,puts him in the category of few social reformers particularlyfrom Maharashtra and some parts of South India who hadlaid emphasis on 'one caste, one well'. Also, he advocatedequality among groups (castes) along with equality amongindividuals. Another interesting point to mention here is thathe perhaps conceived of equality in a broad sense and-that iswhy he made no mention at all, at that point in time, of libertyand fraternity, that is social, justice. We shall come to this alittle later.

However, exactly nine years later in 1936, he conceived ofequality in a much more elaborate form and on a wider plane,particularly outside the Hindu society. In the ambit of Hindusociety or social system, he suggested that a new doctrinalbasis be given to the Hindu religion if the former was to be inconsonance with equality, liberty, and fraternity or democracy.He held this as being practically outside the Hindu belief system,though he had not officially or publicly denounced Hinduismby that time. Though he stood by his earlier reference to equalityas proclaimed by the French National Assembly of 1789, healso accepted the notion of equality as an inherent part of atrinity consisting, besides it, of liberty and fraternity. Hereferred to this in responding to a self-posed question about hisconception of an ideal society in his undelivered butsimultaneously published Presidential Speech under the titleAnnihilation of Caste (1936) and now included in his Dr.Babasaheb Ambedkar: Writings and Speeches, Volume 1 (1979). There, he took note of inequality among men (and women) onthe basis of their physical or biological heredity and socialinheritance or endowment in the form of parental care,education and their own individual efforts. But then he asked,"Shall we treat them unequal because they are unequal?" Andhe answeredby saying that from the individual's point ofview, that was to be so. But in that case equality, in his opinion,would remain confined only among those who were privilegedand it would not percolate down to the underprivileged ones.This was in a way similar to his argument made earlier in 1927. Yet, he pleaded for an expansion or widening the horizon ofequality in which each and every one should be provided asmuch incentive as possible to develop one's social, economicand political power (Ambedkar 1979: 57-58).

The pursuit of equality, in his opinion, was inevitable foranother reason also. He said, "A Statesman (who advocatesequality among all men and women) is concerned with vastnumbers of people. Hehas neither the time nor the knowledgeto draw fine distinctions (among men on the basis of variousattributes) and to treat each equitably, ie., according to needor according to capacity. Howeverdesirable or reasonable anequitable treatment of men may be, humanity is not capableofassortment and classification. The Statesman, therefore,must follow some rough and ready rule and that rough andready rule is to treat all men alike not because they are alikebut becauseclassification and assortment is impossible. Thedoctrine of equality is glaringly fallacious but taking all in allit is the only way a Statesman can proceed in politics which isa severely practical affair and which demands a severelypractical test" (Ibid: 58).

Here, he was perhaps hinting at some incipient policyframework which was to be evolved to achieve equalitybetween the privileged and the underprivileged. Though hedid not say it in so many words, it later became the guidingprinciple of framing the Constitution for free India and forincorporating in it the provisions of the Fundamental Rightsof Individual and the Directive Principles for the State Policy,besides serving as Preamble to the Indian Constitution. In theidiom of equality or social equality, to be precise, these twotypes of provisions in the Constitution have beentermed'equality as a right' and 'equality as a policy' (Beteille1992:192-214). In other words, equality provided under the sectionon Fundamental Rights is the individual's right to equalityand the equality accorded by the Directive Principles of theState Policy to some groups or communities of the individualsunder some specific policy or policies to be evolved for thepurpose is equality as a policy or principle. These two typesof equality have also been termed horizontal and vertical, andformal and substantive equality. More precisely, equalityguaranteed under Articles 14, 15, and 44 of the Constitutionis the formal ensuring of the horizontal equality to all citizensacross their caste, class, creed and gender. Similarly, Articles15(4) 16(4), 29, 30(2), 39(A), 46, 330, 331, 335 etc. promotevertical equality of certain categories of people with those ofhigher castes and classes by providing them special benefitsor concessions. Hence, these promote substantive equality (fordetails, see Galanter 1991: 379-93). However, what Ambedkarconceived of equality, at that stage, was much beyond whatBeteille (Op. cit.) has termed 'equality as policy' or Mill andde Tocqueville had called 'equality of conditions' to be createdfor having equal say in the political governance of a countryor society. In fact, unlike Mill and de Tocqueville, Ambedkarpleaded for creating 'equality of conditions' through evolvingcertain policy for realizing equality or social equality amongmen (and women) of all castes and communities.

The other source-materials wherein Ambedkar gave hisreflections on equality are Volumes 3 and 4 of his Writings andSpeeches published posthumously in 1987. Although it is notclear when he had actually written these manuscripts, in achapter entitled "Essential Principles of the Hindu Social Order"included in Volume 3, Ambedkar replied to the critics of equalityand endorsed the view that inequalities among human beingswere the results of the traditional institutional prescriptions.With the functioning of the initial few years of the constitutionalprovisions relating to equality, he became aware of limitationseven of the democratic institutions. He therefore stated, "TheDeclaration of Independence does not assert that all men (andwomen) are equal, it only proclaims that they are 'createdequal' (1987a: 97). In fact, he added at this stage the dimension of 'morality' to equality which, in his opinion, was located inthe ethical value in which equality was to be understoodetymologically. He said that moral equality " denied that superiorphysical strength has a moral right to kill, eat, or oppress humanbeings merely because it is superior. To talents and wealth, theideal of moral equality makes a similar denial of right. And indeed, few can imagine themselves that to have superiorphysical strength, talents and wealth will withhold inferiorsfrom all moral rights" (Ibid). No doubt, this has nowunconditionally been accepted by all modern societies in theworld, which greatly redounds to his credit.

Civil and Political Liberty

Liberty is another aspect of his scheme of thought whichhad highly been debated in the classical political theory in theWest, especially in Europe, during the eighteenth andnineteenth centuries. Disagreeing with the consensual positionon classical utilitarianism - 'maximizing the happiness andminimizing the pains' or the greatest happiness of the greatestnumber of those affected by human actions and socialinstih1tions (an approach developed by Jeremy Bentham, 1789,1907; David Hume, 1739; J.S. Mill 1859, 1861, etc. thoughwithout referring to their writings), Ambedkar accepted in1936 the term liberty not only "in the sense of a right to freemovement, in the sense of a right to life and limb" but also"in the sense of a right to property, tools and materials asbeing necessary for earning a living to keep the body in duestate of health". More than that he accepted it in the sense ofmaking "an effective and competent use of person's power"and choosing one's profession (1979: 57). One may agree withthe view that Ambedkar's conception of liberty was attunedto the temporal conceptuality wherein the Untouchables orthe Dalits did not enjoy liberty or freedom not only in making use of their worth but also in selecting the profession of theirchoice.

Then, he later expanded his understanding or horizon ofliberty, and classified it into two civil liberty and political, liberty. In civil liberty, he included liberty of movement orfreedom from arrest without any process of law, liberty ofspeech including liberty of thought, reading, writing ana.discussion, and, finally, liberty of action. Civil liberty, in hisopinion, is essential and fundamental. It is a necessary conditionfor intellectual, moral, political and social progress of humanbeings. It makes individual free from exploitation,suppression, unemployment, poverty and so forth (1978a: 98).But ironically, civil liberty at the practice level in India hasremained confined to the movement for freedom from arrestand confinement without completing properly the legalprocedure. The movements organized, from time to time, indifferent parts of country for civil liberty have, in fact, ignoredother aspects such as liberty of thought, reading, writing,action, etc. Had Ambedkar been alive, he would not haveeasily dispensed with the reductionist pursuance of liberty orcivil liberty. Instead, he would have laid emphasis on itspursuance in totality, i.e., liberty of individual fromexploitation and suppression or oppression, of any sort, fromunemployment, poverty, etc.

Further, "Political liberty", in Ambedkar's opinion,"consists of individual's right to share in the framing of lawsand in the making and unmaking of governments". But whathas happened all along in Independent India is that the peoplehave right (though by proxy till recently in the case of weakersections of society), through their representatives, to maketheir governments and even laws to govern themselves asper the constitutional provisions. Yet, they do not have rightto unmake or dethrone their governments if these do notperform well nor protect them. Moreover, they on their owndo not have right to make or unmake a government; rather, itis the state machinery which creates conditions enabling themto avail themselves of such right - a purely political right ofexercising their adult-franchise. Anyway, in Ambedkar'sopinion, "Political liberty is really a deduction from theprinciple of human personality and equality ....Once thesacredness of human personality is admitted, the necessity ofliberty, equality and fraternity must be admitted as the properclimate for the development of personality" (1987a: 98-99). But for the real liberty, certain conditions, in his opinion, arerequired and these conditions are social equality, economicsecurity and knowledge or information to be made availableto all (1987a: 38-39). Quoting Harold Laski in his critique of"Philosophy of Hinduism" in volume 3 he said, "The moreequal are the social rights of citizens, the more able they areto utilize their freedom ...." or liberty (Ibid: 39). Suchconception of liberty has found its full expression in the IndianConstitution where it has clearly been spelt out in the formsof liberty of thought, expression, belief, faith and worship(see, the Preamble to the Constitution of India).

Fraternity vs. Democracy

The pivot around which his philosophy or ideology movesis fraternity which incidentally at present has not drawn muchattention of the planners, policy makers and the people atlarge. A few scholars also, who have recently shown interestin the study of Ambedkar's thought and philosophy, haveundermined the importance of fraternity in his system ofthought. This is because fraternity primarily requires sheddingaway of one's preoccupations, pretentions and self-interestor self-centerdness. Generally speaking, fraternity is acceptedin the sense of democracy. But for Ambedkar, it is more than a mere political democracy based on uniform opinion ofnumerical strength of the population. It is " a mode of associatedliving, of conjoint communicated experience" (Ambedkar 1979:57). He further stated, "It is essentially an attitude of respectand reverence towards fellow-men" (Ibid).

His. Suchunderstanding, in 1936, of fraternity got expanded later whenhe said, "Fraternity is a force of opposite character. Fraternityis another name for fellow feeling. It consists in a sentimentwhich leads an individual to identify himself (or herself) withthe good of others. ..... Individualism (individual's self-centredness)would produce anarchy. It is only fraternitywhich prevents it and helps to sustain the moral order amongmen" (1987a: 44).

Thus, in his conception of fraternity, Ambedkartranscended not only the individual vis-a-vis equality butindividualism as practiced in the capitalist societies because,in his opinion, the latter is an intimate attribute of an individualwhich takes him or her away from the natural endowment offellow feeling. Contrarily, his conception of individualismanchored in societal well-being along with that of theindividual and is much sounder than a conception where it isegotism a passionate and exaggerated love of oneself and "isa mature and calm feeling, which disposes each member ofthe community to sever himself from the mass of his fellowcreatures,and to draw apart with his family and friends, sothat, after he has thus formed a little circle of his own, hewillingly leaves society at large to itself" (de Toucqueville 1974: 118).

Taking the discussion further, we may refer here to twoscholars namely Louis Dumont and Andre Beteille who havewritten on this issue in the recent years. Locating a man bothin traditional and modern societies, Dumont, for instance,views him as a "collective man" - a part whole in the former

and an 'elementary man' - 'a biological being and a thinkingsubject' in the later types of society. In fact, the later type ofsociety, for him, is the means and the life of each man orindividual is the end (Dumont 1974:9). The pursuance of suchend by the individual leads him to individualism as againstholism. Beteille, on the other hand, in an essay entitled"Individualism and Equality" (1986) accepts individualism asa value in a given society and concentrates more on itsrelationship with equality. Yet, in another place he states, "When we say that individualism is a value in a given society,we mean that its people hold the individual to be as importantas, or more important than, clan, caste, estate, race or nation,and they act in ways which enable us to infer that they assignhim such significance. With something as large asindividualism, however, it becomes evident that even in thesame society people hold divergent beliefs and act in divergentways" (Beteille 1992: 217). But these divergent beliefs and ways or acts of individuals or people, in Ambedkar's opinion,need not contravene that of others and are to be largely inconsonance with that of collectivity or society which, in noway, is to override the individuals. In fact, in the third phaseof his articulation of equality or social equality, Ambedkarplaced individual as the basic unit in the new scheme of thingsto be pursued in the independent Indian State and society(see, The Constituent Assembly Debates, 1950:39).

Retrospectively, Ambedkar's idea of fraternity is,however, to be located neither in social subordination andsuper-ordination nor in political mobilization. It is also not tobe seen in an artificial closeness through charity orphilanthropic gestures or contextual compulsion between therich and the poor. But it is necessarily to be located in.cooperation and co-existence in which one cares for others. Inhis own understanding, "The word fraternity is not anadequate expression. The proper term is what the Buddhacalled Maitree" or friendship (Ambedkar 1987b: 283). Thus,he himself traced the root of fraternity in religion, not magicbut Dharma, which not only teaches equality, liberty andfraternity among all human beings but ensures and practicesthese without any conditionality. More precisely, he acceptedfraternity as "the disposition of an individual to treat men asobject of reverence and love and the desire to be in unity withhis fellow beings" (1987a: 97). Further, in his opinion,"Fraternity strengthens socialities and gives to each individuala stronger personal interest in practically consulting the welfareof others. It leads him to identify his feelings more and morewith their good, or at least with an even greater degree ofpractical consideration for it. With the disposition to fraternity, he comes as though instructively to be conscious of himself asbeing one who of course pays regard to others. The good ofothers becomes to him a thing naturally and necessarily to beattended to like any of physical conditions of our existence"(1987a: 97-98).

His conception of fraternity is, thus, much more broad-based and abstract than Dumont's (1974: 232) conception ofholism of 'man as a collective being, man as a society' ofhierarchy or hierarchical order of traditional values, ideas,etc. In fact, in Ambedkar's frame of thought fraternity is all pervasive and it is to be attended to at all cost, if a society hasto advance in forward direction with proper well-being of itsindividual members. Such a concept of fraternity, forAmbedkar, is far beyond individualism but is inclusive ofequality of individuals where each individual is an independententity and treats other individuals on the same level; and bothare related to each other on the fraternal basis.

Then, coming heavily on pseudo-democracy, Ambedkarstated that true democracy was the mental disposition ofindividuals; it was the trait of a human personality. In hisown words, "Democracy is more than a political (voting)machine. It is even more than a social system. It is an attitudeof mind or a philosophy of life" (1987b: 283). Thus,Ambedkar's understanding of democracy is much deeper andmore conscientious than that of de Tocqueville (1974) whoanalyzed democracy as a number game along with civil andpolitical rights of people in the United States of America. It isdifferent matter that India has a long way to go to become atrue democracy envisioned by Ambedkar.

Social Justice vs. Distributive Justice

Justice is another term which Ambedkar occasionally usedin his writings and speeches. In the contemporary debate onjustice vs. merit, the term justice or social justice has becomealmost an oft-repeated political cliche. It appears from theusage that justice is something which is totally opposed to theindividual's merit and efficiency, and is to be accorded to thecollectivity of those individuals who are endowed with lessor almost no merit and efficiency. It is also conceived in thesense of welfare of these individuals, and not necessarily inthe sense of promoting and ensuring merit and efficiencyamong them.

We take note here of Ambedkar's conception of justice atthe end of his scheme of thought on justice and equality notbecause of any less value attached to it by him but because ofits fewer occurrence in his writings and speeches on the subjectunder reference, as stated at the outset. In fact, going by thechronological usage of the term in his writings and speeches,one finds that he had not introduced the term justice or socialjustice in his discourse upto 1936. Nor had he touched upon,by this time, the inter-relationship of the trinity of equality,liberty and fraternity. There are, however, two specificcontexts in which he used this term; in the Preamble, to theIndian Constitution (if the credit is given to him for framing,piloting and vindicating the Draft Constitution) and in hisreflections on the Philosophy of Hinduism (Volume 3 of hisWritings and Speeches). In the Preamble, he used the termwith more elaborate connotations of social, economic andpolitical justice. In his later writings, he used it in a somewhatabstract form. Here, he endorsed that "the principle of justiceis a compendious one and includes most of other principleswhich have become the foundation of a moral order. Justicehas always evoked the ideas of equality, of proportion and of"compensation" .... In short, justice is simply another nameof liberty, equality and fraternity" (1987a: 25).

It is, thus, clear why Ambedkar. did not frequently usethe term justice or social justice in his reflections on the subject.It is also clear that justice is not merely a dole or the Statepatronagegiven to the most needy ones. Instead, inAmbedkar's understanding, it is a proportional compensationsocial, economic and political for the loss suffered both in thepast and in the present time to those for whom justice needsto be accorded. This, in a way, is the precise but limited sensein which he used the term justice. It is this meaning of justicewhich is 110w being forwarded by the more socially andpolitically conscious and articulate sections of the Dalits andthc Other Backward Castes or Classes in different parts ofthe country. But, for Ambedkar, the term justice has also abroader and more essential connotation of realizing equality,liberty and fraternity, as stated above. In other words, justicefor him means evolving an altogether new type of society orsocial order which is a more difficult proposition in view ofthe present socio-political scenario in the country. However, itdoes not lessen the epistemological importance of the termjustice or social justice which, in turn, provides incentives tothe State, society and the individual to pursue the goal ofachieving social justice more vigorously and competently.

Yet, it is necessary to mention two things here: one,Ambedkar used the term 'justice' only, whereas in the present-day socio-political discourses the more frequently used termis 'social justice'. Since the term justice appears in social,economic and political domains in the Preamble to the IndianConstitution, this means, justice or social justice (the term socialis used in the generic sense here) is to be accorded, at thesubstantive level, to the people in general and the weakersections the most needy ones, in particular in their social,economic and political life. Two, justice is also often used withthe modifier 'distributive' and hence, the term 'distributivejustice'. We may see here whether these two-social justice anddistributive justice connote the meanings similar to or differentfrom the meaning in which Ambedkar used the term justice. We have already seen above that Ambedkar used the termjustice in two sense - in the sense of equality and in the senseof 'proportional compensation'. In fact, compensatingproportionately the loss is also, in a way, providing someamount of equality to the victim of any loss through somemechanism to be evolved for the purpose. This n1cessarilymeans distribution of justice; hence, distributive justice withthe specific purpose of realizing, if not in full then at least tosome degree, or equality between the loser and the gainer.

Before entering into the contemporary discourse ondistributive justice and trying to locate retrospectivelyAmbedkar's views therein, a point needs to be mentioned herethat he was of the firm opinion that justice or social justicewas completely absent in pre-Independence India. UnlikeDumont's (1986) arguments about traditional justice – justiceaccorded by the traditional caste panchayat (council) and theofficial justice -justice accorded by the State through its variousorgans (see, pp. 315-343), Ambedkar found justice completelymissing in the unequal social order in the pre-IndependenceIndian society particularly in the Hindu social system at boththe doctrinal and substantive levels. Hence, he articulatedforcefully about justice or social justice and got it enshrined inthe Preamble to the Indian constitution which is not only itsguiding principle but is now the inherent and integral part ofits body-text. In the case of distributive justice, what isimportant in the time and space (Smith 1994: 25) i.e., when andwhere justice is distributed. But what is still more importantis to understand who distributes justice to whom when, andhow much. In other words, what is theoptimal limit uptowhich justice is and can be distributed. The answers to thesequestions are already located in Ambedkar's frame ofthoughts, reflected in his writings and speeches and in thespecific sections of the Indian Constitution.

It is, however, pertinent to examine briefly therepresentative theoretical expositions - Rawlsian andDwarkinian which are in high currency in the contemporarydiscourse on justice or distributive justice. Keeping aside thedetails of these expositions, we may refer here to the essenceor gist of arguments and then try to see retrospectively howthese are similar to or different from those of Ambedkar.Accepting inequalities as given (created or to be created bythe State) and tolerable provided these were to work to thebenefit of the most disadvantaged and advocating 'fair equalityof opportunity' to correct arbitrary inequalities by rejectingmeritocracy, John Rawls (1972, see also 1969) lays emphasison the relationship between equality, liberty and fraternity asthe cornerstone of a just society or social order. In this regard,his argument is quite similar to that of Ambedkar. But thedifference between the positions of Ambedkar and the Rawlson this issue is that whereas the former accepts the existingsocial order as unequal and unjust and, thus he envisions anew just social order, the latter accepts (an inference here) thecontemporary social institutions as just in a 'well-orderedsociety' where its members, with a strong sense of justice,follow the existing rules. Rawls' theoretical premise appearsto be based on the emergent social situations in the wake ofthe Civil Rights Movements, liberation of Blacks, equal rightsfor minorities, issues or social justice incorporated in policyformulations and their execution, etc. specially in the UnitedStates of America. Further, for distributive justice, he relieson fair procedure and social cooperation of the rational personsfor producing the fair result. While the fair or perfectprocedure, in his opinion, is to be worked out, the socialcooperation is to be based on 'reciprocity, mutual benefit andmutual respect" of 'free and equal persons' (Rawls 1985). Yet,what makes Ambedkar's understanding of justice or evendistributive justice quite distinctive from that of Rawls is thatsuch persons are not only deemed to be rational but moralalso and, thus, investing the whole society with a moral andjust social order.

Justice or social justice is both concomitant and antecedentof rights which are to be achieved either through assertion ordistribution or even through inheritance. But if rights are tobe read as social justice, these may be achieved only throughassertion or distribution. Even assertion for achieving rightsvis-a-vis social justice leads to distribution of resources andopportunities. Hence, for Dwarkin (1977), 'Justice as fairness'to the persons is based on the theory of rights which proposesthat it is a fundamental right of persons to (have) equal respectand consideration in the design of the institution that governthem' (cf. Sushila 1996:37). In fact, for Dwarkin, justice notonly leads to equality but also provides rights to the people to have equal resources or equal access to the resources(Dwarkin 1981). He treats social, economic and politicalconditions as an "egalitarian plateau," under which membersof a community or society have to have equal rights and arealso to be treatedequal. Taking the Rawlsian concept of 'socialminimum' and its role (Rawls 1972: 276-7, 284-6) at theimplementation level, Dwarkin (1981) argues that the "socialminimum' is to be fairly as well as highly guaranteed so thatthe people may start off with equal resources. So also, theirsocial handicap, lack of talent and even natural resources maybe socially dealt with. Then, locating Ambedkar's position onboth justice vis-a-vis rights, there could not be any divergencebetween his position and that of Dwarkin, except that theformer endorses the right of assertion or assertive right toequality as well as right to have equal or egalitarian distributionof resources and opportunities. Not only that but new social,economic and political conditions (Dwarkin's 'egalitarianplateau'), for Ambedkar, are to be created as envisioned byhim in his 'new social order' (See, his Writings and Speeches,Volumes 1 and 3).

Social Justice: An integrated Coherence ofEquality, Liberty andFraternity

This brings us to think of sequentiality or sequentialordering, if there could be any of equality, liberty andfraternity - the three essential principles of Ambedkar'sideology or philosophy. In this regard, one may be temptedto go at least for one such sequentiality or sequential orderingespecially in event of significance or value being attached toand emphasis placed on them in the present time. It is a known fact that equality in its form of equal opportunity or equalaccess to opportunity is currently emphasized by the Dalitsand the Other Backward Classes or Castes. The articulationof justice has become synonymous with this form of equality.Similarly, liberty particularly civil liberty is championed bycertain voluntary groups and organizations but the politicalliberty hls already been attained with the adoption of theuniversal adult-franchise, though this fact cannot be overlookedthat some vulnerable sections of rural population have beenprevented till recently from exercising their right to vote atthe national as well as grassroot level. Even a sizable sectionof the urban middle-class people do not enjoy political libertybestowed on them by not exercising their franchise. So also,there .is a huge population of children who are treated asminors, and hence deprived of franchise, and eventually ofthe political democracy. In the process, fraternity has beendowngraded or in the most equated with political democracywhich is beset with its own problems of lack of full andcommitted participation by the people.

Then going by their practical usage, a sequential orderingmay exist in the formof equality (justice), fraternity and liberty.This may be so from the vantage point of the Dalits and theOther Backward Castes or Classes. But, from the non-Dalitsvantage point, the sequential ordering may be in the form ofliberty, fraternity (democracy) and equality (justice), In otherwords, the deprived groups of people concentrate theirattention more on equality or social justice than on fraternityand liberty whereas the privileged ones give more importanceto liberty and political democracy than to equality, justice orsocial justice and fraternity.

But in Ambedkar' s scheme of thoughts, there could notbe any sequential order or hierarchical ranking of justice,equality, liberty and fraternity as stated at the outset. So also,this cannot be inferred from the specific contexts in whichthese concepts have been used by him either separately ortogether. In other words, sometimes he uses liberty first, andequality and fraternity afterwards, and at other times, he usesfraternity first and then equality and liberty. He has donethis in view of the specific reference to his discussion relatedto either of these terms. But in all these cases, he has laidemphasis on their interrelationship. Such relationship betweenequality, liberty and fraternity, for Ambedkar, is wellintegratedin a coherent manner irrespective of their beingplaced in any order. He says, "some equate democracy(fraternity) with equality and liberty. Equality and liberty areno doubt the deepest concern of Democracy. But the moreimportant question is what sustains equality and liberty? Somewould say that it is the law of the State which sustains equalityand liberty. This is not a true answer. What sustains equalityand liberty is fellow - feeling (fraternity.... " (1987b: 283). Then he goes further and says, "Without fraternity, libertywould destroy equality and equality would destroy liberty.If in Democracy liberty does not destroy equality and equalitydoes not destroy liberty, it is because at the basis of boththere is fraternity. Fraternity is therefore the root ofDemocracy" (Ibid).

We wish to add, at this stage, one more dimension toAmbedkar's understanding of equality, liberty, fraternity andjustice particularly at the level of their relationship. Here, wehave gone in a way a little further in our reflections on hisconception of equality, liberty and fraternity and theirinterrelationship. This we have done in an essay entitled"Situating Ambedkar in the contemporary Period"(See Ram1995). It has been stated therein that Ambedkar's ideas ofequality, liberty and fraternity which constitute the core ofhis ideology or philosophy are to be accepted in the form of atrinity. In this trinity all the three, though conceptuallyautonomous entities, are well-integrated and they functionwithin the frame of the overriding principle of justice or socialjustice. But this trinity in itself is not a static entity. Rather, itis a dynamic one and it changes with time and space. In otherwords, as society witnesses inevitable changes through timeand space, and so also, the connotations of equality, libertyand fraternity together with justice may correspondinglychange, thus, making their trinity dynamic or ever changing, but this is a subject which requires altogether a separatediscussion. Yet, what can be said here is that, amidst thecontemporary discourses on equality, liberty, fraternity ordemocracy and justice or distributive justice, Ambedkar' s ideason these are still distinctive and have an increasing relevancenot only in India but also elsewhere in the world.

Conclusion

It is beyond doubt that Ambedkar's ideas and thoughtson equality and social justice vis-a-vis his articulation of thesame are relevant not only for contemporary Indian Societybut societies the world over. Although he articulated these ata critical point in time namely the formation of a modernsociety in India, but the fact remain that his above mentionedideas, in some ways, are qualitatively different and are to betaken to the logical end. This is to be done in view of the factthat an integrated coherence of equality, liberty, fraternityor, in a _word, social justice in each and every sphere, of life isthe ultimate aim not only of all ideologies but also of thenumerous ongoing processes of change in different spheresof life. These have ultimately to result into a uniform societyor social order which every society in the world tends toestablish in due course.

REFERENCES

Ambedkar, B.R. (1979), 'Annihilation of Caste' in *Dr. BabasahebAmbedkar: Writing and Speeches*, Vol.1, Govt. of Maharashtra,Bombay, pp. 23-96. (First published in 1936).

Ambedkar, B.R. (1987a), 'Philosophy of Hindusm" and "The HinduSocial Order-Its Essential Principles' (unpublished writings) in*Dr. Babasaheb Ambedkar: Writings and Speeches*, Vol 3, pp.3-115.

Ambedkar, B.R. (1987b), 'Brahma is not Dharma: What good isBrahma' (Riddle No.22) in his "Riddles in Hinduism"(unpublished writings) in *Dr. Babasaheb Ambedkar: Writingsand Speeches*, Vol 4, pp. 281-87.

Ambedkar, B.R. (1994), *Dr. Ambedkar's Speech at Mahad* (Dec. 25, 1927)in Status of Dalits. Lal Bahadur Shastri National Academy ofAdministration, Mussoorie, pp. 56-61 (translated from Marathiby ChangdeoKhairmode and Ramesh Chandra Sirkar)

Bentham, Jeremy (1789), *An Introduction to the Principles of Morals andLegislation*, Payne, London (republished in 1907)

Beteille, Andre (1986), 'Individualism and Equality', *CurrentAnthropology*, Vol. 27, No.2, pp. 121-128

Beteille, Andre (1992), 'Equality as a Right and as a Policy' in hisSociety and Politics in India - *Essays in Comparative Perspective*.Oxford University Press, Delhi, pp. 192-94.

De Tocqueville, A. (1974), *Democracy in America*, Vol. IISchockenBooks, New York (the English translation appeared in 1840).

Dumont, Louis (1974), *Homo-Hierarchicus: The Caste System and itsImplications*. Vikas, Delhi

Dumont, Louis (1986), *A South Indian Subcaste: Social Organisationand Religion of the PramalalKallar*. Oxford University Press, Delhi.

Dwarkin, Ronald (1977), *Taking Rights Seriously*. Harvard UniversityPress, Maharashtra.

Dwarkin, Ronald (1981), "What is Equality", *Philosophy and PublicAffairs*, Vol. 10, pp. 185-246, 283-345.

Galanter, Marc (1991), *Competing Equalities: Law and the Backward Classes in India*. Oxford University Press, Delhi.

Hume, David (1739), *A Treatise of Human Nature* (Republished in1960).

Ilaiah, Kancha (1996), *Why I am not a Hindu?*Samya, Calcutta

Marx, Karl (1948), *Communist Manifesto*. Progress Publications,Moscow.

Mill, John Stuart (1859), *On Liberty*. London (republished in 1974).

Mill, John Stuart (1861), *Utilitarianism*. London.

Mill, John Stuart (1974), "Introduction" to A. de Tocqueville's*Democracy in America*.

Ram, Nandu (1995), *Beyond Ambedkar: Essays on Dalits in India*. Har-AnandPublications, New Delhi, pp. 45-85.

Rao, M.S.A. (1987), *Social Movements and Social Transformation: A Studyof Two Backward Classes Movements in India*. Manohar New Delhi.

Rawls, John (1969), 'Distributive Justice' in P. Laselett and W.Q.Runciman (eds.) *Politics and Society-IIIrd series*. Basil Blackwell,Oxford.

Rawls, John (1972), *A Theory of Justice*. Oxford University Press Oxford.

Rawls, John (1985), *'Justice as Fairness: Political Nor Metaphysical, Philosophy and Public Affairs*, Vol. 14, pp. 223-251.

Smith, David M. (1994), *Geography and Social Justice*. Blackwell,Oxford.

Sushila R. (1990), *Liberty, Equality and Social Justice*: Rawl's Political Theory. Ajanta Publications, New Delhi.

Srinivas, M.N. (1986), *Social Change in Modern India*. AlliedPublishers, Bombay.

4

Marginalised Groups and the State of Human Rights in India

Generally speaking, human rights are those rights which are the most needed for every human-being irrespective of race or caste or ethnic affiliation, gender, age, creed and so forth. These rights of the people are related to their protection from discrimination and exploitation, promotion of their personality and interests, accordance of justice and equality, and restoration of dignity and respect. People equipped with better resources have better remained traditionally exploited, degraded and deprived of their access to the existing socio-economic resources need the human rights to be accorded to them by the State or society of which they are the inherent part. In a way, these are the people who are members of certain groups or strata which can easily be identified in a graded or hierarchical system of any society and more so in a developing society like that of India. These identified groups or strata may be termed as marginalised groups or strata on the basis of their minimal or least access to the existing socio-economic resources and power or authority.

We shall broadly identify, in this paper, some of the marginalised groups or strata in Indian society and analyse the basis or bases of their being marginalised.

We shall also examine the types of human rights most needed to them. We shall take an overview of the progress made, in this direction, by both the State and society in India. And finally, we shall suggest some ways and means for proper accord of human rights to the marginalise groups and strata, and for elimination of their marginalised status in Indian society.

I

Marginality and the Marginalised Groups in India

Before examining a working definition of marginality of marginal groups and strata, it is imperative to look at a phrase like "marginal man". This is, however, not merely a phrase but the existential location of person either in social structural system or in the cultural and emotional organisation of a society. Such person is practically located 'outside' a group or strata of which he or she happens to be member either by ascription or achievement. This may be so as such person does not conform to the norms prescribed by his or her "in-group" or the strata. But such person may also be marginal in event of his or her being conformist to the "out-group" (not being member of the group by birth) but not being fully accepted in it (Merton 1968: 316-25). In such situation, marginality of a man leads him to live with a "dual personality" or a "double consciousness". Living with two cultures or cultural traditions, he remain a "cultural hybrid" (Stonequist 1961: 145). Whether such person overcomes his marginality through the process of anticipatory socialisation or reference groups behaviour (Merton 1968) is not our immediate concern here.

More specifically, we are concerned here with marginality of groups, both corporate groups with ascriptive status such as caste and non-corporate groups-those formed with persons across the ascriptive status groups. These groups have been extensively studied in sociology and social anthropology. Usually, a group whether corporate or non-corporate with a specific culture or having its own cultural area or boundary is socially and culturally located either in the centre-mainstream (Oommen 1986: 53-74) or at the periphery. A group with its culture located at the periphery is a culturally marginal or marginalised group as it does not enjoy the same esteem as the one which is located in the centre. Such group also suffers from multiple forms of social, cultural or religious, economic and power deprivations. In other words, its access to these avenues is much less in comparison to that of the group of the former type. The access of some corporate groups to such avenues or resources is minimal or almost negligible. Cases of the Scheduled Castes an Scheduled Tribes may be cited here.

This leads us to say that the marginality of groups varies in nature and degree. It ranges from minimal t maximal in which the degree of marginality of the non-corporate groups may be less than that of the corporate groups or strata or communities with ascriptive status. Also, if the corporate groups are consisted of those castes or 'ethnie' or ethnic identities which have remained either traditionally stigmatised or physically isolated, their marginality in any of the aforesaid senses would be much more than those which are otherwise. "Depending upon degree of association of marginal (groups) with or dissociation from the "out group" (here consisting of social and cultural mainstream, power or material resources, etc.) there may be persons (and groups) who will be less marginal with more chances of getting accepted in the "out group", or others may be more marginal with little chance of acceptance in the aspired group. Accordingly, the level of their marginality can be found from the degree of their association with or dissociation from the "in-group" also" (Ram 1995: 205). Needless to say, then that the overcoming of marginality or such corporate groups or corporate status groups is much more difficult than that of the non-corporate groups.

Without going into other details of marginality and marginalisation (a process of being marginalised), it is necessary here to identify some groups, both corporate status (the stigmatised strata or communities) and non-corporate groups (social categories or strata drawn from non-stigmatised communities), which are marginalised in different spheres of life and which are in the most need of protection of their human rights of the various types. The United Nations Commission of Human Rights and the Human Rights Committee have identified certain groups of people all over the world whose human rights they promise to protect. These groups are: women, children, minorities, indigenous people and the refugees-not all of them are corporate groups or corporate status groups. While analysing how these groups are marginalised and need their human rights to be protected, we shall also examine the plausibility of some other groups which are even more vulnerable and which need more protection of their human rights. These groups are Dalits or the Scheduled Castes an Tribes, and the aged people who are marginalised either with their corporate group status or non-corporate groups status but have not drawn attention of both the United Nations Commission of Human Rights and of the National Human Rights Commission in India.

Women as Marginalised group

Women being a little less than half of the total population in India have remained susceptible, till date, to various types of discrimination and exploitation. Having physiological structure different from men and being treated as the most valuable living commodity, they are subjected many a times to sexual harassment and inferior social status. They have been treated unequally in terms of their access to various avenues of life. Hence, they are marginalised group or gender category though they are inherent part of a corporate status group or community which may or may not be marginal marginalised in any of the senses. Their marginality or marginalised status is in comparison to men. It is in this context their human rights need to be protected. However, without contesting marginality of women as a gender category and also a traditionally considered inferior social category, it may be mentioned here that women as such do not constitute a homogenous marginal group. Women are drawn from various hues-there are educated and illiterate; some are socially and politically conscious and articulate but others are subordinated and subdued. The former type of women has produced, in the recent years, a vast body of literature through which they have highlighted the miseries of women as such and have tried to articulate the various types of interests of women to be safeguarded. Needless to say, that a large majority of women live in villages, and slums and squatter settlement in urban areas. Majority of them are illiterate and poor, and are discriminated and exploited. They belong to those corporate status groups or communities which have traditionally remained stigmatised, segregated and isolated. It is these women who are marginalised and susceptible to violation of their human rights. Hence, their human rights-their protection from discrimination and exploitation, their human development, dignity and self-respect need to be protected at all cost.

The world Commissions on status of Women (1946), The United Nations Universal Declarations on Human Rights (1948), the International Covenants on Civil and Political Rights, and on Economic, Social and Cultural Rights (1966), four International women's Conferences held in 1975, 1980, 1985 and 1995, and the UN Decade for Women (1975-85) have declared to protect women against discrimination and exploitation, and promote their equality with men in the pursuits of education, employment, inheritance and owner-ship of property, nationality and suffrage. The latter two have already been accorded to the women in India. In fact, India has already set up a National Commission to protect their rights and promote their social progress, though it has not produced the desired result so far.

Children and their Marginality

Another marginal or marginalised group is of children-the adult and responsible human beings of tomorrow. It may not be possible at this juncture to mention about the total number of children living in the world. But the general impression runs that majority of the children are found in the countries of the third world. According to one estimate, "Overall, perhaps 30million young people are" existing somehow in the slums of Mexico City, Calcutta and New York. Their childhood is "stolen"; often their parents and relatives do not know how best to help them" (Whittaker 1995: 139). In other words, children as a group or social category do not have any political power and their dependence is easily abused by the elders. They suffer from maltreatment, exploitation and even from the basic human rights. Thus, they are marginalised not only in terms of their access to the basic human needs but also in expressing freely their views and getting these properly accepted on the issues vital to them.

Accepting it as it is, it may be remembered that children all over the world are not marginalised in the same way and in the same degree. Instead, their deprivations and marginalised status go along with socio-economic and educational status of their parental family. Children of the better-of families are more comfortable than otherwise. Mention may be made here about the recent trend in a number of in metropolitan cities where children are also consulted in matters relating not only to them but even those pertaining to the whole family. But number of such children and families are very small, and the majority of children both in India and outside are those who are deprived to their access to education, food, health-care, love and affection, development of talent and personality. Hence, they are highly marginalised and their marginality is an inherent part of majority of their parents and also o the corporate status groups or communities which in turn are marginalised.

Children's rights have been protected through a series of resolutions adopted at the international fora. Besides the United Nations' Declaration of the Child (1959) and 1979 as International Year of Child, an International Convention on the Rights of child was held in 1989 in which 139 countries participated and adopted resolution laying " foundation for a system to codify existing laws and tighten new ones: the right to survive, to develop, to be protected and to participate fully in the community" (whittaker 1995 : 140). These rights of children across the world irrespective of their race or caste or ethnic affiliation, colour, sex, language, religion and political opinion (Desta 1994 : 405). In addition to a World Summit for Children convened in New York in 1990, the World Conference on Human Rights organised in Vienna in in 1993 set the target of holding the Children's Convention by 1995 (which had not taken place). Yet, the condition of children of the poor strata specially in third world countries has not improved at all where they are largely deprived of their childhood and in a country like India they continue to work as bonded labour.

The Scheduled Castes

The Dalits or the Scheduled Castes representing about 16 per cent of the total population in India have traditionally suffered from untouchability and numerous forms of discriminations and exploi0tation in social, cultural or religious, economic and political matters. In a word, with their corporate group status being stigmatised for centuries together, they have largely remained below the pollution line and poverty line and have also suffered from gruesome forms of atrocities inflicted by others. Marginality is associated even with their origin as corporate status group or community. In this regard, Jayaram (1993 : 67-68) has referred to two these of their exclusion (relegation) and inclusion (absorption) in the Hindu society. The first thesis though much familiar is termed by Klass (1980) as 'divine plan' theory according to which the Untouchables or the depressed castes initially being integral part of the classical or traditional Hindu society were placed later at the lowest position and were thrown (much later) even out its convention fold of castes or varnas. Hence, their exclusion from the Hindu society. The other thesis, though not much popular in sociology and social anthropology, has been advanced by Ambedlar (1948) according to which the Untouchables were originally broken men (wanderers or unsettled people) – followers of Buddhism who were absorbed in the village Hindu society and assigned marginal status as a result of reconciliation occurred sometimes in the second century, A. D. This latter 'incorporation thesis' (Jayaram 1993 : 68) holds substantial empirical support as their separate hamlets in villages and slums and squatter settlements in cities can easily be seen in all parts of the country.

Thus, their location at the periphery-village outskirt and back lanes and slums in city, their stigmatised corporate group status and practice of untouchability against them, their cultural marginalisation their being upwardly socially mobile though not being fully assimilated in the referent group or strata (Ram 1995 : 200-16), their occupying marginal identity and status even in other religion embraced by them (Jayaram 1993 : 67-80) and over and above their exploitation and unequal access to socio-economic opportunities and political and administrative power – all these either separately or together place them as the most marginalised corporate (status) group or community or strata in the country.

One may argue that in event of constitutional provisions in the form of Protective Discrimination Policy and allied schemes and several other administrative and legal measures under operation for more than last fifty years of so the Scheduled Castes or Dalits have made considerable progress in various walks of life. Hence, they may not be considered as marginalised group(s). True, the Protective Discrimination Policy an dallied schemes different marginalised castes included in the Schedule prepared for the purpose under the Constitution (Scheduled Castes). Order from time to time have benefited from the policy and schemes but the size of this group is very small-say roughly 10 per cent of the total population of the Scheduled Castes. Their vast majority still remains underprivileged and marginalised. Even those benefited from the constitutional provisions and State actions remain relatively marginalised in absence of their equal share in socio-economic resources and power positions. "However, the Scheduled Castes as a whole are regarded marginal in terms of their outcaste image, cultural diversity with structural or positional "inferiority" of their culture and, hence, lack of their full integration (unity) in the Hindu society...." (Ram 1995 : 211). The United Nations Organisation has not paid so far any attention towards them though they are the most vulnerable corporate group in India and are fully qualified for protection of their human rights.

The Scheduled Tribes and Other Indigenous Groups

The Scheduled Tribes of Adivasis in India have remained isolated from the mainstream people for centuries together. They have been virtually located at the periphery –both physical, social and cultural systems. As a result, they have been marginalised in terms of their equal access to education, employment, power and, in a word, the overall development of the country. Like Scheduled Castes, a small of section of tribal people have made considerable progress with the help of the Protective Discrimination Policy and allied schemes but still they remain marginalised in relation to the mainstream people due to their distinct tribal ethnic identity, their continued social and cultural animosity, and prolonged isolation from the mainstream. The vast majority of the tribal people living in different parts of the country remains marginalised even today in almost every spheres of their life. Their marginalised is both qualitatively and quantitatively different from other marginalised groups or strata due to taking away their natural rights over forests and forest resources, continuously being exploited by money lenders and government officials, and thus making them dependent on others even for their human survival.

A controversy has emerged recently over the issue whether tribals in India be considered indigenous people. The specific arguments given against their indigenous group status were based on their not one but numerous groups with distinct nomenclatures, different social moorings, diversified cultural customs, slow disappearance of their animosity and developmental process. Some have gone to the extent of erroneously accepting them as backward Hindus (see for instance, Ghurye 1963 Bose 1961). Notwithstanding, various types of changes occurred among the tribal particularly since independence because of governmental measure, modernisation process and their frequent interaction with caste and community people in different regions in the country. While some of these may be accepted as indications of lessening intensity of their marginalised status, these really do not negate their indigenous origin in the sense that their origin and distinct social-cultural moorings cannot simply be equated even with the most backward people of other castes and communities in the country. Even an international agency like ILO in its Conventions (107 of 1957 and 1969 of 1989) have accepted the tribal or semi-tribal populations in independent countries as indigenous people on account of their descent and social, economic and cultural backwardness (for details, see Roy Burman 1994 : 13-30).

Further, the United Nations has taken note of certain indigenous people, numbering about 300 million persons in different parts of the world. These are: the North American Indians or Red Indians, the Australian Aborigines and the Mooris of New Zealand. Their marginalised status may be attributed to their descent of the "original inhabitants of territory" their unreliable dependence on the patronising goodwill or non-concern of late comers, their being treated as "second-class citizens lacking respect and recognition of inherent rights", and their social, economic and cultural deprivations amidst the process of urbanisation, modernisation, etc. (Whittaker 1995 : 141). If we apply some of these indicators to the tribals of India, we find them being indigenous people in the country. Nevertheless, the UNO had resolved to protect human rights of the indigenous people and declared 1992 as the International Year for the Indigenous People. It has emphasised "the need of their right to preserve, develop and transmit to future generations a sense of ethnic an end to forced integration, eviction and displacement by extensive agriculture and mining concessions. Self-determination was one of the absolute principles of the UN Charter and subsequent legislation" (ibid). This equally applies to the Scheduled Tribes in India whose human rights need to be protected at any cost.

Ethnic and Religious Minorities

One of the major determined or an ethnic or religious community to be considered minority is the numerical number of its adherents or pursuants. This applies to the linguistic minority also, Oommen (199 : 3-11) has talked about six religious minorities in India though all these are not marginalise. These are: marginalised minority (Jains) in cultural and political terms; lionised minority (Sikhs) due to their visible economic prosperity and significant contributions made to the country's developments; duplicitous minority (Buddhists or Neo-Buddhists) in terms of collective assertion, with previous caste identity, for gaining constitutional benefits but otherwise striving to overcome marginalisation and alienation. This equally applies to the minorities like Neo-Christians and Neo-Muslims converted largely from the Dalits. Other minorities are vanishing minority (the Jews) due to substantial decline in the number over all these years; the insulated minority (Parsees or Jorastrians) practising rigorous endogamy and remaining cultural isolate; and intimidated minority

(Bahais) proselytised mostly from the Scheduled Castes and being socially and economically deprived. Members of this last type of minority have adopted a policy of political retreatism. In general parlance, Muslims of India are the largest religious minority in comparison to the Hindu majority though they are marginalised in several ways.

Two points need to be mentioned here. One, mere numerical strength of minority community does not make it a marginalised community or corporate status group as I s evident from religious minorities like Sikhs and Jorastrians. Instead, it is the socio-economic and cultural derivations which make a minority community the marginalised one. The Minority Rights Group- an international organisation accepts a wider connotation of minority and attributes marginalised status to minorities on the basis of their powerlessness (Phillips 1994 : 264-273). Two, the UNO has not yet incorporated in its Charter or any of its Covenants or Conventions the protection of rights of minorities due to resentment of the member countries specially the western ones on account of political reason and internal void or political imbalance. Though the International Convention of 1969 had declared the Elimination of All Forma of Racial Discrimination, all minorities ether in India or in other countries are not racial minorities and they do not always suffer from the racial discrimination. Hence, their human rights against their discrimination of any form, their exploitation and powerlessness need to be protected as emphasised by the Minority Rights Group.

Refugees as Marginal Group

Due to a number civil wars, World War II, war between two nations and partition of a country the number of refugees has gone multiplies during all these decades. Granting the fact that quite a few refugees get rehabilitated in due course, "Throughout all continents there are something like 20 million victims of intolerance, persecution and violence and many thousand more displaced by natural and man-made calamities. Nearly 10,00 people become refugees everyday; their desperation I seen world-wide in newspapers and on television screens.... In international law a refugee is defined as a person who has a well-founded fear of being persecuted (and displaced) in the homeland for reasons of race, religion, nationality, social grouping or political opinion" (Whittaker 1995 : 142). This definition now extended to include those people who are forced to leave their own country due to war and internal civil disorder but it does not take note of those who are refugees in their own country due to internal conflict and displacement due to natural and man-made calamities.

Needless to say that the refugees all over the world are drawn from all races, sexes, ages and countries. They are marginalised groups but their majority belong to the most vulnerable sections or corporate groups or strata of each society. They have, however, been shuttling between the sharing or shifting the burden either by the native country or the host country where they have sought the refuse (for details, see Moussalli 1994 : 338-44; Muntabhorn 1994 : 345-53, and Saxena 1994 : 354-68). The UNO had appointed as early as in 1954 a High Commissioner for Refugees to highlight and resolve their problems and protect their human rights. In had earmarked some budget through its 1993 Vienna Conference. Anyway, the UNO has deliberated on the multiple problems of the refugees and suggested to protect them in three ways: to voluntarily repatriate them to the place of their origin under the favourable condition, to receive them in a host country for a limited period under a determined quota, and to resettle them to start afresh under long-term programmes evolved for the purpose. All the three strategies are in effect related to citizenship status of the refugees and don not pay any attention to protect their social and cultural rights nor to the self-mobilisation or mobilisation by others of those who have become refugees in their own country due to natural and man-made calamities as mentioned above.

Marginalisation of senior citizens

In the last category of the marginalised group are the old people. With the emerging dominant trend of nucleation of family and the self-centredness both in urban and rural areas in India, the old people or the 'senior citizens' have become marginalised in their being whole-heartedly accepted in the family of their children and grand-children. They have also gradually lost their say in the decision making in such families and in the overall society which are being managed largely by the younger generation. Tied with this are the "generation gap" and conflict of old and new values represented by older and younger generations respectively. This may also be seen in the context of tradition and modernity represented largely by them. One may also hold that it is in this sense the Indian society is passing through the transitory phase wherein there is perhaps greater possibility of replacing older values, norms, customs, etc. by the newer ones. Perhaps, this may be taken as a part of the universal evolutionary process of change in vogue all over the world. Thus, in absence of joint family the modernisation process is heading to a state where old people are becoming physically, socially and emotionally uprooted irrespective of their caste, religion and gender background. Hence, their marginalised status.

Besides, this also raises the pertinent issue of human rights where the older people are neglected, sometimes humiliated and harassed also, both within their family and that of children and grand-children and also in the whole society if not directly then at least indirectly. Their problems get aggravated in absence of proper institutional mechanism devised either by the State or society. The due personal and social respect is the basic right of all human-being irrespective of their caste, creed, colour, gender and socio-economic position. Those old people who have been a little careful, in their yester years, about their social security in the old age, they might, be relatively in better position though they also suffer from general neglect, lack of emotional support and from alienation. But majority of the aged people drawn from the vulnerable corporate groups or strata in rural and urban areas are both socially and economically handicapped. Hence, they need their minimum human rights to be protected.

Human Rights vs. Fundamental Rights: Declarations to Implementation

We shall briefly mention here some distinct features of both human rights and fundamentals rights in India and then point out their some in-built paradoxes specially in their declarations and implementations. We shall also suggest some ways and means through which these paradoxes may be resolved. The human rights have been chartered in the UN Universal Declaration of Human Rights to meet certain types of challenges that the humanity has been facing throughout the world. Norchi (1959 : 9-11) has identified three specific types of challenges of human rights that all human-beings throughout the world are facing currently. These are of respect, of well-being and of dignity. The very first Article of the Universal Declaration of Human Rights states, "All human beings are born free and equal in dignity and rights. They are endowed with reason and conscience (which may not be equal in nature and magnitude) and should act towards one another in a spirit of brotherhood (or fraternity)". The respect for others or mutual or social respect, which is the very foundation of the contemporary human rights, means "ensuing the fulfilment of the full range of human values."

Secondly, right of well-being is the right to life and security in terms of combating slavery or bondage and socio-economic exploitation, arbitrary arrest, torture, extra-judicial execution, etc. At a more fundamental level, it includes right to food, shelter, health-care, and in word elimination of poverty. The former type of wellbeing is relatively easier to execute by enacting and rigorously implementing legislations, and bringing offenders in the book but the latter type is more difficult in event of natural or genuine and man-made scarcity of resources and the mal-distribution of the available ones. With the result, most of the governments are in a way evasive of the human rights – the tight of human well-being though they claim for their doing best to endow this right of the citizens in their country.

The crux of the human rights is the human dignity – of men and women which is the third type of human rights. Human dignity perhaps can precisely be explained in absolute and relative terms where in the former case it is to treat all human beings equal within the full range of human values regardless of their race or caste, gender, age and social status. But in the latter case the human dignity is to be seen in the context of regional and cultural particularities though it is devoid of "termination of (UN) prescriptions designed to ensure a modicum of dignity for everyone, regardless of culture, religion, age or gender" (Norchi 1995 : 10). Moreover, human dignity in relative sense may lead to its gradation or ranking in a given regional and cultural context where some may claim for more dignity than others defeating the very basis of universality of rights of the human dignity. What is, therefore, required is to go for commonality of values of human dignity enshrined in the Universal Declaration of Human Rights.

Every member-country of the UNO has its own constitution – written or unwritten based on convention – to govern its populace by providing some fundamental rights to the people and legal – administrative principles to the State for the governance. Thus, the fundamental rights are those rights given to the individuals or citizen of a country to make best use of their freedom within the legal – constitutional framework. These rights of individuals empower them to file suite in a court of law even against the State or the government if their rights are curbed or taken away by it. The fundamental rights of the people in India, as enshrined in Part III of the Indian Constitution, provide the right to equality, freedom of speech and religious pursuance, right to acquisition of property and right to constitutional remedies. The State is also empowered, through the Directive Principles of the State Policy, to formulate its policy or policies and help those individuals to enjoy their fundamental rights who belong to the vulnerable sections of the society. Thus, both the Fundamental Rights and the Directive Principles of the State Policy together protect the human rights of the people specially the marginalise groups o people in India. However, both the Human Rights and the Fundamental Rights suffer from a number of paradoxes which need to be resolved in the require contexts. Some of the paradoxes are : one, the human rights covering a wide range of rights and freedom of individuals appear to be more of a political chicanery than the genuine concern of the world fraternity. Although these rights as declare in the UN Universal Charter reflect the basic needs of the humankind, these are in reality articulations of political elites of the member – countries on behalf of the marginalised people or groups in the world. It is not out of place to mention here that the third world regimes have mostly denounced and violated human rights treating these as something being dictated by economically and thereby politically powerful countries of the West. Hence, instead of setting their own house in order "they are preoccupied with evolving defence mechanisms to shield, themselves against what they perceive to be an unwarranted Western intrusion into their sovereign domains" (Gupta 1969 : 9). This becomes more pronounced in the light of the fact that the Western countries themselves frequently violate proclaimed declarations of human right for their own people. "The decline in the credibility of human rights come about at a time when human rights consciousness is fast spreading across diverse societies, most of whom are experiencing growing scales of state sponsored violation of basic rights. Paradoxically, however, the dialectics of human rights seem to be moving further away from the basic human concerns and getting entrapped into a web of opportunism being created at the global level"(Gupta 1996 : 10). This equally applies to the fundamental rights of the people in India. Thus, in absence of a genuine say of the marginalise groups the declarations of both human rights and fundamental right at least in their case seem to be a mere political rhetoric.

Secondly, since the member – countries of the UNO vary from one range to the other in terms of their social organisation, economic progress and structure of the political governance, the general principles of the human rights have been chartered leaving enough scope for political manoeuvring by these countries in the name of their regional and cultural specificities. Moreover, the economically vulnerable countries of the Third World have always been governed, in one way or the other, by the super – power of the economically advanced countries. Therefore, their concern for human rights many a times appears to be superimposed on them rather than an outcome of their genuine social and political conscience. In such situations the State apparatus in these countries becomes defensive vis – a – vis Western countries, and violative of and offensive to both the human rights as well as fundamental rights of their own people as mentioned above.

Thirdly, there is much wider gap between declarations and actual implementation of both the international human rights and the Indian fundamental rights. This may be attributed mainly to two things: first, the people specially the marginalised groups are not well aware of their human rights and so also of their fundamental rights. Only recently some NGOs have tried to educate and mobilise not all but a few marginalised groups in India about their rights and to democratically fight for their proper and full implementations at various levels. Second, some of the declared rights are so abstract that it is difficult to translate them into practice at uniform level. Even other types of human legality that the would be beneficiaries may not easily follow and try to get them accorded in their favour. Finally, the realisation of both human rights and fundamental rights for the most needy people in any country or society is much expensive and time taking. In view of this the marginalise groups of people may not easily afford to get justice against violation of their fundamental rights. The UNO has recently made the provision of entertaining even individual complaints from one whose human rights have been violated. It has fixed the responsibility to the concern member country to protect the human rights of its people and become accountable to the international fora. The Government of India, on its part, has evolved a number of institutional mechanisms including setting up national commission for redressing the human rights problems of some of the marginalised groups. But the results in both the cased are not very encouraging.

Marginalised groups, Human Rights and Quest for Equality

Out of the aforesaid three major concerns of the UN Universal Human Rights Declarations namely respect or social respect, well-being and human dignity the first and the last are usually emphasised by the marginalised groups or communities though the second one is essential for their human existence. In the present time people of the marginalised groups almost in every society of the world articulate their concern for the accord of self-respect and human dignity. This may be so due to fast changing human values and closeness of the world societies as a result of revolution in the communication systems. This is also because of articulation of their interests by numerous organisations of different fora. But in the case of Dalits, tribals and women in India, each of these groups or social categories aim at achieving equality with rest of the people. No doubt, their quests for equality pass through highlighting their exploitation, deprivations and discriminations of various types. But one thing is quite clear that these marginalised groups are no longer willing to accept their subordination to the socially, economically and politically dominant groups. It is needless to say at this stage that their quest for social respect, well – being and dignity emanates from the global as well as national concern commitments for the same and gets more clearly articulated at the grassroot level.

Another interesting aspect to mention her is that the marginalised groups do not accept the declarations of human rights and fundamental rights as an international or national doles or charity. Instead, they claim for these rights as their birth right which gets reinforced through the hemming of concerns of a number of organisations working at the various levels. Yet, substantially their such claim seems to be rooted in their understanding of the system of various types of exploitation. In other words, their reckoning of marginality is essentially an out-come of their age-old exploitation which may not be easily blurred by the liberal gestures or tones of human rights and fundamental rights. A number of genuine NGOs not only act as catalytic agent of educating and marginalised groups but also mobilising them as mentioned above. They establish necessary links between these groups and the national and international agencies for showing more vigour to resolve the issues at an early hour. Yet, there is a long way to go.

Conclusion

What is need d at this stage is to properly comprehend the varied human and existential problems of the different marginalised groups. It is also required to analyse the main concern of both human rights and fundamental rights from the points of views of the marginalised groups themselves, and to evolve the proper and effective mechanisms both at national and international levels to meet the challenges. But to talk about the future state of human rights and fundamental rights of the people in general and of the marginalised groups in particular amidst the processes of economic liberalisation and cultural globalisation may be only a conjecture at this stage though these rights are still the major focus of concerns at the world level.

There could be both short-term and long-term impacts of economic liberalisation and cultural globalisation on human rights vis – a – vis fundamental rights specially of the people of marginalised groups and communities. In case of India these processes begun recently have aroused considerable degree of fear – psychosis among the people to be swayed away by the economic and cultural systems to be created by the multi-national corporations. As a logical corollary, the local as well as national entrepreneours will be cornered and the status of already marginalised groups and communities will be further marginalised. What would be the nature of their further marginalisation and how much time would it take? Whether marginalised groups and communities would be assertive for full realisation of their human rights as well as fundamental rights? All this would depend on the intensity of liberalisation and globalisation on one hand and mobilisational capability of the people, on the other, to counter excessive impact of these processes. As far as short-term impacts are concerned, the economic liberalisation is based on the main premise of growing the national economy at rapid pace and trickling its benefits down to the grassroots. But by its own logic, the capitalist economy is guided by the profit motives and it develops in some sectors even at the cost of underdevelopment in other sectors as was experience during the 1970's and 1980's in many Latin American countries. Though the very idea and steps of economic liberalisation have been accepted in India with some degree of resistance by certain section of population, what impacts it makes on the government's concerns and the people's strives for realisation of both human rights and fundamental rights would be known only in years to come.

On the issue of cultural globalisation the Indian government has been fumbling on formulating a cultural policy for the people.

It has opted for modernisation of material culture and, in some ways, retention of traditional norms, values, etc. ignoring their symbiotic relationships. People on their own, remain lured by both material and non-material cultures of the West and the members of marginalised groups and communities also drag their legs towards that. Amidst all this the fait accompli of people's concerns for human rights as well as fundamental right may not be readily known at the present juncture.

REFERENCES

Ambedkar, B. R., 1948, *The Untouchables*, Amrit Book Company, New Delhi.

Bose, N.K., 1961, "Hindu Method of Tribal Absorption" in his Cultural Anthropology, Asia Publishing House, Bombay.

Desta, Mangista, 1994, "Rights of the Child" in K. P. Saxena (ed.) *Human Rights: Perspectives and Challenges*, Institute of World Congress on Human Rights, New Delhi.

Ghurye, G.S., 1963, *The Scheduled Tribes*, Popular Prakashan, Bombay.

Gupta, V.K., 1996, "Conceptualising Human Rights: A Search for New Identity," in his (ed.) Perspectives on Human Rights, Vikas Publishing House, New Delhi, pp. 3-21

Jayaram, N.1993, "Emancipation through Proselytism? Some Reflections on the Marginal Status of the Depressed Classed", *Sociological Bulletin* 41(1-2).

Klass, Morton, 1980, *Caste*, Institute for the Study of Human Issues, Philadelphia.

Merton, R.K., 1968, *Social Structure and Social Theory*, Amerind Publishing Company, New Delhi.

Moussalli, Michele, 1994, "Measure and Strategies for protection of Refugees in Countries of First Asylum in Transit and in Receiving Countries" in K.P. Saxena (ed.) *Human Rights: Perspectives and Challenges*.

Muntabhorn, Vitil, 1994, "Refugee Problems and Developing Countries: Between Burden Sharing and Burden Shifting" in K.P. Saxena (ed.).

Norchi, Charles H., 1995, "Human Rights in the Post – Cold War Era", *Span* (36 : 9).

Oommen, T.K., 1986, "Insiders and Outsiders in India; Primordial Collectivism and Cultural Pluralism in Nation Building", *International Sociology* 1(1).

_________1991, "Religious Minorities and Indian Polity: Towards a Policy Framework" *Religion and Society* 38(1).

Phillips, Alan, 1994, "Minorities Rights and International Response" in K. P. Saxena (ed.).

Ram, Nandu, 1995, "Marginalisation and Social Mobility Urban India" in his *Beyond Ambedkar: Essays on Dalits in India* Har-Anand Publications, New Delhi.

Roy-Burman, B.K., 1994, "The Indigenous peoples and the Problem of Human Rights", *The Administrator* 39(2).

Saxena, J.N., 1994, "Problems of Refugees in the Developing Countries and the Need for International Buden – Sharing" in K. P. Saxena (ed.).

Stonequist, E.V., 1961 *The Marginal Man: A Study in the Subjective Aspects of Cultural Subject,* Russel and Russel, New York.

Whittaker, D.J., 1995 *United Nations in Action.* University College of London Press, London.

5

Genesis, Mechanism and Growth of Caste System in South India

I am honoured in getting invited by RC-09: Dalits and Backward Classes of the Indian Sociological Society to deliver the First Professor C. I'arvathamma Memorial Lecture at its 32nd annual conference held at Chennai, Tamil Nadu during 27-29 December 2006. My first acquain- lance of late Prof. Parvathamma goes back to 1973 when I read her research paper on "Dr Ambedkar and After: The Scheduled Caste Classes and Masses", published in the Eastern Anthropologist. Then, I met her at I IT Kanpur in 1978 and at Meerut in 1980, and discussed a number of academic issues, especially pertaining to caste system and location of the Dalits or the Scheduled Castes (SCs) in it. Subsequently, we also met at least twice during 1990s at her residence, in some selection committee meeting. Through these meetings and reading her publications, I had found in her a fine brain, brilliant scholar and a very meticulous researcher, endowed with straightforwardness, elderly affection and Fine personality. Prof. Parvathamma proved herself to be a lone crusader, after llaba Saheb Ambedkar, against the vulnerable position of Dalits through her academic pursuits. This lecture is a modest tribute to her unforgotten memory and an inspiration to young social scientists, specially sociolo-gists and social anthropologists, pursuing the theme presented forthwith.

Indian society is said to be caste-ridden in whatsoever form caste exists, whether in old or new or even newer. The sociological and social anthropological studies undertaken so far testify that the caste exists as a major social structural and cultural institution (Weber, 1958), with its well-knit organization or system. It exists not only among the Hindus but even the non-Hindu communities in India have also adopted this system at least at the level of social interaction and commensal relations, though they reject its adoption as an ideological basis of their social structure and belief system. Hence, a few sociologists and social anthropologists (e.g., Dumont, 1970) have accepted it as a pan-Indian phenomenon like the varna system. Contrary to it is the view of a few scholars that caste system, in their reckoning, persists in India not only as a cultural organization and social structural system but remains a purely localized structural reality (Mencher, 1974) or at least an adaptive structure (Berreman, 1979) where it has necessarily imbibed in itself the characteristics of other non-Hindu communities, including the tribal communities. In the same vein, there is lack of unanimity among the indologists, historians, ethnographers, and sociologists and social anthropologists on the varna/jati model of the Hindu society or system, i.e., of the two—varna and jati—which came first in its social formation. Also, there seems to be lack of unanimity among scholars about the varna model being structural reality at all at any point of time in Indian society. In fact, the varna system, in their opinion, never existed as a social structural reality; instead, it was an ideal or ideational construct in which the numerous castes and sub-castes were hierarchized and ranked as superior and inferior, along with ranking in superiority and inferiority of the four varnas.

Genesis of Caste System

Some are of the view that during the Vedic and later-Vedic periods, the Aryans (who later got identified as Hindus) were divided into four varnas. In fact, the varna was a technical term used for the then existed four major castes (Muller, 1883; Ambedkar, 1979; Weber, 1958) or classes or social categories, which split later into numerous jatis and up-jatis or castes and sub-castes or sub-sub-castes, due to multiple reasons. Some of these were imposing or superimposing endogamy over exogamy, the Brahmin's initially adopting a policy of closing their doors of commensality or commensal relations, including marital alliance, with others, which subse-quently was followed by the latter groups or varnas (Ambedkar, 1979), pursuing specific types of occupations as well as customs and belief systems by different groups of people, and so on and so forth. Opposed to this is the view heralded by a number of social scientists and foreign travellers who had visited India before the first millennium AD. Such view accepts the presence of numerous groups, not varnas or castes, of the people pursuing different types of occupations, customs, belief systems and also having heterogeneous types of social organizations, interaction patterns, commensal relations, etc. Then, the extended view is that the four-fold varna model was, as mentioned above, an ideal devise or scheme of the Aryans under which the already existed numerous groups of the people were supposedly or notionally fitted. It is a well-accepted fact that quite a few groups did not strictly fit in that, and yet others were either forcefully kept out or they themselves refused to get fitted in and opted out of the scheme. Such groups of people have obviously been termed either indigenous or aborigines or tribals, Dravidians, Antyajas, Antyavasins (Ati-Shudras or untouchables), etc. In other words, the varna system was an idealized version of social organization or social structural arrangement of the then existed population of the Aryans, but in reality the people at large were living in numerous well-organized or loosely organized groups or social categories. Not going here into further details of historiography of origin of caste or the caste system and also its major characteristics or attributes like hierarchy, separation or repulsion and interdependence (see Bougie, 1971), we may buy the argument, for the time being, that the impression-istic view about the varna system being the pan-Indian phenomenon or accepting the four-fold varna scheme at all-India level prevalent during (he ancient period gets falsified by the facts that are available through the archaeological excavations, historiographic interpretations of inscrip-tions, interpretations of and inferences drawn from the scriptures written or complied in vernacular languages of different regions, and the ethnographic surveys done about the structural arrangements of almost all groups of people, including their customs, belief systems, commensal relations and occupations practiced in different parts of the country. This then simply means that the ideal devise of the four-fold varna scheme was conceived of by the ancient sage-scholars and was ideationally or notionally operative within the Indo-Gangetic basin, though the exerting connived power did try, in some cases successfully but in many cases unsuccessfully, to instal the scheme or system by transplanting the people of some varnas from the Indo-Gangetic basin to the other regions of the country as they were indigenously not available there.

Contrary to this, the caste system, either in the form of collectivity of l he numerous occupational groups or a well-structured system of social groups, as erroneously projected by some social scientists, has had ever existed at the pan-Indian level though its structural arrangement varied from locale to locale or region to region. It may also be stated that the caste system as a unitary structure or a well-bounded social organization never existed as a static entity; instead, numerous permutations and combina-tions have ever been in operation within it, making the system relatively complex and yet a dynamic one. Hence, the caste system is not only a localized social structure but the latter has evolved several types of caste systems (and thus there are caste systems) in India, though all of these supposedly operate within the frame of an idealized version of uniform hierarchy of caste system (see Dumont, 1970). Needless to say, such version of the caste system projects its resemblance with the varna system, though the numerous castes and sub-castes are not uniformally well categorized and are unqualifyingly accepted within either of four varnas in the varna system, or there exist even more caste categories placed in altogether different type of hierarchy of castes operative at the local or regional level. Yet, it cannot be denied that the numerous castes and sub-castes have been trying both successfully and unsuccessfully, especially since the colonial period, to get them accepted in the higher ranked castes within the varna scheme. In other words, the process of synchronization of the discrete caste categories (caste and sub-castes) has been going on in a continuous hierarchy of the caste system (Gupta, 1993: 110-42), though the continuous hierarchy or continuity of hierarchy is not of traditional ranking of all castes and sub-castes in the descending order to the Brahmin, Kshatriya or Rajput, Vaishya, Shudra and the untouchables.

There is, however, no dearth or empirical evidences to suggest that in their day-to-day life people in different regions have not only downgraded but even denied the ritual or religious supremacy of the Brahmins or of their numerous castes or sub-castes. Contrary to it, it has been said that a Brahmin in a village is considered the superior most, irrespective of whether he possesses the traditional (ideal) attributes prescribed in the scriptures (Mandelbaum, 1972: 24). In certain areas, even the traditional supremacy or dominance of the Kshatriya or Rajput caste, with its sub-castes, has been challenged by the people of the economically, politi-cally and numerically middle level dominant castes. Thus, one finds the earlier formulations easily contestable on the basis of the emergent empirical social realities in different parts of the country. A few such contestable formulations are like, sanskritization leading to positional change or change in the social position or social status of the lower castes hut leaving their ranked position vis-a-vis the hierarchical structure of the caste system intact (Srinivas, 1966), the top (Brahmin) and the bottom (the Shudra castes and by extension the untouchables) ranks of the hierar-chical caste system remaining intact or immobile and all permutations and combinations or changes occurring only in the middle ranks or orders (Bailey, 1964), and, as stated above, villager knowing fully well about the men of the Brahmin jati (caste including its sub-castes) of his village as being neither scholars nor trained priests yet accepting their highest ritual status or rank traditionally decreed on them (Mandelbaum, 1972: 24).

Mechanism and Growth of Castes

There are five main theses on the mechanism (s) and the

consequent growth of caste system in a region and from one region to the other over a period of time. Its growth is to be understood in terms of growing its number and consolidation of attributes prescribed to it in a given hierarchy of castes found in a region. How and by whom these attributes were evolved and prescribed to a caste and how were these accepted or contested by its members are not our immediate concerns here. Rather, we wish to state briefly the basic tenets of these theses and examine criti-cally their being valid ones on the mechanism for the growth of castes and the caste system.

The first thesis is of the policy of exclusion which means exclusion or throwing away or boycotting permanently members from a caste. Such policy has remained in operation since the early period of the Indo-Aryan and later Hindu society in India. This operates even today, especially among the lower castes in rural society, though it is applied generally on temporary and not permanent basis. As stated earlier, Ambedkar formu-lated his thesis in 1916 (published in 1917), about the genesis of caste as an outcome of the superimposition of endogamy over exogamy (as form of marriage) which he considered as one of the mechanisms for the genesis as well as growth of caste. As part of his thesis, he referred to marriage of surplus men (widowers) and surplus women (widows) outside their group or caste as growth of and one of the mechanisms for the genesis of caste into numerous other castes. The final point that he made in his thesis is the closing door policy. In his conceded opinion, Brahmin, Kshatriya, Vaishya and Shudra were initially four classes and not castes, and the varna, with the Aryan origin, happened to be a technical term given to each class. The Brahmin, according him, was a class and its members first became a caste through coining and implementing the policy of closing their door for members of the other classes. In other words, the Brahmins adopted endogamy and closed their door of marriage and commensal relations for members of the other three classes. Thus, they first became closed in and then closed for others. "... while making themselves into a caste, the Brahmins, by virtue of this, created non-Brahmin caste; or, to express it in my way (says Ambedkar), while closing themselves in they closed others out" (Ambedkar, 1979: 20). Being guided by the notion of 'pure self and impure other', they might have done this to make themselves as of pure blood and distinctive from others. Later, others imitated them and closed their own door still for others; and, hence, became endogamous. In the words of Ambedkar, "It is 'infection of imitation' that caught all these sub-divisions (non-Brahmins) on their onward march of differentiation and had turned them into castes" (ibid.: 18). Ambedkar's thesis, though not widely acknowledged in socio-logical and social anthropological analysis of caste in India, stands on its own merit of logical argumentation and empirical verification even in the present time as numerous castes and sub-castes are said to have origi-nated and grown through such mechanisms.

The second thesis on the origin and growth of castes and sub-castes is about the mechanism or process of inclusion which, as the face of it, appears to be contradictory to the above stated thesis. Notwithstanding the invalidated contradiction between the two, the thesis of inclusion explains numerical strengthening and consolidation of castes and sub-castes since the early times in the history of genesis and growth of castes in India. It is evident from the socio-anthropological and historiographical analysis of the various segments of population of the indigenous and Indo-Aryan society of the ancient period that the people, as a whole, including Aryans, classified into Brahmin, Kshatriya, Vaishya and Shudra varnas, were tribal in their beliefs, customs, taboos and totems, etc. (see, Risley, 1908; Weber, 1958; Kosambi, 1956; Dutt, 1986). More precisely, they were mixture of both Aryans and non-Aryans or native people (Kosambi, 1953, 1956, 1962, 1965). This was found not only in North India but also in South India where there was a total absence of such classification of people of the Indo-Aryan society. In fact, some people, especially with the nomenclature of Brahmin and Kshatriya or Rajanya from north, were transported and inducted in the south, besides recruitment of the local people to these classes or varnas. Anyway, without going into details of their induction process and recruitment patterns, we wish to reiterate here that the policy or process of inclusion of outsiders, especially tribals (Kosambi, 1956; Dutt 1986), into a class and later caste, was approved and legitimized by the then existed power and authority for l lie purpose of organizing and regulating society of a sort with its own ongoing tradition and civilization of procreation as well as orientation.

It is, however, worth noting that as the system of caste happens to be a system of graded inequality (Ambedkar, 1979), wherein each caste is ranked higher or lower with unequal ranked status and with cumulative social and ritual inequality with the other, the inclusion mechanism was operative in the vertical and not horizontal fashion. This means, the newcomers—both individuals and groups—were included in a particular class or varna with lower ranked status (sub-caste) yet with the nomen-clature of the same class or varna or with the independent ranked status (caste) in the hierarchically arranged system and thereby spreading at length and breadth of the caste system. However, there continued to be asymmetrical relationship among all of them, especially in terms of marriage and commensal relations, ritual purity, etc. It is also true that the independent ranked statuses or castes, not being satisfied with such partial or differential inclusion in the caste system, had all along been contesting for their complete inclusion in the idealized yet socially and religiously accepted system of distinctively ranked upper classes or varnas. Thus, this thesis stands valid as the mechanism of inclusion and the resultant contest can easily be seen even in the present time.

The third thesis is of the transformation and spread of clans into castes which we will be discussing, in detail, in the following section. Here, we shall look briefly at the nature and composition of clan and the mechanism it adopted to get transformed into caste by changing its tenets or attributes and switching over to that of the caste. This thesis was initially formulated by Kosambi (1962) as a part of his larger explanation of formation of society and culture as well as of civilization in Indian sub-continent, especially in the peninsular India. He has done this on the basis of the archaeological and historical evidences. Since the people of different stocks or groups observed clan (gotra) exogamy and married people of the other clans within the group, this gave birth to caste, and the clan subsided through the passage of time. This thesis has, in recent years, been discussed, in details, by Morton Klass (1998), who has explained bow, in the past, clan got transformed into caste. Referring to l.cvi-Strauss' (1963) two structural type words 'bear' (totem) and barber' (caste system), Klass has accepted totemic groups as clans practising rule of exogamy opposed to caste rule of endogamy. "Each 'clan', however, obeys the rule of exogamy: a male and a female of the same clan may not marry each other (as they are treated as brother and sister because of their supposed origin from the same descent), and so the spouse for each member of the society (clan) must be sought in a 'clan' or 'section' other than his or her own' (Klass, 1998: 139). This, in a way, supports Kosambi's thesis of 'marriage commune', consisting of a number of clans living in a single region or circle or caste (ibid.), though he has not specified whether such 'marriage circle' is territorially confined among the members of the same commune living in a single region or outside it. He has further added two more characteristics to his propositional thesis: 'equalitarian clans' and 'absolute surplus'. In the case of equalitarian clans, he says that, "the galaxy of societies and social groups making up the precaste (clan based) South Asian milieu exhibited, to a significant degree, endogamous clusters of exogamous, unstratified, stipu- lated-decent, 'equalitarian clans', and that it was this galaxy—this total social and economic milieu - that was transformed into the stratified socio-economic system we know of as 'caste system' (ibid.: 158).

Similarly, Klass' thesis or sub-thesis of 'absolute surplus' meant the continuous production of surplus, rather absolute production of food grains, which was obviously more than that required for subsistence. Compared to those whose food production or items produced from hunting and gathering was for the bare subsistence, the producers of 'absolute surplus' emerged as separate castes, though their clan affiliation remained the same (Klass, 1998: 155-56; see also, faiswal, 1998: 4-6). This does not mean that castes originated only among those who had 'absolute surplus', rather those being less fortunate with bare subsistence production and rendering services, especially labour, to the fortunate ones as well as those being hunters and gatherers of the forest produces and living in the adjoining eco-zones also formed castes through their inter-action with the former. Interestingly, this thesis subscribes to the view that the mechanism of clans to castes, within different eco-zones, was operative simultaneously throughout the whole South Asia, including India. Needless to say, all these castes were neither placed horizontally nor had equalitarian relations among them due to their differential position in the economic structure with whatsoever meagre form it existed. Then, at a much later stage, these castes vis-a-vis their system got legitimized with the introduction of ritual purity and impurity or pollution as well as ranking assigned to each one. Still another thesis, related to origin and growth of castes, is that of die occupational affiliation or division of labour which has been greatly emphasized in sociological and social anthropological studies on the subject, though Ambedkar (1979: 47—48) considered it, with his substantive argument, as division of labourers. In a simplistic sense, as (here existed differential forms of occupations, both skilled and unskilled, pure and impure, the labourers or the people performing these occupa- I ions either voluntarily or by traditions or birth were treated as separate castes, or were ranked higher and lower in the order or system. This thesis, not being convincing one, was criticized by Ambedkar (ibid.) on lire ground that had the division of labour been the source as well as mechanism of origin and growth of castes and caste system, these could have equally been found in all the civilized societies of the world wherein division of labour is a necessary feature, but this is not the case as the castes, with their system, are found only in India and nowhere else. Secondly, since a person changes his occupation at one time or the other (in most of the cases, the people have changed their traditional or caste specific occupations in the present time), his caste affiliation could also be changed but this has never happened. Hence, the division of labour or occupational pursuit could never be the basis and mechanism of genesis and growth of castes and the caste system as well.

The last thesis about the genesis, mechanism and growth of castes in India is related to the religious Sanskritic texts which subscribe to the view that all the four varnas of Brahmin, Kshatriya, Vaishya and Shudra—the four categories or classes of Aryans—were of the divine origin, of meeting of the Purusha (male) and Prakiti-nature (female), or of the four organs—body parts of the Purusha himself. All the four varnas had to perform four distinct functions and were assigned specific ranks or status—higher and lower or superior and inferior—and any violation of these was subjected to punishment specially in the form of ex-communication. In the idiom of varna, if a male and a female of two different varnas had intimate relation and produced a child considered vamashankar—mixed breed, they as well as their progeny were thrown out of the either varnas. Such persons, with their progenies, formed caste or castes, which could not be fitted in the varna scheme. As a critique of this thesis, it may be said that it does not stand on the logical argument as no creation of a living being is possible through the body organs other than the particular one. Then, this may be accepted as an ideological legitimacy to the classification of population, in India, into various social categories or classes or varnas being higher and lower or pure and impure in the hierarchical scheme. Since the miscegenation or intimate sexual relation between males and females of two different classes or varnas has all along been discouraged and punished appropriately by the system, the condemnation of such persons, along with their progeny, and their formation of separate caste, can be accepted as a valid part of this thesis.

Anyway, it may be said here that there is no unanimity among the theses, cited above, on the mechanisms and growth of castes and caste system in India as each thesis emphasizes one mechanism and does not take cognisance of the other. Yet, one may agree that castes originated from tribe and its clan, within its totemic structure, through switching from exogamy to endogamy and getting legitimated by ideological elabo-ration at later stage. Such ideological elaboration was anchored in the divinity for the universal acceptance of castes and the caste system with the double check through enactment of specific rules and regulations relating to rewards and punishments to the adherents or practitioners and violators respectively. Such rewards and punishments were directed to the upward and downward movements as well as excommunications, in certain cases, of the persons and the groups concerned, within the status scheme that ranked higher and lower along the attributes or guna of quality, fate, rebirth, purity and impurity, superior and inferior occupation, etc. One thing is clear that the scheme was evolved by keeping in view the privation of some and deprivation of many in the matrix of the existing ranked statuses, and social interaction and social relations covered under it.

Caste System in South India: From Clan to Caste

In view of the traditional aspect of the caste system, one is generally informed about its rigidity, both in its structural and cultural forms, lived with by the people in South India. Such impression is not merely based on the heresay but is well substantiated by the scriptural texts as well as similar literature written, in local languages, about the local folk-traditions, historiographic interpretations, ethnographic surveys, census monographs and a few independent monographs, and research articles published by historians, and sociologists and social anthropolo gists, on the society of the South Indian states. But, the more important issue is to know briefly whether the caste system originated indigenously there or had travelled all the way from north to south India and got rigidified there with all its structural attributes as well as cultural practices with firm ideological grounding among the indigenous groups of the people. In doing this, it is also obliquely necessary to probe the possible reasons for the later.

We have stated above that the castes originated simultaneously throughout India. There are, however, four distinctive views about the origin, mechanism and growth of castes and caste system in South India. The first view speaks of origin of caste or castes simultaneously in different parts of the country, including the peninsular India. For instance, Kosambi (1956: 25) accepts the rules of endogamy as survival of the pre-Aryan or non-Aryan tribal practices in the Harappan civilization (around 2000 BC) and finds their fusion as the foundation of the caste system, specially after the developed form of division of labour among the people, as mentioned above. But Kosambi is silent on whether that had happened simultaneously in all or only in specific parts of the country. It is, however, clear from his elaborate narratives about what he spoke more or exclusively of that in the northern India, and he covered, for the purpose, utmost the central and western India. Here, his arguments are inclusive of both the materialist and textual analyses of archaeological as well as living evidences found in these regions. The second view is of Klass (1998) who provides, on the contrary, an exclusive material basis for the origin of caste. As already stated, he speaks of a number of 'equaiitarian' endogamous social groups (like those described by Kosambi) in the hunting and food gathering stage (pre-historic times) living in the numerous eco-zones, but he does not call them tribals. Later, these groups or at least some of these succeeded in producing 'absolute surplus' of the food grains and, thus, were 'prosperous' compared to those engaged in producing or collecting food grains, forest produces, or hunted animals for their subsistence. These groups were also having equaiitarian exogamous clans, constituting of a single 'marriage circle', and sharing together both prosperity and misfortune. But, with the development of new agricultural technology, those groups which possessed cultivable land turned to be in advantageous position and the deprived ones became labourers to them at the communitarian (group) level. Thus, there emerged a hierarchical ranking of both the advantaged and the disadvan-taged endogamous groups, with their exogamous clans, leading from 'clans to castes'.

But treating Kosambi's thesis as a tentative probing, Jaiswal (1998: 3) is of the view that the entry of the tribal groups into the 'general society' is a racial explanation of caste. According to her, if we accept this formulation that the different endogamous tribal groups (with their supposedly racial origin) formed castes or caste system, then it would have formed race or racial system and not the castes or caste system. Notwith-standing the tribe as a race, the origin of caste has also been attributed to tribe by Dutt who says:

In this matter the aborigines (tribals) contributed more than the Aryans .... The Aryans when they came into India had outgrown this stage of tribal economy, ... From what we find among non-Aryanized aborigines of India we can believe that the practices of totemistic exogamy and tribal endogamy were practically strong among the Dravidian peoples of India, which kept the various tribes asunder like so many castes .... Again, even before the coming of the Indo-Aryans, there had been great cultural differences among the natives of India, probably between the civilized Dravidians and the savages pre-Dravidians, between men who dwelt in towns and forts and had well-developed political organization and systematized creeds, and men who still dwelt in forest and caves, and had not advanced beyond the hunting and fishing stage of culture. These differences had raised a wall of separation between the two types, and each avoided contact with the other. These tribal and cultural divisions of society could not be shaken off by the natives even after their conquest by the Aryans, and under the changed circumstances, they became hardened into caste divisions. Hence, the curious fact that the caste rules are more rigid among the Dravidians of the south, not only between the Brahmans and non-Brahmans but between the various sections of the non-Brahmans, between the touchables and the untouchables, than among the more Aryan peoples of northern India. Thus, the practices of the conquered aborigines (tribals) contributed as much to the development of caste as the racial class preju-dices of the Aryan conquerors. (1986: 18—19)

It is, thus, clear from the above lengthy quotation that prior to the origin of castes and the caste system, the various types of differences existed among the native or aboriginal or tribal people which supple-mented and complemented to the origin and growth of the institution of caste introduced and legitimized by the Aryans in India over a period of time.

Similarly, Klass' formulation, as stated above, also does not hold ground as in many regions the tribals had a well-developed peasantry but, at the same time, retained their distinct tribal social structure and identity, and had not transformed it into that of a caste. But, in certain cases, some tribal groups transformed themselves into caste only after introduction of the Brahmanical culture and ideology (Jaiswal, 1998: 5-6). We shall come to this a little later. We may, however, be tempted to accept, for the time being, Klass' general formulation but this applies largely to the latter part of the colonial period up to the country's political independence, though the study of Nagaraju (1995: 8-23) supports, in a way, this formulation as ihe tribals of the Rayalseema of south-western Andhra Pradesh gained tribal chieftaincies through their role in the wars between the Chalukyas and Pallavas in the 8th-9th century AD. Later, they adopted the varna/jati (caste) model either at the middle or mostly at the lower level in the local caste hierarchy. But it has also been said that a few castes found in the early South Indian society were both structurally and culturally different from the Brahmanical institution of caste—with differential ranking and system of hierarchy based on the notion of purity and impurity or pollution. According to Gurukul (1995: 245), "Most of the views in early historiography of South India confused the problem of caste by taking clan surnames for caste suffixes and juxtaposing them with the varna system. It has been clarified that the institution of caste was yet to charac-terize early Tamil (South Indian) society and what has been listed as castes by scholars in the past are clan names". Yet, like Kosambi, Klass also talks about the general process and ignores the regional specifica-tions, including those found in the South Indian society.

But, the most pertinent question may be raised about the authenticity of the thesis of the tribal endogamy, emphatically emphasized in both the above mentioned formulations. In fact, in absence of any authentication, these are either conjectural probings or extrapolations in view of the well- accepted fact that at the initial stage of the societal evolution, human groups the world over were living a primitive life or, even during the later ancient period, were not only exogamous but also matriarchal, though the matriarchy practised among them was qualitatively different from that practised till recently in the society of some south as well as north-eastern I ndian states. It is also a fact that over a period of time matriarchy has been replaced by patriarchy and exogamy by endogamy. Even then, the reminiscences of the earlier practised exogamy are strictly adhered to both among the castes and the tribes throughout the country as the marital alliance within the same gotra (clan) is a taboo and totally prohibited in both the cases. In fact, the remnants of clan are also found among most of Ihe Dalits or SCs in South India even in the forms of their avoidance of eating flesh of some reptiles such as tortoise, snakes and birds like crows, fowls, and revering and worshipping them. They also avoid cutting of a few trees, creepers, etc. All these are totems for them and they are supposedly originated from those, or these are treated as their siblings. The tribes and castes, including SCs, are discrete social segments and are originated from various clans which are "named after or otherwise identified with a particular animal, plant or insect. They claim to be descended or otherwise derived from it (clan), and are customarily forbidden to eat the totemic object, although they are free to eat the totemic objects of sister groups of their own society" (Klass, 1998: 138-39).

The third view about the origin and development of caste in South India relies again on clan but derives its strength exclusively from the ancient texts composed and compiled during the contemporary period. More precisely, most part of South India, i.e., Tamilakam was divided, during the ancient period, into five ecological or eco-zones, which were known as tinai. These five tinais were the Kurunchi (hilly backwoods or forests) inhabited by the vetars and kuruvars or hunters and shifting culti-vators, the Palai (parched areas) lived in by the marwars or warriors, the Mullai (pastoral tracks) occupied by the itayars or pastorialists, the Marutam (wetland) occupied and cultivated by the ulavars or ploughmen or agriculturists, and the Neital (the littoral or ponds) settled in by the paratavar or fishing community. But, in those areas where two tinais merged, the people, with their respective social groups and forms of subsistence, appeared to be mixed (see, Gurukul, 1994: 23; also Jaiswal, 1998: 7-8). These were dominated by the tribal chiefdoms (Champakalakshmi, 1975: 269). Besides the ecological and resultant material aspects, the ancient Tamil heroic poems, representing a people and their culture and social organizations as well as relations, were recited by a number of poets as a part of oral tradition of that period. Then, an academy of scholars collected and compiled these poems into ten anthol-ogies, known as Sangam Literature, during 300 BC to 300 AD.

According to Gurukul (1995: 242), these anthologies about the five tinais have also been accepted as efforts made towards "mechanical compartmentalization of nature into five divisions, symbolically denoting the historical evolution from the primitive to the civilized in south India". What is interesting to note here is that the people inhabited in the tinais were divided into several occupational groups and were dependent on kins, except Brahmin households (which were different from the Brahman households of the Brahmanic tradition transplanted much later in South India) for production of agricultural and other goods. Not only the production of these goods overlapped in several tinais but there were also frequent movements and social interactions of people of one tinai to the other.

With regard to the origin and growth of caste in these tinais, it is said that four kutis (castes) of panam,paraiyan, tutiyan and katampan existed in a tinai during the period of Sangam literature but is has also been mentioned that a kuti, in reality, meant a settlement of people or a family of people, and not a caste. It has further been stated that the four castes of parpar (seers), aracar (kings), itaiyar (cowherds) and kuruvar (hunters), and not the four stated above, were living in the tinai. Yet, at another place, other names of the four castes as antanar, aracar, vanikar and velalar have been mentioned. Even then, it has been clearly stated that these four castes were entirely different from the four castes and classes or varnas of the varna Brahmanic ideology in the North India (for details, see Gurukul, 1995: 245-46).

Finally, the last view on the origin and growth of castes and caste system in South India derives its strength from the adaptation process. This means, the Brahmanical version of castes and caste system were adapted, from the north, in South India during the post-Sangam literature period. This was, in other words, operative during the period of 400-600 AD and during 600-900 AD—the period of the dynastic rules of the Pallavas and Pandyas, respectively.

Then, there were three specific mechanisms through which such adaptation was carried out. One, the earlier undertaken visits, from the north of the [aina Shramanas and later of the Buddhist monks through the routes of the eastern coast, were directed towards spread of the message of ahimsa (non-violence) but these also resulted in their cultural inter-action with the people of the south. According to Thapar (1998: 132), visits of the Buddhist monks and cultural interaction between them and the people of south were possible during the rein of Ashoka (268—232 HC), the Maurayan ruler. Since both the Jaina Shramans and the Buddhist monks were largely opposed to the Brahmanical caste system in the north, was out of question of their carrying caste system with them to the south for the purpose of its induction there, though they had their establish-ments (mathas, viharas) there. But it is also stated that several traders I rom the north travelled later, through this route, to the south and carried castes and the caste system with them and transplanted these over there through their interaction with the local people. Both castes and the caste system in South India subsequently got legitimacy by the local chieftains or rulers of the local regions. The same or similar trade and commerce mechanism of the origin and growth of castes and the caste system in South India was through the route of the Dakshinapatha to the south during this period. This southern trade route of the Dakshinapatha was stretched from Magadha (in Bihar), the capital of the Mauryan empire, in the north upto Paithan at the north of the river Godavari in Deccan, in the south via Kashi (Banaras or Varanasi), Ujjaini (present Ujjain) and Maheshwar at the bank of the river Narmada, Bhilsa (now a district) in Madhya Pradesh. More specifically, Paithan, the southern end of the Dakshinapatha, was located in the southern part of present Maharashtra bordering north of Karnataka. But interestingly, the Dakshinapatha never touched the south—rather southern Karnataka and deep south, the Tamil country. According to Thapar (1999: 120), "The route was not only a channel of communi-cation between north and south but also the vanguard of the exploration of the (southern) peninsula by the states of the north, intensified under the Mauryas". Also, through this route, the trades in shells, diamonds, precious stones, pearls and gold were carried out (Ray, 1995: 143). However, for the purpose of the present discussion, the Dakshinapatha was important in terms of penetration of the Brahmanical form of caste, along with its systematic arrangements, culture, customs and rituals, and religious legitimacy during the Maurya regimes, as mentioned above. In other words, the traders from the north were castemen and believers of the Brahmanical caste and religious ideology. Hence, they had played signif-icant role in induction of the Brahmanical caste system in the south. It first got its anchorage in the Kanarese country (the present-day Karnataka) from where it spread to Tamil country consisting of major part of the present Tamil Nadu, southern part of Kerala in west, and the west of Andhra Pradesh in the north-west. Besides the trades reached to South India through both the routes, a few Brahmins from the north were also persuaded by the local rulers to travel over there during this period perhaps initially to perform certain religious rituals and later to introduce the caste system with the Brahmanic ideology under the state patronage. Thus, the Brahmanical form of castes and caste system had reached there through both the east coast and the Dakshinapatha during this period and got crystallized there up to the beginning the medieval period.

The second mechanism of adaptation of the Brahmanical caste system in South India was rooted in the Hindu religious sects and cults formed and practised in the north. According to Kosambi (1962: 82-109), specially the Mother-Goddess cult has spread though the primitive tracks (hilly regions and forests) of the Dakshinapatha and the trade routes. The forms or names were obviously different from those in North India but the forms of their reverence and worship were, more or less, similar everywhere. But his analysis is more about the north than the south, and in the case of south it goes utmost to the Deccan, through the Dakshinapatha—the southern trade route, and not beyond that. However, a number of Shaivite and even Vaishnavite sects already spread by that time over major parts of South India, and the Virasaivas of Karnataka, adopted obviously from the north, had attacked the Jaina Sharmanas, the images of Mahavira Jaina, and the establishments set in his name from the 7th century onwards (Thapar, 1999: 73). This was equally true in the case of the images of the Buddha, and the Viharas set up for the Buddhist monks during that period. The Brahmins, travelled from the north to the south, had also started yajnas (sacrifices of animals and forest produces) on the Rigvedic patterns. All these together were instru-mental in introduction and adaptation of the Brahmin form of the castes and the caste system, first in the northern part and then in the entire South India during the 300-600 AD and even till the period, as stated earlier.

The third and final mechanism through which the caste system spread throughout South India is related to the Aryan or Hindu religious scriptures, especially the epics like Ramayana, written in the major vernacular languages of region, during the early period of the first millennium AD. These scriptures were mainly supportive of the Brahmanic philosophical tradition (s), culture, religious rituals and rites, vegetarianism, etc. Moreover, these legitimized and installed the Brahmanic system of castes and varnas with well-knit ideology and hierarchy of pure and impure as well as of superior and inferior or higher and lower ranks of both varnas and castes, enthroning obviously the Brahmins at the top and the Shudras, including untouchables, at the bottom of the vertical scale. It may, however, not be agreed that the scheme of ranking of the local population on the North Indian model was a smooth sailing there without any dissention or resentment, as stated earlier. Yet, the ideological induction of varnas and castes was well accepted which continues even in the present times, of course, with regional specification of ranks or ordering of statuses of different castes and their sub-castes.

Tribe-Caste Continuum

Keeping aside the pre-tribe and post-cas-te special formations, the focus of our discussion, in this section, is on the process of continuous change, along with change in the nature of the process itself from tribe to caste over the passage of the historical evolution of the society, specially in South India. The continuum hypothesis, opposed to that of the dichotomy, proceeds with the premise that the two extreme poles or points or stages on a given scale remain constant, and the continuous change occurs from one stage to the other without any abruption. Such changes also occur along the consistent parameters broadly drawn from the socio-cultural attributes or characteristics of the societies supposedly prevalent at both the extreme stages and poles. Another important point to mention here is that it is assumed in the continuum hypothesis, that through the passage of the continuous changes, the society, with its distinct socio-cultural attributes or characteristics, of the first stage foregoes completely its existence and is replaced by another advance form of society evolved at the subsequent stage. But, the gradation of change or form of changes at the stages located in between the two extreme stages is continuous, i.e., every subsequent grade or form of change is necessarily superior or advance to the previous one. Anyway, without going into the critically or validity vis-a-vis invalidity of the hypothesis, which empha-sizes change in the unilinear direction, we may accept it at its face value but subscribe to the view that some socio-cultural attributes or character-istics of the first stage are always present through the continuum process and are distinctively visible along with those found at every subsequent pole or stage, irrespective of whether these are viewed significant or insig-nificant. It is, however, equally true that through the passage, these characteristics or attributes themselves undergo both qualitative and quantitative changes or alterations to the degree of their permeability and acceptability at the extreme or 'last' stage.

In the previous section, we have discussed, in detail, the formation of caste from tribe, specially in the ancient South India. Since the focus of our discussion has been on the formation of castes and caste system from tribe, we have undermined the presence of certain attributes or character-istics or elements of tribe in the caste, and have also not ascertained the side by side existence of the tribe there. Yet, as our immediate concern, in this section, is to trace the tribe-caste continuum not in the ancient past but in the immediate present-day society and culture in general and among the SCs in particular, we shall accept the latter as an example to verify the validity of the tribe-caste continuum hypothesis. More specifically, we shall examine how the various SCs in South India live, even today, with certain socio-cultural attributes or characteristics of tribe, in spite of their being an integral part of the Hindu caste society, though placed at the lowest rank of its hierarchy. But, before doing that, it would be necessary to have an overview of the validity of this hypothesis in the larger context of the continuum of tribal elements in the caste as perceived by a few social scientists in India. Also, contrary to the two extreme stages being polar opposite or the separate monolithic hole, we have to accept them as being diversified at their existential levels, though this latter one may not be relevant for the present discussion.

For the present discussion, both tribe and caste, having separate social and cultural institutions and systemic arrangements, may be placed at the two extreme poles or stages of the continuum hypothesis. There are a few sociological, social anthropological and historical studies on the relationship between tribe and caste in India. Some have talked about change or transformation of tribe or tribe clan, as a unit, into caste (Beteille, 1997: 57-58; Klass 1998) but through transformation to lineage to hereditary occupations (Gurukul, 1993-1994) in ancient period, absorption as well as hierarchy consisting of higher and lower ranks (Bose, 1994), tribe-caste interaction, tribe in transition (Majumdar, 1961), tribals as backward Hindus (Ghurye, 1963), tribe-caste conver-gence (Bara, 2002), etc. Without explaining the merits and demerits or strong and weak points of these formulations, we may state here that these indirectly endorse, either fully or partially, the continuum hypothesis, though not referring to it. Yet, the point relevant here is that those tribes or their segments, who were absorbed especially at the lower or lowest level in the caste system through the passage of historical evolution, have not asserted for reviving their tribal identity or even elements of that unlike those tribes who have remained out of the caste-fold. Moreover, the former ones have formally been absorbed in the caste system but they substantially retain some attributes or characteristics of tribes along with those of castes, even after thousands of years of their leaving the tribal-fold. Thus, the tribe-caste continuum hypothesis is fully 'valid' in these cases, yet its full validity would be proved only when the socio-cultural attributes of tribes such as the structure of social control and the rituals and belief systems are completely absent among the castes.

The above point can easily be substantiated by giving examples of a few SCs from South India. Almost all the SCs there maintain the tradi-tional caste panchayat (council) headed by the elderly members of the respective castes. The caste panchayat, in its structural organization and functions, resembles with the tribal panchayat whose membership is obligatory or is accorded by birth for men of the respective caste or tribe. Such panchayat has traditionally been an effective mechanism for exerting social control especially over those members who violate the caste norms or indulge in such activities which bring disgrace to the caste. Yet, the forms of social control imposed by the caste panchayat over the deviants are temporal and worth compliance, and some of these are temporary excommunication or social boycott—throwing away from the caste but revoking that after paying the imposed fine, undergoing purification ceremony and hosting the caste or community feast. It is also a fact that the caste panchayat has traditionally been operative as an effective mechanism of social control among the SCs as well as the Shudra castes or the OBCs. Since it has proved to be less or even least effective mechanism among the younger educated generation of the SCs and also the Shudra castes, who are socially and economically better and more powerful compared to the former ones, it also suggests that even upper castes, not only in south India but all over the country, might have adopted caste panchayat as a mechanism for controlling deviances in the respective caste but discarded it earlier, through the passage of time, to make them distinctive from the castes placed at the middle and lower ranks in the local caste hierarchy. In other words, the process of casteization from tribe, initiated much earlier among them, may be accepted as complete one compared to that of the lower castes.

Another consistent parameter of the continuum between tribe and caste in the case of SCs in South India is a set of customs related to their life cycle, and their religious beliefs and practices. Some of their customs are related to birth, marriage and death in the family, and their religious beliefs and practices pertain to reverence and worship of local deities, gods and goddesses, ancestors, totems symbolizing clans, etc. While a few sets of customs, and religious beliefs and practices, are those prescribed to the caste and are drawn from the wider Hindu pantheon, others are neces-sarily anchored in the tribal system though perhaps with their modified forms. For instance, the custom of preparing separate huts by maternal uncle for an elaborate celebration of the first puberty of girls among some SCs. These are remnants of the earlier customs of tribals of the respective areas. In the case of marriage ceremony also, most of the SCs, in South India, follow the customs, rituals and ceremonies which largely resemble those of the erstwhile tribal customs. For instance, payment of nominal bride price, marriage through elopement, widow remarriage, etc. are some of the marriage customs and practices which remained within the confinement of the tribals of the regions and which are still followed by some of the SCs there.

Thus, the religious beliefs and cultural practices, which are remnants of tribes and are presently found among many SCs in South India, are not the outcome of the tribe-caste interaction but of continuum. This simply means that these SCs were initially tribe and got absorbed in the caste system at some later stage. More specifically, some of their religious beliefs and cultural practices, which they adhered to even in the present time, are their reverence and worshipping of village and regional deities like Maramma or Mariamm, a Ponniamma, faith in omens, demon worship, pacification of ghosts and spirits through reverence and worship, devil dances, sacrifices of goats and fowls, playing musical instruments, on festive occasion, made up of animals or forest animals, ancestor worship and so on and so forth. Since they are Hinduized and part and parcel of the Hindu caste system, they are also staunch believers of gods and goddesses of the wider Hindu pantheon. Even they celebrate Hindu festivals of a calendrical year and other auspicious occasions with other caste people of their respective regions.

Untouchability and the Untouchables in South India

Before we attempt to trace the period and involved mechanism of the origin of untouchability in general, and in South India in particular, it is necessary to distinguish, at the conceptual level, between untouchability and impurity or pollution or defilement, which are often mixed up and used synonymously. The notion of pollution or impurity stands opposite to purity and is generally used for the temporary defilement, which can easily be removed through performing some purificatory rituals. Contrary to it, purity is an abstract notion or entity that remains merely a point of reference and exists only in degrees, along with certain defining elements or attributes or substances. Unlike the dominant view attributing to the notion of purity to have ever worked as the guiding principle in situating an object or a person or a group or community in the Indian culture and civilization in general, and in the Hindu caste system in particular, it is the impurity which, in actuality, has all along enjoyed primacy or absolute authority over purity in terms of determining varying degrees of the former. Louis Dumont (1974) also has placed both pure and impure as binary opposites, which simply means that these exist as a paired concepts and the purity is necessarily opposed to impurity. He has stated further that, "... in the setting of the opposition between pure and impure, the religious division of labour goes hand in hand with the permanent attri-bution to certain professions of a certain level of purity. From this it should not be inferred that the religious division of labour cannot arise in another setting" (ibid.: 49). Thus, the two poles—the Brahmins (pure) and the untouchables (impure)—are equally necessary, though both being located at unequal levels, simply to maintain for others because the execution of impure tasks by some is necessary (ibid.: 55). This implies that the two—the Brahmin (pure) and the untouchable (impure)—being inflexible or rigid extreme poles, for Bailey (1963), are not only necessary but also complementary to each other in terms of their functionality—of course, the former's function being considered superior to that of the latter. This is what Dumont also has called complementarity between pure and impure (1974: 53-53). But his understanding of complementarity of the two is partial and partisan wherein the untouchable takes away the temporary impurity of the Brahmin, who for Dumont is never impure permanently, by removing his dirts, and the Brahmin, in turn, removes the untouchable's notional impurity temporarily by prescribing specific purif-icatory rituals for him. But as in his scheme of thought the untouchable is permanently impure, removal of his impurity, even temporarily, does not arise. It is the people of the non-Brahmin castes, other than the untouchables, whose temporary impurity or defilement is to be removed through the ritual purification. However, there exists a duality in relationship between the temporary impurity of the pure and the permanent impurity or untouchability of impure in the sense that the touch of the latter to the former makes it impure only temporarily and not permanently, whereas the temporary impurity and the permanent impurity of the latter one is removed only temporarily through undergoing some purificatory rituals prescribed by the former, as stated above. This implies that the existing contradiction between the two needs to be removed.

Thus, in the words of Dumont, "... the (permanent) impurity of the Untouchable is conceptually inseparate from the purity of the Brahmin. They must have been established together, or in any case have mutually reinforced each other, and we must get used to think of them together" (1974: 54). But, as stated above, such relationship does not exist in strict sense of the term; instead, it is some sort of working relationship as the former exists only among the equals or near equals, and not among those who are placed at the two extreme positions in the system—here, caste system. More so, as the Brahmin has an absolute 'repulsion' or repulsive attitude and behaviour towards, as well as, complete 'separation' from the untouchable (for details, see Bougie, 19 71), the complementarity between the two is not possible. It may, however, be mentioned here the Dumont's understanding of complementarity between purity and impurity simply explains the presence of the two in which they exist as autonomous entity without their being co-related, i.e., less impurity means more purity. But, in actuality, it is impurity which provides purity to certain object or person by absorbing his/her impurity in itself. Hence, the centre or rallying point is impurity, and not purity, as located in the mindset of the Hindus as well as the social scientists such as Dumont. Contrary to this, in their understanding the central reference in the status ranking of castes in the caste hierarchy is the purity, e.g., the Brahmin, irrespective of his impurity of temporary nature as well as all sorts of vices is taken as a reference for defining and determining the rank position of rest of the castes in the caste system (for details, see Mandelbaum, 1972).

On the other hand, the permanent impurity in the institutionalized form is untouchability, which is hereditarily attached with an individual as well as his/her caste or community. More so, it is attached with a caste or community; and as an individual, in Indian society, especially in the Hindu social system, is an inherent part or a member of it by birth, the untouchability is inevitably transmitted to him or her from generation to generation even if the individual is far away from the ambit of the criteria applied for determining the nature and magnitude of the permanent impurity or untouchability. In other words, once the members of that caste are made to be associated temporarily with impure occupation or to deal with an impure object on some occasion(s), they are considered to be impure forever, unlike the Brahmins and others who remain impure temporarily. Even if they dissociate themselves from that, the stigma of their occasional impurity or untouchability remains forever simply because of their membership with caste labelled as impure and untouchable. This simply means that, it is not the association with impure occupation or touch with an impure object which makes a person an untouchable but it is his/her membership with a caste which is treated as untouchable caste forever. This also means that, unlike the temporary impurity, the permanent impurity or untouchability is not easily removable due to its institutionalized form as a social-religious institution does not easily die down. It is, therefore, to be abolished both legally and socially, and legally it has already been done away with the promulgation of the Constitution of India.

Our intention in doing somewhat elaborate analysis, at the outset of this section, of the purity and impurity, including untouchability, is simply to demonstrate the fact that the ancient society in both north and south India was consisted of the numerous tribes in which there was no sign of permanent impurity or untouchability in the day-to-day life of the people, though the temporary impurity had existed there. Since the caste as well as the caste system had already been emerged and some adoption of that from the north was also made in South India during the later part of the period, untouchability originated and it not only got associated with certain types of occupations and other related practices and customs but also those, who pursued and practiced these, and were classified into separate caste groups and treated as untouchables. To make this simple generalization into somewhat complex analysis, it may be said that the tribals in India practise, even today, some forms of impurity based on violation of certain totems and taboos, customs and rituals, religious practices, observance of purity on various occasions such as birth, menstruation, death, etc. This is not to be constructed as juxtaposition of the present over the past or of caste traits to that in tribe, but such practices had prevailed among the tribals even in the remotest past or the early ancient period in Indian society—both in north and south—as is evident from the interpretations of the archeological excavations and the historiographical explanations of life of the people of that period. Such practices of impurity and purity were both structurally and functionally different from the permanent impurity or untouchability associated with certain groups of people during the later part of the ancient period of evolution and growth of society in South India.

The Dalits or untouchables have a long history of their origin and that of their untouchability and other forms of discrimination, exploitation and subjugation. One may argue that both the untouchables and their untouchability are synonymous and they originated together, though Ambedkar (1990: 237-379; see also Thapar, 1999) differs in this regard. Such argument is certainly attuned to a thesis of the simultaneous origin of four varnas or classes or castes from the divine power. Keeping aside the mystic origin of the institution of varna or caste or, by extension, even of untouchables and their untouchability, we shall discuss below a few these, which are universally applicable to the origin and mechanism of untouchability both in north and south India. The thesis of Ambedkar, with inherent empirical evidence, of the origin of untouchability, is that it originated sometimes during the 4th century AD, and was an outcome of (he last reconciliation arrived at between the settled communities of the Aryans, divided into the four varnas or classes of Brahmin, Kshatriya or Rajanya, Vaishya and Shudra, and the broken men, who were primitive tribes and virtually outside the system of the settled communities (see Ambedkar, 1990). That means, there was already a class of people—the broken men or the unsettled communities—who were living as wanderers or people with unsettled life. Because of the unavoidable situational compulsion on part of both the settled communities and the wanderers as well as more vulnerability of the later, the reconciliation took place. This resulted into the subordinated co-option of the broken men and imposition of the various types of ignominies on them by people of the settled communities. Also, they were to live in separate yet nearby settlement and were part-apart of the social arrangement of the already settled communities (ibid.). In other words, they were, in principle, not part of the socio-religious or ritual hierarchy of people of the settled communities but were dependent on them for rendering their labour and earning livelihood from that. Vivekananda Jha (1975: 14-31) has opined that though untouchability began to take "firm and definite shape with respect to a few groups" upto 2nd century AD, it was also present even during the Vedic period. In fact, he has mentioned about four phases in the early history of untouchables: the first phase ending upto 600 BC with a number of tabooed sections of society during the Vedic period; the second phase extending upto 2nd century AD; third phase ended by 600 AD during which the practice of untouchability was intensified but it was also resisted by the untouchables themselves; and the fourth phase extended upto 1200 AD and beyond during which the ranks of the untouchables swelled by incorporating several other castes, and untouchability reached at its peak. But, the trouble with such formulation is that it is all based on the Hindu religious texts, leaving no room for empirical verification except their reinterpretations and reformulation of the thesis as there seems to be absence of unanimity among the early such texts on the subject.

Still another thesis, which could be, in a way, an extended derivation of the first one, is that the Shudras, last or the fourth of the four varnas, were divided into Sat (with substance or cleanliness) and Asat (without substance or uncleanliness) or Shudras and Ati-Shudra classes or categories. Members of the first category were engaged in clean and of the second in unclean types of occupations. Those engaged in the unclean occupations were termed untouchables whereas those with clean occupations as clean castes but below the Brahmins, Kshatriyas and Vaishya or the merchants and traders. Though this thesis is very much in line with the origin of caste or castes from labour or occupation and, hence, the origin of the caste system based on the division of labour, but the trouble with it is that it fails to get ground in event of absence of caste or caste system in non-Hindu society wherein division of labour, in the form of clean and unclean occupations, is inevitably present. It also ignores the fact that religion—in the form of unconditional faith in super-natural power, and the related notion of ritual purity and pollution—has remained the sole basis of binding together the traditional society in India. Secondly, it fails to ascertain the issue of when, why and how the Shudras got divided into Sat and Asat or Shudra and Ati-Shudra groups or categories, and whether the socio-religious ignominies were imposed on the Asat Shudras only or on both the Sat and Asat Shudras, as prescribed primarily in the Manusmriti compiled during the 2nd century AD. Related to this are two different views: one, the socio-religious ignominies were imposed on the Shudras—a category or varna of people as such, irrespective of their sub-groups or categories. Two, this view holds ground as there seems to be absence of such categorization at the level of self-conscious assertion before the middle of 19th century. Although during the later part of the 19th century lyotiba Phule tried to bring both the Shudras and Ati-Shudras or Sat and Asat Shudras together on account of commonality of their exploitation by clean castes and this categorization has remained distinctive till date in spite of the sporadic efforts made for bringing them to a common political platform. Such efforts manifest, at present, in the form of Dalit Bahujan or Bahujan Samaj, and remain a mere rhetoric or political articulation in absence of socio-cultural intermixing of the Dalit castes and the OBCs. In fact, the distinction between the classes or castes and the untouchables or the SCs or Dalits has sharpened during all these years due to unwanted superim-position of former over the latter. This has happened due to the fact that after acquiring economic and political dominance, the OBCs have undergone transformation through the process of 'sanskritization' (Srinivas, 1966) by claiming their notional ritual superiority and newly acquired economic and political dominance over the Dalit castes. Their economic and political dominance and caste status superiority has often manifested in their practising untouchability, and committing heinous forms of physical violence and atrocities on the Dalits, especially in rural areas. Retrospectively, the relevant question to be asked here is that why were the various forms of social and religious ignominies imposed on the broken men or the Shudras, specially the Asat category of Shudras, after their co-option in the settled life of Aryans? What was responsible for that—was it their impressed need of getting co-opted in the settled life at any cost or was it their vulnerable economic position of living, as a wanderer, with unsettled life? Or, was it the continued risk to their life from the bewilderness or some other reason responsible for that? From the status quoist point of view, since there was functional necessity of some ones to render free labour and perform the most degraded menial jobs for the settled people, the broken men or the Ati-Shudras (of course, this nomenclature emerged much later after their 'co-option' in the system) were co-opted for the purpose at the cost of their getting located them at the reasonable physical and socio-religious distance. But, such a view point does not explain why the various forms of social and religious ignominies or disabilities, practised in the form of untouchability—the severest form of ignominies—were imposed on them once they agreed to get co-opted in the system of the settled people. That means, there could have been some other valid reason for the same. In fact, Ambedkar has provided the most justified reason for it. Accepting both the settled communities and the broken men initially being members of the primitive society and living life of the nomadic tribes and the former getting trans-formed into settled communities earlier, Ambedkar has stated that: When some (nomadic) tribes became settled, the tribes that remained nomadic found more advantageous to concentrate their fight against the settled tribes. It was more paying than a war against other nomadic tribes. The nomadic tribes had come to realize that the settled tribes were doubly wealthy. Like the nomadic tribes, they had cattle. But, in addition to cattle, they had com which the nomadic tribes had not and which they greatly coveted. The nomadic tribes systematically organized raids on the settled tribes. The third fact is that the settled tribes were greatly handicapped in defending themselves against these raiders. Being engaged in more gainful occupation, the settled tribes could not always convert their ploughs into swords. Nor could they leave their homes (and their lands and crops as well as cattle) and go in pursuit of the raiding tribes. (1990: 275)

Hence, there was a compromise between the tribes: those with the settled life and those with nomadic life. Since the settled tribes wanted to live peaceful life through finding new defenders and the nomadic tribes were also tired of their continuous raids on the settled tribes and wanted to live a settled life, the compromise was beneficial to both of them. But, the latter, being raiders on the former, had to pay the cost in terms of being asked to get settled at a distance from the main settlement and also getting various types of social and religious ignominies imposed on them, including the practice of untouchability against them which came in existence much later. Ambedkar has further stated that the practice of untouchability against these nomadic tribes or broken men, with their late settled life, started sometimes in the 4th century AD because they had accepted Buddhism, opposed to Hinduism, and continued to eat beef—the flesh of the dead cattle—which the earlier settlers—the Hindus—had already left. That means it was contempt of the Hindus against these Buddhists which caused the practice of untouchability against them (Ambedkar, 1990: 311-20).

With the above theoretical explanations, it is imperative here to venture into the origin and growth as well as adopted mechanism(s) of untouchability in South India. More precisely, we wish to probe when and how it originated, grew and got institutionalized there. Whether the same mechanism (s), as suggested by Ambedkar, worked for that or some others were operative, which were entirely different from that in North India. Then, with regard to the origin and mechanism of untouchability in South India, particularly in Tamil society, Subramaniam (1997: 154) makes sweeping narratives by saying that in the process of Dravidianization (with the Dravidians coming from outside the land during the most ancient period) "... the aboriginal tribes, the primitive people, were driven to the hills and the more amenable ones reduced to a state of helotry. The practice of untouchability and habit of treating one part of the society as 'low class' (ilicinar) prevailed there as it did in the north. There is no reason to suppose that untouchability was introduced into Tamil Nadu by immigrants from the north; it was a cultivated attitude of supreme snobbery (of the superior towards the inferior ones) which obtained in both places—north and south India. To substantiate his argument, Subramaniam gives the examples of the Kuruvar, Panar, Paraiyar (Pariah), Tutiyar, etc., listed now as the SCs, who were considered the 'low class' people in South India. A point may be mentioned here that as the helotry universally remained an outcome of a considerable degree of resistance and subsequent defeat of a native people to the invaders, the helots or slaves had always to face the contempt of attitude and behaviour of the victorious ones. Hence, it was not the snobbery but contempt of the winners towards the defeated ones in the game, which was in the root of the origin of untouchability in South India. This, in a way, also supports Ambedkar's thesis (1990) of the origin of untouchability sometimes during the 4th century AD but not in the too remote period of evolution of society in south India, as suggested by Subramaniam. This is supported even by Thapar's brief mention about untouchability in south India in her relating it to the persecution of the Jaina Shramans and the Buddhist monks, since the 7th century AD onwards, by the Saivites. In her own words, "Untouchability was also a form of religious persecution (like persecution of the Broken Men or some primitive tribes—the Buddhists in Ambedkar's thesis), for this exclusion was common to Brahmanism as well to some Sramanic sects, the candala (Chandala) being a category apart" (Thapar, 1999: 74). With whatever period and the involved mechanism of its origin, the untouchability had got institutionalized even in rural Tamil Nadu and other parts of south India during the period of Rajaraja I, the Chola king, who had ruled the Chola-Mandalam, the territory from the Kaveri delta to the extreme south of the Indian peninsula, from 985 to 1016 AD (Karashima, 1997: 21-30).

We may enquire, at this stage, into the question whether both the untouchables and their untouchability in South India originated simulta-neously or the former had originated earlier and the latter got associated with them afterward. We will deal with this question by examining, first, their origin in Indian society as such and, then, attempt to trace that in the case of South India. The reference may again be made here of Ambedkar's (1990) thesis of the broken men who had existed in the form of a section of the primitive tribes since the early age. They were not only Buddhist in their faith but were also eating beef (flesh of the dead animals), which the settled tribes had already left. Since both the broken men and people of the settled tribes reconciled due to their situational compulsion, the latter developed hatred and contempt against the former, who had not accepted initially the faith and the cultural practices of the settled tribes. Rather, a large section of the broken men continued to eat beef even after the recon-ciliation not because of their habit but simply because of lack of a stable source of their earning and utter poverty. Needless to say, they had to face the highest degree of hatred and contempt of the settled tribes for their continuing beef-eating and belief in Buddhism.

At the regional level, particularly in the case of South India, Subramaniam (1997: 198-206) has stated that the local purohitars (Purohits), rulers, merchants and labourers could be roughly equated with the classical four classes or varnas of Brahmin, Kshatriya, Vaishya and Shudra of the Aryavarta situated in the north-western part of North India. Then, during the ancient period (3C0 BC-600 AD) in South India, other communities were the Eyinar (hunters), the Umanar (the salt sellers), the Marawar (the martial community), the Konar, Itaiyar (cow-herds), the Utavar (peasants), the Valainar (fishermen), the Kuyavar (potter) and the Ilicinar (the low-class or low-caste people), besides a few other categories of people who were associated with the low- level unclean occupations or manual works, and the numerous tribes. It is the last category of people—

the Ilicinar—whom he has considered the untouchable, who lived in their segregated cheris (localities or settlements or hamlets) in both the rural and urban areas. But what is interesting to mention here is that in his entire narratives, Subramaniam does not explain how and exactly when the Ilicinars and their untouchability had originated, except his inference from their association with the unclean occupations.

There seems to be no unanimity among the scholars, specially histo-rians, on the exact or even approximate date and involved mechanism about origin of the untouchables and their untouchability in South India. Hence, we are left with two options: one, since castes and the caste system originated there from the numerous tribes and their social relations over generations during the ancient period, these got crystallized and revitalized at a later stage due to justification from the Brahamanical social order based on the notions of purity-pollution and superior-inferior ranks, adopted from the North India. Accordingly, not only the impurity or defilement was treated as permanent attributes of people of the inferior ranks but all their activities and associated objects were considered to be impure and defiling the pure and the superior ones. This all happened during the periods between 4th and 7th century AD. Then, the second option with us is to accept the thesis that those considered to be impure had not accepted their imposed permanent impurity without showing a considerable degree of resistance to the superior ones with both power and ritual purity. Thus, they became victims of the winners in the game and thereby had to bear the maximum degree of hatred and contempt of the powerful ones. There could be numerous evidences to this effect, both before and after the 4th century AD, but ironically these have not been properly and systematically recorded by the historians, including those from the South India.

The Statutory Position of Scheduled Castes and Criteria for their Scheduling

The Scheduled Castes (SCs), as a nomenclature for the erstwhile depressed classes, appeared, for the first time, in the

British Government of India Act, 1935, where it was used for those Hindu castes, and their sections converted to Buddhism, Jainism and Sikhism, who were ostra-cized and exploited for centuries together. Consequently, the first order named The Government of India (Scheduled Castes and Scheduled Tribes) Order was issued in 1936 iiself. But in what concrete manner the ostracization as well as exploitation of the depressed classes was spelt out and how many castes from all over the country were included in the schedule or list at that time and in subsequent years is not easily known at this stage. Yet, perhaps the same criteria, along with more emphasis on the practice of untouchability, were adopted in the Constitution of free India, and the list provided by the states was approved by the President of India. The first such order named The Constitution (Scheduled Castes and Scheduled Tribes) Order, with the assent of the President, was issued 1950 itself, which was modified as The Scheduled Castes and Scheduled Tribes Order (Amendment) Act, 1976. The latest amendment as The Constitution (Scheduled Castes) Order (Amendment) Act 1990 also includes those SCs who have converted to Buddhism.

At stated above, we may also explore briefly here some of the socio-demographic criteria for inclusion of certain castes in the list of the SCs, particularly in South India. But before that it is necessary to have a look at the number of castes included in the list in South India, consisting of four states of Andhra Pradesh, Karnataka, Kerala and Tamil Nadu, and the union territory of Pondicherry. Going at the face or the mere number, there are 60 castes in Andhra Pradesh, 102 castes in Karnataka, 69 in Kerala, 75 in Tamil Nadu and only 16 in Pondicherry included in the list of the SCs in these states. Thus, the total number of the SCs in South India has remained 322 in 2001. Hardly any new caste(s) from any state or the union territory in South India has been included in the list in the recent years. But it is also true that a number of SCs notified in one state are also notified even in other state (s) and the union territory. For instance, the Adi Andhra and the Adi Dravida, which are originally found in Andhra Pradesh and Tamil Nadu respectively, have been notified in all the four states and the union territory of Pondicherry.

Similarly, there are a sizeable number of castes which have been notified as the SCs in all the four states or in three states and in the union territory, a few others only in two states and in the union territory and still a few in two states. Thus, on an average, there are around 295 castes notified separately as SCs in South India, although their exact number is only 112 only due to synonyms of a large number of SCs in these states and the union territory. The total number of persons of these castes, according to 2001 Census, in Andhra Pradesh is 1,23,39,496, in Karnataka 85,63,930, in Kerala 31,23,941, in Tamil Nadu 1,18,57,504 and in Pondicherry 1,57,771. Hence, the total number of people belonging to SCs in South India is 3,60,42,642 and nearly 80 per cent of them live in rural areas.

Then, going by the socio-demographic criteria for notification of these castes as the SCs in South India, we find that merely the size of population has not been taken into consideration, where a large number of population of a caste perhaps would amount pressure for getting it included in the list of the SCs. It is evident from the fact that the total number of persons belonging to SCs in Karnataka and Kerala is less than those in Andhra Pradesh and Tamil Nadu but the number of castes included in the list of the SCs in the state of Karnataka is higher than that in these latter states. Similarly, if we take untouchability and various other forms of discrimination as the criteria for listing a caste as the SC, then, we also find that all the castes notified as SCs in South India have not suffered from the stigma of untouchability even in the past. Some such castes are Bariki of Andhra Pradesh, Kakkalan of Kerala and Tamil Nadu, Maila and Mavilan of Karnataka, Kerala and Tamil Nadu, Koliyan and Vathiriyan of Tamil Nadu, and several such castes in these states. But, in the case of all these castes, their population size is also less than 10,000 persons in the states where these are found. The majority of the castes smaller in population size (numbering 218), having less than 10,000 persons (large number of them having even less than 1,000 persons), also do not have even effective leadership of their own to articulate the issue of and exert pressure for their inclusion in the list of the SCs. Hence, instead of subscribing to the view of vagueness in the criteria adopted for the purpose, we emphasize here that a complexity of criteria are in operation for identifying and listing a caste as an SCs in a state.

We have already stated in the earlier section that a number of tribes or a section of them had transformed into caste in South India even during later part of the colonial period, which could not be included in the list of the STs. Since they had already Hinduized yet away from the traditional religious system of Hinduism as well as devoid of the practice of untouchability and other forms of discrimination, they largely remained socially and educationally backward. They also remained deprived of the dignified and sustainable self-resource of their livelihood. Had these castes come into closer contact with the caste Hindus, especially in the traditional system of jajmani (patron-client) relations, they would have certainly faced the frenzy of untouchability and other forms of discrimi-nation. Hence, a relatively prolonged isolation, and practice of untouchability as well as other forms of discrimination, coupled with socio-economic and educational backwardness, have been the major criteria for notifying and listing a caste as the SC. It is this socio-economic and educational backwardness, which occasionally instigates some sections of caste Hindus or even upper castes to acquire false certificate of an SC and claim for the benefits of the provision of reservations, though they have never experienced any forms of untouchability and other related discriminations.

Ethnic Identity and Origins: Role of Myths

Generally speaking, the ethnicity as a concept has broad connotation, and is inclusive of caste, race (being now discouraged both in principle and in usage), class, religious affiliations, region, political ideology, etc. Being a cultural construct, it thus cuts across the castes, race, class, and religious affiliations, religious, regional and political ideological boundaries and relies largely on the cultural markers like language, customs, food and dress patterns, festivals and alike, besides a strong emotional 'we feeling'. It has its own notional cultural and structural boundary within which members are supposed to pursue the varieties of activity, but in no way violative of its cultural code of conduct or the opinion of its leaders. Initially, an ethnic group or community originates in a particular region, with specific climatic environment, and then it moves out along with movement or migration of its members but it largely retains its cultural markers and interacts as well as integrates with cultures of other host groups and communities. What is more important to mention here is that the members of an ethnic group or community invariably identify themselves with it, hence, their collective identity, though they may cherish a few more identities based on their individual achievements in the secular domain of life. Being originated initially in the European continent sometime during the 1960s and used for the immigrants from several countries, it has travelled since then to India also and is adopted frequently in the academic writings—particularly in a few social sciences like sociology and social anthropology, political science, history, etc. But, in the case of India, it has also been used for castes and tribes where each caste or tribe has its own distinctive identity. Since castes have been arranged as superior and inferior on the basis of their ritual purity and impurity, in a specified hierarchy, there are certainly a number of castes which are stigmatized with their impurity, hence, their stigmatized caste or ethnic identity (Berreman, 1979).

During the recent decades, specially after independence of the country, members of the stigmatized castes or ethnic communities have been striving for overcoming the stigma of their collectivity (caste or ethnic community) as well as of their own. Since they are engaged in looking for alternative self and collective or group (caste) identity, they have been making use of two courses of action, rather than social processes, which have remained in vogue in Indian society: one, making use of achievements in secular domains like education, caste-free occupa-tions or white-collar jobs (economic), and power or authority. But all these three, in actuality, do not replace or obliterate their traditionally stigmatized group or caste identity. This is to be understood in terms of what Ambedkar has said as early as in 1917 (see Ambedkar, 1979) wherein achievement or merit of an individual in the caste system goes along with the merit or demerit of his/her caste. As the lower castes have traditionally been attributed to demerit or non-achievement, the achievement or merit of their members has not yet succeeded in overcoming the stigma of their group or caste. As all the traditionally stigmatized castes have constitutionally been called the SCs, with their traditional nomenclature being intact at the local level, the merit or achievement of their members is considered to be sponsored by the state through its policy of reservation or compensatory discrimination. On the other hand, the merit or achievement of the persons belonging to the non-stigmatized upper and middle level castes is considered to be their individual attribute, yet it has not motivated or inspired them to shelve their caste affiliation. In fact, the self and group or caste or collective identities of people belonging to both the stigmatized and non-stigmatized caste groups go hand in hand, in spite of some apparent changes occurred in the caste system in all these years.

The second option—course of action or process—available to the members of the stigmatized castes or ethnic communities, other than the achievement one, is the myth related to the origin of their castes or communities. It is true that the myths are self-created, but it is equally true that these are interpreted by the people in the manner that suits them. But these take longer time, rather centuries, to get them crystallized and then followed by the large section of population. Broadly speaking, myths are cultural attributes and markers of identity of a person or group or caste, and they play significant role in shaping one's personality as well as providing pride to him/her, besides his/her group (caste). Most of the myths in the caste system are generally anchored in the Hindu mythology and these centre around the personalities or mythological heroes of high origin and their projected achievement. Hence, people of the lower castes also adopt them for the said purpose, though this process cannot be gener-alized at the universal plank. For instance, a large majority of the people of the lower castes in north, west, central and east India hardly believe in the Hindu myth about their origin or that of their castes. So also, they do not derive any inspiration from these for shaping their personality and targeting their achievement. At the most, they refer to the heroic historic personalities, particularly from their own caste or community, for their immediate gains in the secular domains of life and juxtapose that to their primordial affiliations or castes.

On the contrary, a majority of people of the lower castes (ex-untouchables) in South India have adopted several Hinduized myths to trace the origin of their castes, although their orientation towards secular achievement is hardly guided by that. In few cases, the name of their castes also goes along with these myths. For instance, the Arundhatiyas/Arunthathiyars of Andhra Pradesh, Karnataka, Kerala and Tamil Nadu trace their origin from Arundhati, a female goddess of the Hindu mythology. Similarly, the Jambuvulus of Andhra Pradesh, Karnataka, Tamil Nadu and Pondicherry claim their descent from the Rishi (sage) Jambvant of Hindu mythology. Likewise, Pallans or Pallars of Tamil Nadu, where their caste name is also known as Devendrakulathan, claim their ancestry from Devendra, the superior Indra of the Hindu mythology, though they do not do so in Karnataka, Kerala and Pondicherry, where they are in minority or less in number. Besides, a sizeable number of SC people in South India also claim their descent either from goddess Parvati, the wife of Lord Shiva, or from the Rishi Jamdagni or Lord Parashurama and a few other personalities of the Hindu mythology. A point may be mentioned here that their claimed ancestry does not go along with their claimed gotras who are generally revered at the time of mate selection or solemnization of marriage. But they hardly remember their descent or ancestry in their daily routine. Further, quite a few SCs in all the states in South India also follow the gotras and practise totems and taboos, which are either tribal in origin or at least resemble to that. This certainly contradicts their claimed decent from the Hindu mythology, though their belief system and cultural practices are largely drawn from the Hindu pantheon.

Still, one more process has remained at work, in recent years, among the lower castes in South India. Quite a few such castes as Arundhatiya and Jambuvulu of Andhra Pradesh; Arunthathiyar, Chakkiliya, Jambuvulu and Pallan of Karnataka; Arunthathiyar, Chakkiliyan and Pallan of Kerala; Arunthathiyar, Chakkiliyan and Pallan of Tamil Nadu; and Chakkiliyan and Pallan of Pondicherry have started adding a letter or alphabet at the end of their name. Thus, they call themselves Aundhatiyar or Arunthathiyar, Jambuvuluru, Chakkiliyan and Pallar as (or original) name of their castes particularly at the places of the origin. They do this to add respect to their castes like Aiyanagar and Mudaliyar of upper castes; Chettiyar or trading castes; and Nadar, Thevar and Vellalar of the middle level peasant castes of South India, particularly of Tamil Nadu. Such minor addition to the caste's name or change of name of the castes, articu-lated by their socially and politically conscious members, certainly provides two advantages: one, supposedly it places the caste in relatively higher esteem of respectfulness in the local hierarchy of caste system. But unless it is reinforced by the adequate socio-economic and political dominance as well as mobilization of its members, it does not serve the purpose. Two, it inspires and motivates the members to achieve their worth in the secular domain of their life. However, in both the cases, the traditional low rank or status of caste and the stigmatized caste identity of its members often come in the way of defacing the prejudiced attitude and behaviour of the upper and the middle level castes as well as taking the socio-economic achievement and the assertion of the lower castes to the logical end. Hence, the present continuation of untouchability and infliction of violence vis-a-vis atrocities by the former against the latter in South India and elsewhere in the country, though the state often inter-venes ineffectively through its police administration and judiciary.

Social Structure and Social Relations

It is often said that the caste system in South India is more rigid than elsewhere in the country. Though this needs to be empirically verified, a fact, however, may be stated here that the restructuration process of the earlier social system on the line of the Brahmanical system of castes vis-a-vis varnas began in South India since the 6th or 7th century AD and continued till the beginning of the colonial rule. As stated earlier, a number of Brahmins from North India were inducted there who, in turn, helped the local rulers in the process by providing the considerable degree of legitimacy and justification through the existing Dharmashastras and even creating or writing new sets of Sanskritic literature for the purpose. All this means that as the caste system or the Brahmanical caste system in South India is newer in its origin and structuration than that in North India, its relatively more rigidity is to be there compared to that elsewhere in the country. The caste system has been functioning there through all these years with its 'demonstration effect'. Since our concern here is to look at the nature of the existing social structure, inclusive of economic and political structures, in South India and the type of social relations among people of the various castes there, we shall briefly examine that, especially the one, which has come into being since the mid of the colonial rule in India.

Generally speaking, social structure, being abstract at the conceptual level, manifests concretely in the forms of various institutions, organiza-tions, and roles and relations of their members, besides their status or position either ascribed or achieved one. It also consists of differentiation of roles and statuses or positions in their respective existing hierarchy or the overall system of social stratification. Moreover, social structure is operative at local level, hence, localized social structure, which in many ways exists as a replica of the generalized or even abstract social structure. Needless to say that social structure either in its abstract form or as a living reality is inclusive of economic and political power or authority, cultural and personality structures, with their well-defined regulatory mechanism (s). In the way, it also resembles with social system, though at the conceptual level the latter one is not only different from social structure but even its defining properties are separate from that of the former. For instance, a social system may consist of several structures or social structures and their role-relationships. Since our frame of reference of social structure in India, particularly in South India, is limited to caste system with the explicit hierarchy of castes and of status or rank of each caste in it, and both traditional and modern or present role(s) of its members, their achieved and ascribed statuses as well as their incon-gruence, their belief system and cultural practices, and their future aspirations or psychic mobility, we shall explain briefly here how the localized social structure has functioned over the last hundred years or so, and what kinds of changes have occurred in it in all these years.

As mentioned above, the social structure in South India, as elsewhere in the country, is localized in the sense of requirements of people in various regions, yet it largely derives inspirations and even dictates, though more at the psychological level, from the religio-philosophical justification from the Sanskritic texts in whatsoever forms these are known or informed to its members—both literati and laity. In such social structure, people of the upper castes like Brahmin had not only enjoyed the superior most rank in the caste hierarchy but they also remained much better in socio-economic and religious positions than the people of the middle and lower castes till the early 20th century. While this was true in the urban areas, the situation had completely changed in the rural areas since the 1970s because of the earlier adopted Land Reforms Act of the 1960s, followed by the imposed ceiling on the size of the landholding per family. Prior to these land-related legislations, almost all land was in the possession of the Brahmins, former princes or rulers, big landlords, etc., and people of both the middle and lower castes, including Dalits or the SCs, were not only associated with land in their capacity of rentiers and landless labourers respectively but they were also under considerable degree of dominance of the former. With the adoption of the stated legislations, the situation became topsy-turvy at least in the case of the middle level castes, who became the owner-cultivators and also increased the size of their landholdings subsequently through their own efforts. So also, due to the manpower available in the family required for cultivation purpose, they flourished financially and captured power at the local as well as state levels because of their numerical dominance (for Andhra Pradesh, see Rao, 1975, Rao, 1998; for Kerala and Tamil Nadu, see Menchar, 1975; for Karnataka, see Srinivas, 1987).

But, the lower castes or Dalits largely remained unaffected by the said legislations, and were pitiably forced to change their master from the Brahmins and other upper castes to the middle level castes. This brought two significant changes in the rural social structure in South India: one, a sizeable number of Brahmins moved to urban areas and got engaged in white-collar jobs. Those who remained in villages, depended, as and when needed, on favour of the middle level castes for their sustenance and well-beings. Two, the landowners of the middle castes became more tyrants or tyrannical to the lower caste agricultural labourers. They became reluctant to pay required wages to the labourers, mostly Dalits, and started practising untouchability and other forms of discrimination, both overtly and covertly, against them in more stringent fashion. However, such practices did not go unchallenged as the lower castes in rural areas started showing considerable degree of resistance (see Mencher, 1975; Rao, 1998; Yagati, 2003; Viswanthan, 2005; Ramaiah, 2007), resulting into large-scale caste violence and atrocities against them. The situation has, however, remained somewhat different in urban areas where the Brahmins and other upper castes, although in numerical minority, continued to occupy the top positions in bureaucracy, various professions, and in religious and political organizations. While the trading castes managed the economy through trades and commerce, the middle and lower castes were engaged in sundry occupations, besides their employment in lower level bureaucratic jobs, professions, vending, in the unorganized sector of economic activities and so forth. It is only since the last few decades, especially the 1970s, people of the middle castes started showing their presence in bureaucracy, politics and various professions as well as in educational institutions. The educational achievement, employment in white-collar jobs and political participation, in case of the lower castes or SCs in urban areas, are mostly state sponsored through its policy of protective discrimination or reservation, which of course has reached a small section of their population living in both rural and urban areas. A point may be mentioned here that a relatively flexible social structure has emerged in urban areas during all these years, but it has not shelved completely its relation with the traditional social structure based on caste and communal considerations.

On the whole, some fluidity is visible in the structure of society and culture in South India, though crystals of the traditional social structure are definitely found even in day-to-day social interaction of the people drawn specially from the Brahmin and other upper castes as well as from the middle level castes with those of the SCs. These are seen in the attitude and behaviour of both educated and uneducated, rich and poor. But, the fluid social structure as well as social relations among the various castes are found more in urban than in rural areas, where social classes or status groups exist along the achievable attributes like education, occupation and power or authority positions, income and consumption, etc., though these generally do not transcend the traditional caste and communal or community lines in close interaction among the people, as stated above. On the contrary, some flexibility in agrarian social structure has also occurred, but that is confined mostly to the upper and lower castes, as stated earlier. A few classes like upper and lower castes, as classes, along the size of landholding and income level, have emerged in the agrarian social structure, but these again are within the upper and middle level castes where caste still remains a cementing 'barrier in brining these two

caste groups together along their similarity in the class position (Beteille, 1965). Though a large majority of the Dalits or SCs in rural areas fit in the lower class, there is hardly any class affinity between them and others placed in the same class as caste again comes in their way in establishing same class identity, commensal relations and other such close interaction. However, it is mostly the socially and politically conscious people of the SCs who have been striving for bringing some quantitative and qualitative changes in the existing social structure in rural areas by articulating the idioms of social equality, liberty and fraternity, besides that of self-respect, dignity, and social justice—the very dictum of the Constitution for a free society in independent India.

Social Change and Mobility

Being a neutral or value-free term, social change moves in forward or backward direction and has both positive and negative attributes, though in the general usage the former enjoys primacy over the latter. At the concrete level, both development—inclusive of social, economic, political and cultural as well as of human personality—and social structural and cultural modernization, besides cooperation and conflict, are forms of social change. Then, at the social relational level, change in interpersonal and inter-groups relationships is also termed as social change, both in the narrow and broad senses, respectively. In either case, change or social change is both time and space specific, i.e., both quantity and quality of change is visible distinctly at two different times and spaces. Similarly, social mobility as a concept simply means shift from one status or social status to the other either in vertical or horizontal direction. Although social mobility is examined in a given system of social statuses, which is further examined in a given nature, it has also been analyzed extensively along a single status, or unit of status, like occupation, in the western societies, which are relatively open in nature and where occupation plays the most significant role in determining one's income, expenditure pattern, authority, lifestyle, and in a way, social class position. But, in Indian society, it is caste or other such primordial unit that has ever enjoyed the sole primacy in determining one's social status in the system of given social stratification, and occupation and other units of status or position are only the additional inputs to it. Hence, social mobility in the western sense is possible, in Indian society, only in the case of shift of these status units or positions but such society mobility is only partial and not total (for details, see Ram, 1988), unless the entire group or corporate status group like caste or caste-like primordial unit moves either vertically or horizontally. It is not out of context to mention here that either vertical or horizontal move/mobility of an individual also does not help much as he/she is necessarily an inherent part of a caste or such primordial unit. Yet, mobility or social mobility in his/her case takes place along a single or even multiple status units, and it has also drawn attention of a few social scientists, especially sociologists and social anthropologists, historians, etc., in their study of present as well as past society in India, though some studies of social mobility of the entire corporate status group are also available.

There are two more interesting aspects of social mobility in Indian society, particularly the Hindu caste system: one, social mobility through social movement and, two, through the state sponsorship, the former being operative since the early times and the latter, of course, being the creation of the post-independent period. Since the early period of the colonial rule in India, a few untouchable castes, like Izhava of Kerala and Shanan of Tamil Nadu, had organized strong social movement for their elevation in the hierarchy of caste system in the respective states. As the frame of reference of their upward social mobility happened to be the caste system, they succeeded in getting them elevated to the level of middle castes. Consequently, the Shanan adopted the nomenclature of Nadar but the Izhava retained the same nomenclature, though with the higher rank in the caste hierarchy. Besides, there have been several other castes tradi-tionally middle ranked like Kamma and Reddy in Andhra Pradesh; Lingayat and Vokaligga in Karnataka; Nayar in Kerala; and Thevar, Vannier and Vellala in Tamil Nadu, which have claimed their status or rank at par with the traditional Kshatriya caste (which had never existed in South India) due to their economic, political and numerical dominance in the respective states. But, such claim, if there was any, of majority of the untouchable castes or the SCs had never succeeded due to their traditional impure status as well as their economic and political vulnerability. Inter-estingly, the social reformers of the medieval period as well as the political leaders and ideologues of the colonial period had always condemned the caste system and emphasized social equality through the fair and equalitarian deal in the secular domains like education, employment, political power or authority, and social interaction and social relations with others. For the purpose, they had organized numerous social movements and made several petitions and submitted memorandums to the government. Needless to say that they succeeded to some extent, but looking at the huge population size of the untouchable castes, and the limitations of resources and the various types of social constraints of the government, their efforts could not produce the desired results. Moreover, the counter-forces or the status quoists resisted to any meaningful initiatives towards the required radical change or shift, in the then existing social order, to produce the desired results. All such initia-tives yet paved the way for realizing limited upward social mobility within the frame of socio-economic status or loosely termed as class or social class, which in itself is problematic at the operative level, not being exclusive of caste or such other primordial unit, as stated earlier.

However, the limited upward social mobility, in the case of SCs, STs and now the OBCs within the framework of socio-economic status or social class, has been sponsored by the state, through the policy of reser-vation, as stated above. But such social mobility is confined only to a tiny section of the entire SCs all over the country, although the size of such section of the upwardly mobile SCs varies from region to region and from one SC to the other. In fact, the binary concept of sponsored and contest social mobility is distinctively visible as intertwined, rather, overlapping in the case of the upwardly mobile SCs where for the state's sponsorship of limited positions or status sets, there is contest among thousands of persons of these castes. The sponsorship is based on the individual's achievable attributes or merits, which could have proved them to be upwardly mobile even without the state's sponsorship, provided there was fair chance. Also, the upward social mobility of the SCs, at both the individual and group levels, is definitely inspired by the positive references of upwardly mobile individuals as well as groups drawn from the same or other such social background. It is also reinforced, though distantly, by several social movements organized for the purpose in the past. Then, both social change and social mobility together contribute significantly to bring about change in the social relations at micro-as well as macro-level social structure by making the latter relatively fluid.

Then, social change and mobility among the SCs or Dalits in South India is to be analyzed within the social structure operative at both the micro and macro levels. Within the micro or village level social structure, it may be said that not much significant change has occurred among them over the last hundred years or so. For instance, their traditionally low status continues to exist in the local caste hierarchy in villages. The practice of untouchability and other forms of discrimination in their day-to-day interaction and social relations with people of the other castes and communities still exist in rural areas and small towns, though their conditions are, in some ways, better in cities. Not much qualitative and quantitative change is seen in the agrarian wage structure, and consequently the greater number of younger generation of SCs or Dalits has become urban oriented during all these years. At the social relational level, greater degree and amount of tension and conflict has emerged between the SCs and non-SCs as is evident from the large number of caste conflict between them and the atrocities inflicted on the former in rural areas. Such change or social change is to be perceived as a corollary of the growing nature and amount of social consciousness and awareness, and also their assertion for dignity, self-respect and social justice among the SCs or Dalits on one hand, and intolerance and suppression of the non-SCs towards the former on the other, in rural south India, as stated earlier. However, a fact may be mentioned here that such form of social change is witnessed among only those SCs whose number or population size is large and who are more oriented towards achieving upward social mobility in the given social structure in rural areas. By implication, they also intend to alter or bring about qualitative change in that, which is resistibly retained by the non-SCs.

The social structure is also to be understood in terms of intra-caste arrangement where each SC has been regulating its internal affairs through the mandatory caste panchayat. The caste panchayat has all along exerted its control over the deviant behaviour of caste members through assigning punishment either in the form of cash or kind or community feast as well as temporary boycott or ex-communication of offender from the caste, depending upon the nature and degree of offence. The caste membership of the offender used to be restored after fulfilling or meeting out the punishment. Sometimes, the caste panchayat has also mobilized the members to forgo the customary practice and bring about social reform among them. As the caste panchayat used to be constituted either hereditarily or by elderly persons of the caste, irrespective of level of their education and social consciousness, the younger generation started, in modern time, looking at it as oriented towards backwardness of the caste; hence, they invariably flouted its decision or arbitration, resulting into its irrelevance or absence among majority of the SCs in rural South India. Hence, the contemporary social structure among the SCs in South India, particularly in villages, remains amorphous, though traditional structural attributes are still present in preponderance and their relevance may not last long. The emergence of new social structure or restructuration of the existing one in rural South India in general, and among the SCs in particular, which is forcefully resisted by the upper and middle level castes, is a time-consuming process, and its concrete nature and form lies only in future. Needless to say that the initiation of such process has been made by younger generation of the SCs as it improve their life chances vis-a-vis social status in both social and caste hierarchies at the macro and micro levels.

Finally, limited social mobility has taken place among the SCs, both in rural and urban areas in South India, through both sponsorship, including contest, and social movement—the former being available in more systematic form since the independence of the country and the latter remaining a continuous process at least since the beginning of the 20th century. Without going into details of these two processes, it may be surmised here that both intra- and inter-generational social mobility is visible among them more in urban than rural areas. It is found in the forms of educational achievement, white-collar and other non-traditional employment, and limited amount of power or authority. Not only their income level is relatively improved, but they have also acquired greater degree of awareness and consciousness, besides their being assertive and more identity conscious. In rural areas, the limited upward social mobility is witnessed in the form of their being conscious and aware of the individual as well as collective identity, its suppression, oppression and exploitation and so forth, irrespective of their educational level and sources of livelihood. However, their consciousness vis-a-vis psychic or psychological mobility has not sailed without unequivocal resistance from the upper and middle level castes. Their such psychological mobility, yet, continues to draw inspiration from their better-off brethren in urban areas and an overall awareness and consciousness emerged in all these years in

Indian society as a whole in which the state initiatives, along with the existing socio-political leadership as well as of civil society or voluntary organizations, have also contributed to some extent.

REFERENCES

Ambedkar, B.R. 1979. "Castes in India: Their Mechanism, Genesis and Development" (First published in 1917), in *Dr. Babasaheb Ambedkar: Writings and Speeches,* Vol. 1, Government of Maharashtra, Bombay.

________. 1990. "The Untouchables: Who Were They and Why They Became Untouchables?" (first published in 1948), in *Dr. Babasaheb Ambedkar: Writings and Speeches,* Vol. 7, Government of Maharashtra, Bombay.

Bailey, F.G. 1963. "Closed Social Stratification in India", *European Journal of Sociology,* 4(1), pp. 107-24.

Bara, Joseph. 2002. "Tribe-Beast or Man: Case for a New Concept of Tribe", *Social Action,* Vol. 51, pp. 121-33.

Berreman, G.D. 1979. "Self, Situation and Escape from Stigmatised Ethnic Identity" in his *Caste and Other Inequalities,* Meerut: Folklore Institute, Meerut, pp. 164-77.

Beteille, Andre. 1965. *Caste, Class and Power.* Delhi: Oxford University Press.

________. 1997. "The Concept of Tribe with Special Reference to India", in his *Society and Politics in India: Essays in a Comparative Perspective.* Delhi: Oxford University Press, pp. 57-78.

Bose, N.K. 1994. *The Structure of Hindu Society.* New Delhi: Orient Longman.

Bougie, Celestin. 1971. *Essays on the Caste System in India.* Cambridge: Cambridge University Press.

Champakalakshmi, R. 1975. "State and Economy: South India Circa A.D. 400-1300", in Romila Thapar (ed.), *Recent Perspectives of Early Indian History.* Bombay: Popular Prakashan, pp. 266-308.

Dumont, Louis. 1970, 1974. *Homo Hierarchies: The Caste System and Its Implication.* Chicago: The University of Chicago Press.

Dutt, N.K. 1984. *Origin and Growth of Caste in India.* Calcutta: Firma KLM Private Ltd.

Ghurye, G.S. 1963. *The Scheduled Tribes.* Bombay: Popular Prakashan.

Gupta, Dipankar. 1993. "Continuous Flierarchies and Discrete Castes", in his (ed.), *Social Stratification.* New Delhi: Oxford University Press, pp. 110-42.

Gurukul, Rajan. 1995. "The Beginnings of the Historic Period: The Tamil South" in Romila Thapar (ed.), *Recent Perspectives of Early Indian History.* Bombay: Popular Prakashan.

Jaiswal, Suvira. 1990. Caste: Origin, Function and Dimensions of Change. *New Delhi: Manohar.*

Jha, Vivekanand. 1975. "Stages in the History of Untouchable", *Indian Historical Review.* Vol. 2.

Karashima, N. 1997. "The Untouchables in Tamil Inscriptions and other Historical Sources in Tamil Nadu", in H. Kotani (ed.), *Caste System, Untouchability and the Depressed,* New Delhi: Manohar, pp. 21-30.

Klass, Morton. 1998. Caste: The Emergence of South Asian Social System. *Manohar, New Delhi: Manohar.*

Kosambi, D.D. 1953. "The Brahman Clans", *American Journal of Orientalist Society,* Vol. 73, pp. 202-08. *1956. An Introduction to the Study of Indian History. Bombay: Popular* Prakashan.

_______. 1962. Myth and Reality: Studies in the Formation of Indian Culture. Bombay: Popular Prakashan.

_______. 1965. The Culture and Civilization of Ancient India in Historical *Outline.* New Delhi: Vikas Publishing House Pvt. Ltd.

Levi-Strauss, Claude. 1963. "The Bear and the Barber", The Journal of the Royal Anthropological Institute of Great Britain and Ireland, *93(1), pp. 1-11*

Majumdar, D.N. 1961. *Races and Cultures of India.* New York: Asia Publishing House.

Mandelbaum, David. 1972. *Society in India.* Bombay: Popular Prakashan.

Mencher, J.P. 1974. "Cases System Upside Down: The not-so Mysterious East", *Current Anthropology,* Vol. 12, pp. 191-209.

_______. 1975. "Agricultural Labour Movement in their Socio-Political and Ecological Context: Tamil Nadu and Kerala", in B.N. Nair (ed.), *Culture and Society.* Delhi: Thompson Press (India) Limited, pp. 240-66.

Muller, Max. 1883. *India, What Can it Teach Us?* London: Longman, Green and Co.

Nagaraju, S. 1995. "Emergence of Regional Identity and Beginnings of Vernacular Literature: A Case Study of Telugu", *Social Scientist,* Vol. 23. Nos. 10-12, pp. 8-23.

Ram, Nandu. 1988. *The Mobile Scheduled Castes: Rise of a New Middle Class.* Delhi: Hindustan Publishing Corporation.

Ramaiah, A. 2007. *Laws for Dalit Rights and Dignity.* Jaipur: Rawat Publica-tions.

Rao, B.S.S. 1975. "The Land Reforms and their Impact: Study of a Coastal Andhra Village", in B.N. Nair (ed.), *Culture and Society.* Delhi: Thompson (India) Ltd., pp. 370—23.

Rao, N. Sudhakar. 1998. *Organised Power and Unorganised Resistance.* New Delhi: Aravali Books International.

Ray, H.P. 1975. "Trade and Contacts", in Romila Thapar (ed.), *Recent Perspectives of Early Indian History.* Bombay: Popular Prakashan, pp. 142-75.

Risely, H.H. 1908. *The People of India.* Calcutta: Thacker, Spink and Company.

Srinivas, M.N. 1966. *Social Change in Modern India.* Berkeley: University of California Press.

_______. 1987. The Dominant Caste and Other Essays. *New Delhi: Oxford* University Press.

Subramaniam, N,, 1997. *Tamil Social History.* Vol. 1, Chennai: Institute of Asian Studies.

Thapar, Romila. 1998. *Asoka and the Decline of the Mauryas.* New Delhi: Oxford University Press.

_______. 1999. *Interpreting Early India.* New Delhi: Oxford University Press.

Viswanathan, S. 2005. *Dalits in Dravidian Land.* Chennai: Navayana Publishing.

Weber, Max. 1958. *The Religion of India.* Glencoe: Free Press.

Yagati Chinna Rao. 2003. *Dalits' Struggle for Identity: Andhra and Hyderabad 1990-1950.* New Delhi: Kanishka Publishers & Distributors.

6

Studying Dalit Movements, Protests and Social Change: Some Theoretico-Methodological Issus

It is widely known that over the last few decades a substantive number of writings have been published on the issues. Some of these have portrayed the pitiable socio-economic conditions vis-a-vis plights of the Dalits – Scheduled Castes (SCs) and Scheduled Tribes (STs) in the country. While a few have addressed the ongoing perpetration of untouchability on and the various forms of discrimination practiced, especially against the SCs, who are even singularly addressed as Dalits, the others have analysed the various types of atrocities committed on both the Scheduled Castes and Scheduled Tribes. Still, a very few studies have explained the social development taken place among them along with the relative progress in their educational achievement, employment position, especially in the public sector, and political empowerment through their representation in Parliament, State Assembly and Panchayati Raj Institutions. However, not many studies have been conducted on the issues related to the numerous movements orgainsed by the Dalits against the commission of atrocities on them and, so also, on the issues related to their assertion for accord of a dignified and respectful social identity for them. Then going by the critical assessment of all these studies, one finds that while these contribute, in one way or the other, to understand the various issues related to the Dalits, most of these also suffer, at the same time, from a number of misgivings or misreporting. Interestingly, such misgivings have crept in these writings of both academics, the journalists and the social activists, perhaps due to the lack of their full understanding about the ground reality pertaining to the Dalits and more so due to the lack, in their writings, of certain specific framework(s) to analyse this reality in a systematic theoretico-analytical perspective supported by a proper methodology for the purpose. This may also be so perhaps due to their etic rather than amic views on the Dalit issues. It is also not out of context to mention here that these misgivings are rooted in the very understanding of certain concepts which are often in usage these days as well as in the lack of conceptual differentiation between the terms Dalit, and Dalit movement and Dalit protest. The Dalit as a concept or conceptual category is used in two senses – in the narrow sense and in; the broad sense, and the concepts of Dalit movement and of the Dalit protest are often used interchangeably. Another misgiving about the antecedents of both of these concepts is that, as a process, these always lead to social as well as physical conflicts of one type or the other between the Dalits and the non-Dalits resulting into disturbing the social harmony or social equilibrium, as if in absence of that Indian society or, more precisely, the Hindu social system remains properly cohesive and fully integrated. But contrarily, such social system, on the ground reality, is completely incoherent and highly divisive from within, though in principle it does not appear so from outside. Moreover, one also forgets the fact that the conflict or more appropriately the social conflict has been viewed, in sociological literature, as functional and it brings a type of social change qualitatively different from the one emanated from the usual functioning of the structural elements of the social system. Still another misgiving related to this is that the social change resulted from Dalit movements or even from Dalit protests vis-à-vis conflict or social conflict has all along been equated with social justice assuming as if both such social change and social justice have negative connotations and are undesirable from the existing systemic point of view. But the disciplinary requirement of social sciences in general and sociology in particular needs to examine the

Dalit movements and social change in a perspective to be evolved though converging both the structural-functional and the conflict approaches of studying a social phenomenon. In other words, there is a need to examine the contemporary Dalit movement vis-à-vis social change accepting these not only as isolatory happenings or separate units of analysis, but also to analyse them in a coherent manner particularly in relation to the society and culture that has existed in India. This also needs to understand the given socio-economic and political scenario in which Dalits are motivated, either voluntarily or under compulsion, to organise their movements or protests often resulting into conflict or social conflict and thereby producing social change of several varieties, of which one variety might be the movement or the protest itself organised by them.

My intention in this paper is not merely to clarify the above-mentioned misgivings and thereby to redefine the concepts of Dalit; Dalit movement, protest and social change as they have been understood particularly in sociology and social anthropology, but also to examine how Dalit movements contextually and even theoretically (if there could be any) are different, in some ways, from social movements of general nature. The paper also aims to enquire into the concept of protest and to examine the nature and degree of social change that a Dalit movement or even a Dalit protest produces either directly or indirectly and its role in comprehending it as such produced by the state and other agencies. In the end, the paper also suggests some theoretico-methodological perspective or framework for studying Dalit movements or protests and social change not in isolation but in totality whereby it may enable the scholars to study afresh the Indian society, polity, economy and even cultural system(s) in a coherent manner with which every section of population might identify both emotionally as well as substantially in whatsoever manner it could.

From the structural-functional point of view anchored in maintaining the systemic status-quo, any movement or protest has been regarded as aberration. So, the analysis of the nature and degree of social change which Dalit movement or protest produces seems to be either undermined or engrossed largely with such consideration, of its being aberration, in the ongoing academic discourses both in India and abroad. Without endorsing the movement or protest, or for that matter, the Dalit movements and Dalit protests as aberration in the existing society or social system in India, we intend to clarify here the concepts of Dalit movement and Dalit protest, and then to go into explaining other properties of the issues under reference.

There is no denial of the fact that a few studies done in sociology on the Dalit movements have invariably made reference to the concept of social movement. Even the concept of Dalit protest has been analysed with reference to the concept of protest or social protest (for details, see Oommen 1990; Jogdand 1991; Gore 1993; Ram 1995). This simply means that no exclusive effort has been made so far to conceptualise the term Dalit movement or Dalit protest without making reference of movement and protest extensively studied in sociology and social anthropology. The reasons for this could be of two-fold; one, the studies in sociology of Dalit movement vis-à-vis protest started quite lately. This may be attributed to the fact that the Indian sociology, for about half a century, was involved in studying the institutions primarily of family, village and case. These institutions were studied not only through the structural-functional approach or perspective, but even living with these institutions by the Dalits was either ignored or was accepted obliquely similar to that lived with by the non-Dalits. Secondly, studies in sociology did not accept the Dalits as a separate social category, although they accepted them as a separate conceptualisation of the movements and protests organised by Dalits. It is, therefore, imperative to conceptualise the Dalits as a separate social category and so also to conceptualise separately the movements vis-à-vis protests organised by them.

We have mentioned above that the term Dalit has two different connotations of which no distinction is made in usage in the contemporary academic discourses and so also in the non-academic reflections. Keeping aside a third connotation or definition of it being synonym to class which was formulated in the early 1970s but could not percolate to the level of usage in the masses, the first conceptual understanding of the term Dalit is to be seen in the sense that it is used by socially and politically conscious youth of a particular Scheduled Caste living in a particular region for the people of their own caste. It can be said here that with such usage, the Dalit as a concept or a conceptual category has neither percolated down to the masses of; the same caste nor has it been accepted by others within the same region. In the second sense, the concept of Dalit has a broader connotation where it is used by all the socially and politically conscious youth not only for the various Scheduled Castes as a unified social category, but also for the numerous Scheduled Tribes. It is a different matter that at the level of ground reality, the different Scheduled Castes and Scheduled Tribes do not fully endorse and use it in their day-to-day social interaction and social relation. The reason for this could be located not in their national and socio-cultural differentiation, but in the lack of a wider level of their socio-political consciousness especially about their uniformity or even near-uniformity in their socio-economic deprivations. However, as a matter of fact, the process of uniform use of the term Dalit with its broader connotation is increasingly visible for them and among them.

What is important to mention here is that such usage of the term Dalit, with its broader connotation, represents not only all the scheduled castes and tribes and thereby it relies on their socio-economic deprivations of various nature and degree, but it also brings them closer even if their closeness is merely a notional or emotional one. However, if one intends to view such unification as a process of class formation either in Marxian or Weberian sense, then it is not free from the problematic. The simple reason for this is that the term Dalit with its broader connotation accepts them (all the Scheduled Castes and Scheduled Tribes) as a unified entity only in terms of their uniformity in the context of their various types of deprivations such as their economic exploitation, social subordination, absence of assertion for their cultural autonomy and so forth, in spite of their differential social and geographical location. Yet, their such closeness cannot be easily dismissed in accepting them as a social category, or even as a conceptual category for that matter, particularly in event of enormous degree of uniformity in their deprivations in spite of retaining their distinctiveness of being caste and tribe. Such proposition for redefining the term Dalit, with its broader connotation, is of course in the process of making.

Then, it is logically imperative to define or even redefine the Dalit movement wherein it could be somewhat different from the definition accepted so far by the sociologists, journalists, social activists and so forth. We have stated above that the Dalit movement has been treated as one of the many types of movements or social movements organised by different segments of population for different purposes. So has been the case with the definition of the term Dalit protest. In the existing sociological literature; protest has been defined in the sense of an ideology and social movement in the sense of a mechanism "through which men attempt to move from the periphery of the system to its enter" (Oommn 1990:30). It has also been said that "movements are the conscious efforts on the part of men to litigate their deprivations and secure justice" (Ibid).

Briefly speaking, movement or social movement is a collective action on the part of men as well as women for achieving certain goal with the help of an ideology, mobilisation of its pursuant or participants and its (of collective action) durability or a time frame (Rao 1984; Oommen 1990, Jogdand 1991). This also means that once a goal is achieved, the movement or social movement is terminated. Contrary to this, a social movement has also been viewed "as a pattern of socially meaningful behavior at the level of objective consequences" (Gore 1993). In this sense, a social movement has been seen as an ideology created even to recurrent phenomenon whose objectives may be to bring out certain change in the existing system or to change the same and set up a new social system or social order (ibid). All such definitions of a movement or social movement may be helpful in understanding, to a great extent, the concept of Dalit movement as well as Dalit protest. But in view of the fact that Dalit as a conceptual category has both the narrow and broader senses, the existing definition of social movement or protest may not be sufficient to fully comprehend and conceptualise the Dalit movement or even Dalit protest. What is needed, then, to add the specific attribute of Dalitness, on one hand, and both the social deprivations and cultural distinctiveness of Dalits for ascertaining a complete or near complete definition of a Dalit movement or protest, on the other.

It is not out of context to mention here that a protest as an act of behavior of an individual or collectively is for a limited purpose and for a short period. Besides, it may remain successful or unsuccessful in achieving its goal or objective. But a movement may be a broader issue to address – be it getting rid of deprivations of the group or collectively by having its access to the given resources, finding a proper place through correcting he inconsistencies in the social system or to completely replace the existing social system by advocating for a new one. Since the goal or objective of movement is wider and so also vital to the existing social system, it may not only invite greater degree of resistance from the existing system or the opposite forces in the system, but it may also take longer time to achieve its goal. Therefore, it may reoccur or get organised again and again till its defined goal is achieved. Broadly speaking, the major objective of the Dalit movement is not only to have the Dalit's access to the existing resources and to correct the inconsistency in the given system, but also to change the existing social system or order in Indian society wherein the Dalit may get accord of a dignified and respectful social identity. So, the Dalit movement, both at the definitional and operational level, is to be qualitatively and quantitatively different from a general movement as such.

Similarly, in the case of protest, I may hasten to clarify that while agreeing with Gore's (1989:3) view on protest involving "rejection, confrontation and conflict: the protest is to be accepted as a temporal phenomenon which may occur for a short period and subside with or without fulfilment of is goal(s). It is, however, clear from a few writings on Dalit movement and Dalit protest that both the terms have been used interchangeably, as stated earlier. But one has to make a distinction between the two, especially along with the nature of the pursued goals and the time-span covered by them. In other words, the Dalit protest may be of short duration with a relatively less important goal(s)which may or may not be fulfilled through the protests organised by the Dalits. On the other hand, the

Dalit movement may be longer duration with the mobilisation of a greater number of people and, thus, may continue for a longer period especially till the goal is achieved fully or even partially.

Another aspect less frequently referred to in studying Dalit movement or protest is the social change brought but it. This can, however, be easily identified in the form(s) of achievement of the goals of the movement or protest and, in turn, the social change that it brings out in the existing society or social order. But as stated above, the social attention of the scholars who have studied Dalit movement or even Dalit protest in sociology, with both its positive and negative connotations, has extensively has been studied specially in the form of development and modernisation. A few studies have also analysed social change taken place in India society, both in the single and multiple directions. It may not be exaggerations to say that both the social structure and social change have extensively been studied in sociology in relation to the ongoing change in the structure and culture in Indian society. But the smaller number of studies conducted on the social change produced by Dalit movement or protest can be attributed to the lack of serious or even less serious attempt made by the scholars in their study of Dalit movement. This also means the lack of serious concern on the part of scholars particularly sociologists in studying Dalit movement and protest, in spite of the fact that, according to Oommen (1990:31-32), the collective action or social movement is one of the several roots to bring change in the society.

Although the question remains as to why certain sections of people, particularly the less endowed one, opt for movement for bringing change in their own life conditions vis-à-vis in the existing social order particularly in the event of the efforts made by the government, civil society, etc. The answer to this could easily be located in the fact that the nature and degree of social change produced by the state or the civil society is to be at the full satisfaction of the socially and economically deprived sections of the population namely, the Dalit inclusive of Scheduled Castes and the Scheduled Tribes. Hence, in the absence of that they are often compelled to organise their movements or even protests to achieve the desired type and degree of social change in their present-day life conditions. But more than that their movements are targeted, albeit, to bring out a total change in the society or to set up a new social order. Yet,the frequency of their organising such movements and even their commitment to these needs to be seriously and systematically examined. This is necessary in view of the fact the Dalit movements and protests often die their premature death either after getting their short-term goals fulfilled or due to bickering in leadership including factionalism in their organisation, especially of gratification along with co-option of the movement leaders in the existing counter-forces or social order. This present state of affairs the Dalit movement needs to be examined seriously by converging both the amic and ehic views in the study of Dalit movement.

Looking at the issues addressed by the Dalit movements, one finds that these more often address to the issues related to the day-to-day life conditions of the Dalits. But these also address latently to evolve a new type of social order in which the perennial deprivations of the Dalits could be resolved. This has clearly been articulated by Oommen (1990:32) who has come with the theory of social movement by suggesting the interlocking of past, present and future. In his own words, "At a deeper level the framework (implying past, present and future) implies that men make history, and constantly learn from their historicity. Movements are neither mere accidents nor entirely resultants manipulations by leaders and demagogues but the consequences of conscious effort of men to change system in the light of their past experiences, avoiding its pitfalls. Finally, the continuous occurrence of the movements implies that manis not imprisoned by present structure and no moratorium on his creativity can be imposed" (Ibid). This equally implies in the case of Dalit movements which relied on the experiences of their present-day deprivations that they address and strive to get it resolved. But in the given situation when they find it difficult to achieve their goals, they invariably look for evolving a new social order in which their existing social deprivations could be removed fully with faster rate and, so also, they can achieve a dignified and respectful social identity.

Then at the methodological level, the pertinent question arises as how to study the Dalit movement in a systematic manner. Reflecting on the methodological problems in studying social movement, Oommen (Ibid:41) has encountered with the problems related to a scale of movements and the issues related to the units and levels of observation as to how far a movement has succeeded in achieving its goals. In the case of a scale of the movement, he has talked about the number of participants whether large or small – in the movement, the time-span of the movement – whether for a short period or a long period, and the social composition of the participants in a movement. Similarly, in the case of observation about nature and result of the movement, he has suggested to study the social movement, both at the micro (local) and macro (in different regions) levels. In his opinion, both the number of participants, their mobilisation and degree of their commitment to the goal of the movement depend on the geographical region it covers. This also means that a social movement may be bounded by a specific geographical territory based on the issues which are purely localised and it may also be open-ended, involving several regions due to nature of the issue(s) which it covers.

This methodology may be equally applicable in the case of study of a Dalit movement and protest. Yet, what is to be added to this is that as in the case of Dalits, their socio-economic deprivations may apparently look distinctive, it may, therefore, be said that a Dalit movement or protest may be organised purely around such deprivations which may, of course, be termed as the immediate factor or reason for organising their movement. There may, however, be the approximate reasons or factors which may be found, more or less, in the similar nature and degree in other regions. Therefore, while studying Dalit movement a scholar has to look into both the social composition of its leadership and also its commitment. It is true that the leaders of the Dalit movement come generally from the socially and politically conscious sections of their population. It is altogether a different matter that their commitment may be more pronounced to the immediate goal set by the Dalit movement. But its far-reaching consequences may not necessarily be confined to taking the movement to the local level. Its leaders may also be grappled with the process of their getting gratified or accommodated through their relatively easy access in the existing system itself. Therefore, what is needed at the methodological level is to enquire into the net result a Dalit movement or protest produces in a short or long time-span.

In sum, the Dalit movement and social change are to be studied in a framework, of the cause and effect(s), irrespective of the fact that whether this effect or change is really operative or not in evolving a new social order. Even if it succeeds in making any little alteration in the perennial socio-economic deprivations of the Dalits, it may be given some credit for its successful or even unsuccessful delivery. The students of a Dalit movement have necessarily to take note of the fact that the Dalit movement is to be understood in a sequential manner not only implying the trajectory of past, present and future wherein the nature of Dalits' deprivations may or may not vary, but they have also to go for a well-defined method of study where they have to accept that the Dalit movement is also prone to change in its nature and composition. Besides, it acts as an agent of bringing about the desired change in; the existing society and, so also, of evolving a new social order, depending upon its persistent occurrence.

7

Dalit Movements and Changes in the Caste System in India

Caste system in India is a system of graded inequality wherein numerous castes and sub-castes are vertically arranged in a hierarchy which is considered primarily to be sacred or religious in nature. Such vertical gradation's or claims for that exist even among those castes which are found to be horizontally placed in the hierarchy of the caste system. The institution of caste has remained in existence over thousand years in the Indian society with its varied social structure and multiple functions through different times and spaces. It is still lived with by over three-fourth population of India. Caste exists in the sense of popularity and has, thus , acquired its own systemic form or even forms in different parts of the country. All along, there have been two opposite views on the issue of caste. One view has always justified the legitimacy of caste or caste system . On the ground that it reinforces to and is helpful in smooth functioning of the society particularly the Hindu social system. The adherents to such view generally hail from those castes which have been considered *dwijas (* twice born) and are placed at the top ______ of the caste hierarchy. These castes have been ranked along with the three upper *varnas* of Brahman, Kshatriya and Vaishya though ranks of these castes vary considerably from the ranks of these *varnas* in different regions in the country. These castes have availed both the ritual and secular privileges of the caste system. Even those sociologists and social anthropologists who have functionalist orientation in their perspective emphasize indirectly on legitimacy of the caste through their analysis of the structural-functional organisation and imperatives of the caste system.

The opponents to this view are those who belong to those castes which are placed at the lowest rungs of the caste hierarchy. These are generally the lower castes of the lowest *Shudra varna* and the untouchable castes which are said to be outside the pale of the four-fold division of the varna system or are members of the fifth varna if the traditional varna system is extended to the five-fold division . They have been opposing both the varna system and the caste system since the early time as they have found these systems most exploitative and favourable to members of the upper castes and varnas only. These systems have imposed numerous ignominies and social and religious disabilities of those who happen to be placed at the lower and the lowest echilons. Their opposition to the varna system and more to the caste system is based also on the fact that these systems are divisive and segmentary because the privileges of few and the disadvantages of many have not only fragmented the population from being cohesive but have also generated growing degree of tensions and conflicts among the different segments (castes and sub-castes) of poulations. The caste system negates the many principles of equality, liberty, fraternity and social justice; hence, it is to be annihilated . Caste system in contemporary India is not the same as it was say about hundred years ago. This does not mean that in the earlier times caste system was a monolithic system and was operative for all the times , in equal fashion all over the country. Instead, there existed considerable gap between theory and practice of the caste system and also if the varna system (Manuel ___1972:22) . This gap identified various types of changes in the system. Such change in the caste system have remained gradual and have been possible due to number of forces operated in the past besides the dissensions, protests and oppositions launched both in the organized and unorganized forms by those who were opposed to it. The changes have been accelerated in hte contemporary period due to the process of modernization, urbanization and industrialization

, economic development, educational advancement, occupational diversification, state actions and so on. Even today, there are people specially belonging to the lower and the lowest castes – the Dalits who are opposed to the caste system because they find it as a system of inequality and hence, dysfunctional for achievement of the most cherished goals of equality, fraternity and social justice. They also find the caste system undesirable promoting functionalism and bickering, and sharpening the prejudices and hatred of one caste against the other . In brief, they have been carrying out movements though not always against the caste system but quite often against the evils and dysfunctionality of the caste system.

We shall try to examine , in this article, the types and the extent of changes in the caste system caused by the Dalit movements carried out , specially after independence, in different parts of the country. We shall enquire into the genesis and the phased development of the Dalit movements and analyse the issues raised and fought by them. Finally, we shall look into the future prospects of the Dalit movements and their roles to be played in bringing about some notable changes in the caste system in years to come.

Nature of Dalit movement:

Before we analyse the nature of caste system in contemporary India and changes occurred therein due to the impact of Dalit movements, besides of other processes, it is necessary to briefly explain the nature of and issues before the Dalit movements in the present time. It is also significant to view these movements in a wider socio-political cultures prevailing in the country. Whether the afitations , versitences and protests shown by the Dalits against their exploitation and harassment can be termed as movement or not needs to be examined. The term Dalit has a much wider connotation. It has been used for the Scheduled castes or classes , minorities , women and the poor of upper castes in the Hindu Society. As such, its characteristics are those of a class or social class. We have used this term , in this article, only for the Scheduled castes of the Hindu caste system and for those Scheduled castes who have converted to Buddhism, Christianity, Sikhism and Islam in India.

As the Scheduled castes of the Hindu faith and those converted to other religious faiths are scattered on every villages, towns and cities in the country and the latter are known as neo-Buddhists, neo- Christians , neo-Muslims etc., and they have been carrying out their agitations and movements all over, there is nothing like- "Dalit Movement" . Instead, there are Dalit movements of distinct variations which have been carried out time and again by the Dalits for the purposes of wage increase, veseuting against their social and economic exploitation, and their self-respect and dignity, equality and liberty both in rural and urban areas in different parts of the country. These agitations protests, etc. , of the Dalits are movements as they fulfil some, if not at all, characteristics of a movement.

Conceptually a movement or social movement in an organized effort made by some persons, group or community as such for a specific purpose. In their words, " a social movement is an organized attempt on the part of a section of society to bring about either partial or total change in socially through collective mobilization based on an ideology" (Rao 1978:2). The ideology of the Dalit movements is the ideology of protest against their exploitation and harassment and also against the caste system as a white of which the unequal treatment with their is a part. Thus, their movement is a social movement "with wider social objectives, carried out by the Dalits themselves for their complete liberation from the stronghold of the caste system" (Jogland 1991:9). It is further said, " As a matter of fact, the quest of the Dalit movement is the levelling up the status of people and it is the real manifestation of a new consciousness among them (the Dalits). This new awaking has not only provided them basis for establishing self-respect, self-determinism and honour among them, but also a means for protesting against the domination of upper castes and classes in the society. Those groups who have joined the movement have a sense of self-respect and feeling of unity , an urge for improving their social and economic status and a political awareness which may be of significant in the solution of India's age-old problem of untouchability" (ibid:14).

In fact, Dalit movements are protest movements which are directed to certain social collectivities, groups, communities and also to social norms, values ,,system etc, as these are considered to be inimical to the goal of social equality, liberty and fraternity. The protest of Dalits " is also directed against the governments attitudes which, in their opinion, are passives and sometimes partial and even partisan especially on issues like implementing properly certain constitutional measures and protecting them from both social and physical violence committed on them by other" (Ram 1988:129). It is necessary to clarify that all protests do not qualify to be called protest movements . For instance, an individual Dalit labourer protests against his exploitation by his master but that does not mean that he carries out a movement. Then for a movement or a protest movement a collectivity or collective mobilization is must and it would have a specific ideology for attaining certain goal. Moreover, the unrest, agitation and protest movements of the Dalits also aim to oppose their age-old deprivations and the privations of the privileged groups or communities. It is argued that" The disadvantaged persist in seeking change to escape the privations of the *status quo* more often than not in full awareness that the likelihood of achieving that change is slim. It is testimony to the depth of their disadvantaged, as well as to their courage and the pervasiveness of resistence to oppression, that they persist in the attempt to throw it off" (Berreman 1979:226). Nature of the Dalit movements varies from issues to issues and contexts to contexts. Some are militant whereas others are active resistence to the economic exploitation and social harassment. In the words of Berreman, "the poor and oppressed in India have recently mounted a number of militant movements whose aim is fundamental social, cultural, political, economic, and sometimes religious changes. These essentially revolutionary movements focus on emancipation from the consequences of low caste and class status through revolt against the entire system which reverses wealth, power and privilege for the few at the cost of poverty and oppression for many. Their means are often regarded as drastic, but those who employ them are convinced that only drastic means hold the possibility of success"(1979:244).

As is evidenced from the results of a number of Dalit movements carried out in different parts of the country that the

Dalits co-front with caste Hindus who are basically opposed to their (Dalits) assertion for justified demands of self-respect and dignified status. "Sometimes, their (Dalits) protest also gets transformed i9nto a conflict between them and caste Hindus and others, causing the loss and damages to both this sides. In any case, their protest movement at present is governed by Dr. Ambedkar's ideology based on the principles of equality, justice, freedom, dignity and self-respect" (Jogdand 1991:10). No doubt, Ambedkar-s ideology has generated new sense of awakening among the Dalits which ofcourse is not uniform among them in different parts of country. The Dalits living primarily in the rural areas have perhaps been lacking, since early time, a tradition of well organized and well regulated protests or protest movements. This is so as "A tradition of protest refers to a continuous, not just occassional, stance of opposition to the established power when this is experienced as oppressive" (Devalle 1992:111). Nonethless, they had perhaps a tradition or traditions of protest against the isolated events of discriminations, exploitations and atrocities committed on them over a period of time in various parts of the country. This , however, does not mean that they had in the past, well organized 'culture of protest' which means "the existence of a consciousness of opposition and resistence". In the ' culture of protest' are to be found "the ideas that book political actions, their emergence and development, that means to channel protest in daily life and at the special times of overt rebellion(ibid:112). The tradition of protest or more appropriately culture(s) of protest is to perceived against the 'culture of torture' or 'culture of oppression' against the weak or disadvantaged sections of population which has been crystallized in the form of a deep rooted tradition in rural India. In fact , this is to be seen as "the most significant and basic manifestation of a culture of protest, the other side of pervading oppression"(ibid:193). Thus, the 'culture of protest' is directed against the 'culture of oppression' (ibid:197) and may be accepted as a case of culture conflict.

This is also to be seen in the light of 'culture of terror' pervading especially in the rural areas where the upper and even dominant middle castes create terror, through commiting various types of atrocities on the Dalits or scheduled castes, to tame them and to stop their assertion for their constitutional rights and privileges and to continue to accept unconditionally the traditional and even some new dictates of the former and remain within their 'limits. The intentions of the upper and middle level castes are also that the Dalits should continue to accept the traditional and even newly acquired status-superiority of the former within the traditional frame of caste hierarchy operating at the local level. No doubt, Dalits continue to oppose in many ways , the status – superiority and dominance of the upper and dominant middle social position and thereby achieve social equality,. But whether they accept *status-quo* and justify the legitimacy of the caste system is an interesting enquiry. There seem to be three distinct views about this. One, the scheduled castes or Dalits accept the caste system and their lowest position in it as godly ordained. (But this may be true only in those cases where they are illiterate, economically poor and are bonded to the landed gently in the country sides, though a considerable degree of socio-political consciousness has grown even among them against such view in the recent past). Hence, their movements, if any, are directed towards their upward social mobility in the existing caste hierarchy through secular means and not through questioning the legitimacy of the caste system and their t......

But this is a very simplistic view and cannot be swiftly accepted particularly in events of growing tensions and conflicts between the upper and middle castes on the one side and the lower castes on the other. Second , they accept the caste system but not their low or lowest position in it. That means, they assert for superior status in the caste hierarchy and emphasize less on social equality by opposing the graded system of castes (Berreman 1963:Moffatt 1975:111-122). Third, those deprived in the caste hierarchy oppose both the legitimacy and existence of the caste system and also their lowest position in it. They emphasize solely on social equality in all aspects of social life annihilation of caste system and also of systems of other distinctions including the clase structure (Gough 1960; Mille ....) We have stated earlier that not all Dalits-the scheduled castes and the converted Buddhists, Christians and

Muslims –are equally agitated and involved in carrying out protest movements. Instead, then are some Dalits-the scheduled castes and converted Buddhists who have been carrying out movements of various types along with various issues. "In the case of scheduled castes, the movements were invariably oriented towards status mobility at the initial stages. Thanks to their partial emancipations from the clutches of traditional ritual degradation due to social reforms and social legislations and the state patronage extended to them through the policy of protective discrimination, the scheduled castes have become increasingly aware of the need to continuously fight for their economic and political benefits, which triggers off several movements among them. However, the active groups in this context are only a few, such as the Mahars of Maharashtra, the Chamars of Uttar Pradesh and the Pulayas of Kerala"(Oommen 1990:177).

Dalit movements are rooted in multiple types of the Dalits. These are mainly ritual or religious , social, economic and political. Dalits have been considered ritually impure; economi9cally they are poor and politically they do not hold power through a small section of them have improved their economic position due to their representation especially in the lower level bureaucracy. Still, a few others enjoy political power in their capacity of legislators, ministers, etc. However, the Dalit masses are engrossed with various types and levels of consciousness of their social , economic and religious exploitations. They are reminded of these exploitations separately in specific contexts but otherwise their consciousness id of their total exploitation. Oonmen makes reference of two types of arguments around the Dalit consciousness. These are proletarian consciousness and caste consciousness. These are based on their being economically poor and lowest in the caste hierarchy. Therefore, their struggle for liberation have been termed as class struggle or caste struggle. "But the advocates of both these positions ignore that first, all Dalits are not 'proletarians' (though a large majority of them are) and at least a small sub-stratum among the traditionally underprivileged have undergone a process of embourgeoisement; and, second, the Dalit consciousness is qualitatively different from the proletarian or caste consciousness.

If proletarian consciousness is essentially rooted in material deprivations and caste consciousness is mainly anchored on status deprivations, Dalit consciousness is a complex and compound consciousness which encapsulates deprivations stemming from inhuman conditions of material existence, powerlessness and ideological hegemony (Oonmen 1990:255-256). No doubt, their such consciousness is more distinctively visible today where Dalits perceive their deprivations in totality through for the sake of convenience and due to limited means available at their disposal, they fight against these deprivations separately at the local level.

Issues and styles of protest

There are many issues which the Dalits face at present. Some of these are related mainly to their social, religious, and economic deprivations. At the social level, they face the problems of untouchability and discriminations though these are legally abolished. A majority of them often become victims of various types of atrocities and physical violence commited by caste Hindus. Their literacy rate and educational level is lowest in the country. Their social status is still downgraded and the social relations between them and caste Hindus are not free from traditional caste prejudices. They are dependent largely

Faced by Dalits but along these the main issues are their caste status, educational developments, atrocities , social and religious disabilities, economic exploitation etc. Over and above, the most important issues before them, at present, are of their respectful identity and dignified social status for which they agitate and carry out various types of movements. Then instead of describing separately a member of Dalit movements carried out in the modern times in different parts of the country and also analysing issues addressed and styles adopted by them , we shall try to classify them into several categories and examine briefly their maining tanets and the resultant consequences.

We have already mentioned some of the issues addressed by Dalit movements. But more precisely, the main issues with which the Dalits have been involved and thus carrying out movements-with both successes and failures are related to their religious degradations as Hindus, their stigmatized social identity: their negative imagery portrayed in the existing literature, their assertion for self-respect and social dignity, liberation from exploitation and of bondage. They are concerned with not only their access to but also capture of political power, proper and full implementation of constitutional provisions relating to their welfare, development and physical and social protection from the caste Hindu reactionary forces. Finally, they urge for equality , fraternity and distributive justice through their due share in the resources existing in the country. Though it may not be easier to classify the various types of Dalit movements. In different parts of the country due to overlap of the issues, yet efforts have been made to classify them. For instance, Omvedt and Patanker(1979) have classified them as caste based and class based movements. Shah(1990:107-120) has categorised them into reformative and alternative movements. He further classifies the former into a) Bhakti movements; b) neo-vedantik, and c)sanskritization movements ; and the latter into i) conversion movements, and ii)religious or sevulor movements. Yet, the Dalit movements can be classified as 1)search for social equality through religious conversion movements, movements for religious revivalism and a respectful placement therein 2)literary movement, 3) movement for self-respect, social dignity, and respectful identity, 4) movement for liberation from economic exploitation, 5) strife for democratic political participation and acquisition of political power, 6) movement for proper implementation of special constitutional provisions , and 7) movements for proportionate shore in existing resources in the country. We shall analyse briefly these movements and their consequences for the Dalits at large in the country.

1)Religious movements:-In the words of Ambedkar (1989:409), "Religion emphasizes, universalizes social values and brings them to the mind of the individual who is required to recognize them all his acts in order that he may function as an approved number of the society." He says further that "___ religion exists not for the serving of sowls but for the preservation of society and the welfare of the individual" (ibid 420-21). The Dalits have adopted religion in this sense. Broadly speaking, the Dalits had been associated with several types or religious movements during the late nineteenth and in the present centuries. Some of these were initiated by them and some by others in which they were proselitized. The proselitizing religious movements were Arya Samaj movement in north-western India and conversion movements to Christianity, Islam and Sikhism, in north and other parts of the country. The religious movements initiated by the Dalits have been Satwami movement in chhatisgarh region in eastern Madhya Pradesh, the Ravidas and Shivanorain movements in Uttar Pradesh, the Adi-Dharm movement in Punjab, and Buddhist conversion movement in Maharashtra and also elsewhere. More precisely, the Arya Samaj movement, which was initiated among Dalits by the Dwija caste Hindus and later carried out by Dalit themselves, got involved, in the early years of this century, in proselecting the untouchables like Jatavas (Chamars) of Agra city in which they accepted vedic varna system (and discarded the caste system) as their reference for upward mobility and claimed their status to that of Kshatriya varna (Lynch 1974). This helped them only to claim the dominant status of Kshatriya but did not facilitate them in having their free interaction and intimate social relations not only with Kshatriyas but even expected relations with people of the rest of three varnas or numerous castes and sub-castes. Thus, there was no wider social acceptance of their newly acclaimed status and this also did not help them in acquiring political power and improving their educational and economic positions. Consequently, they almost left their claim of kshatriya status since early 1930's and, as a scheduled caste, positions and acquiring political power (Lynch 1974:66-128).

The Arya Samaj Movement was also active, since late nineteenth century, in Punjab where the prime motive of the movement leaders was not only persuading the Hindus to go 'back to vedas' but also to follow the varna order instead of caste system. Being in the stream of the religious reform, the Arya Samaj tried to convince the ex-untouchable castes of Punjab (who were converted to Sikhism and a few to Muslim and the Christianity) to come back to Hinduism especially within its varna system (and thereby to accept inadevertantly the theories of *karma* (deeds of the previous and alos of present life) and *punarjanma* (rebirth and thus transmigration of soul). No doubt, a sizeable number of untouchable castes of Punjab accepted the classical Hinduism but the most interesting aspect of the movement was that it was confined mainly to the reconversion , through a strategy of *Shuddhi* (purification) particularly of those untouchable castes which had converted earlier to Christianity and Islam as mentioned above. Bit the evidences show that except achieving the symbolic nights of reading *Vedas* and putting on sacred thread, the untouchable castes in Punjab have not succeeded in improving them social status and fully getting rid of them stigmatized caste identity (Pimpley and Sharma 1985:86-101). Thus , in both cases of Jatavas in Agra city and many untouchable castes in Punjab the Arya Samaj Movement which could be easily accepted as the process of *Sanskritization* (srinivas 1966:1-45) failed in getting their claimed or even partially accorded status improved either in the varna system or in the caste system.

The other religious movements concerning with proselitizing the untouchable castes or the Dalits were associated with their conversion to Christianity, Islam and Sikhism, as mentioned above. Reflecting on the genuineness of religious conversions, Ambedkar states, " The conversion of the untouchables if it didi take place would take after full deliberation of the value of religion and the virtue of different religions. How can such a conversion be said to be not a genuine conversion? On the other hand, it would be the first case in history of genuine conversion. It is therefore difficult to understand why the genuineness of the conversion of the untouchables should be doubted by anybody" (1989:404-405). In any case, their conversion to these religions was caused by their most downgraded status in Hinduism untouchability practised against them and their various types of exploitation by caste Hindus. Hence, their rejection of Hinduism and conversion to other religions for achieving social equality. Their conversion to Christianity before four-five generations ago was confined mainly to the South Indian states like Kerala, Tamil Nadu and Andhra Pradesh . Later , it spread in other parts of the country. (For the accounts of Dalit Christians and their conversions in different parts of the country, see Webster

1992). However, their social and physical segregation continued and they did not succeed in getting rid of their stigmatized caste identity. They are still known as 'neo-Christians' or low caste Christians (Alexander 1972:153-161: Caplan 1978:193-218). Not only that but hey are segregated even in churches while offering their prayers and worshipping the Christ. This was confessed in the Bienmial catholic Bishops' conference of India convened in Nagpur in Jan 1991; and it was felt to help the Dalits in their struggle for liberation, (see a report by Andrew S.Wcitor in *Times of India*, Jan 23 1991). But ironically they have not raised any movement for this purpose. Similar has been the state of affairs regarding their conversion to where they are still known as 'neo-Muslims' and they cannot have close and intimate relations with other sections of Muslims. In fact, there are clear social distinctions between Muslims of foreign descents, the upper castes convert Muslims and the untouchable convert Muslims. Both categories of Muslims practise considerable amount of social distance in terms of marriage, social intercourse , commensality , etc. With the untouchable convert Muslims (see Singh 1973:74; Ansari 1960:50,58). Thus, in both the cases they occupy the lowest ranks in social orders of the respective religious communities.

Similarly, Sikhism sprang from Hinduism, during the sixteenth century, as a protest movement rejecting social distinctions among different varnas and jatis and remained confined mostly in the North-Western part of India. People from the middle castes and even some untouchable castes embraced this religion with the hope of redeeming from all socio-religious distinctions practised against them in Hinduism. But with the passage of time these distinctions remained and got structured , more or less, similar to those of Hindus . Some untouchable castes like Chamars, sweeper ,etc who had converted to Sikhism succeeded in getting their economic position improved but they became identified as Ram dasias and Mazhabis they not only occupy the lowest position in the social orders of Sikhism but also cannot have close and intimate relations like marriage, commensality, etc with the traditionally higher social ranks in the Sikh community (Singh 1958:479-503; Mandelbaum 1972:539-544). One interesting thing to note is that the untouchable converts in all the three cases are not happy with their low status in their respective religions and are grapped with various types of agitation, tensions, etc.

The religious movements started exclusively by the Dalits are Ravidas movement, Satnami movement, Adi Dharm movement, Shivanarayan movement. Buddhist conversion movement, etc., as mentioned above. The movements like Satnami movement, Ravidas movement, Shivanarayan movement; in the name of Shivanarayan, a de-caste Rajput-the founder of the movement emerged in earlier centuries and became more effective upto the beginning of the present century . These have continued in their goals and orientations largely in the Bhakti tradition of the medieval period in the Indian history. In the same sequence, the ascetic and Ideological moorings and their corroboration with day today problems of self-identification, social and personal realities, their perceptions of freedom, equality and social justice and finally evolving social and political actions or strategies of the Chamars of Lucknow in Uttar Pradesh can be also seen (khare 1984). The Satnami movement has emphasized on one God, the true name-Satnam (Babls 1972:143-151) by reconstructing rituals and practices, symbols, mythic tradition(s) etc. (Dube 1992:121-158). The Shivanarayan Movement has also laid stress on one god who does not discriminate among the people of various castes, varnas, creeds, etc. The believers of these religious have discarded old traditions, customs, life styles, food habits, etc., of the Hindu religion and become tectotelers, vegitarians. In a way, they worship one god who does not possess any concrete image. There are three interesting aspects of both these religious movements. One, these have been primarily reformist movements in which the chamars or Madhya Pradesh and of Uttar Pradesh wanted through reforms in Hinduism and in absence of that they rejected various rituals worshipping of Hindu decities. Two, these movements emerged as rebellious against the orthodoxy of Hinduism both in its principles and practices(see fuels 1965). And finally, these have provided them an identity separate from caste Hindus and have also motivated and mobilised them to improve their socio-economic status and power position besides then psychological satisfaction of being liberated from human degradation in Hinduism.

The last two movements of Adi Dharma movement in Punjab and the Buddhist conversion movement concentrated move among Mahars in Maharashtra and chamars in Northern India are entirely distinct in their goals and orientations. The Adi Dharma Movement originated in the early 1920's in the rural central Punjab and its founders were a few young moderately educated but financially secured chamars who were earlier associated with the Arya Samaj. Though in its teuor it was also a protest movement which emerged against the dominance of the upper castes and classes in the Arya Samaj which emphasizes on the classical Hinduism but in essence it tried to establish the supremacy of the Adi Dharma over Hinduism and other religions in which its reckoning originated which later and had been alien is this land and its people. In their understanding, the untouchables were not only the original people but also ruler in India who were outclassed by the Hindu invaders through the passage of time (later this because the main basis of Ambedkar's arguments about origin of untouchables and the practice of Buddhism by them in the early time.) Anyway, the untouchables were a separate the people , the community. The movement emphasized on individual liberation, fellowship and equality and advised its followers to adopt and practise the teachings of untouchable saints like Ravidas, Balmiki, etc and discard idol worship, caste system or superior and inferior practices. Interestingly, they adopted Adi Dharma as a strategy of both socio-economic and political changes, to be brought among them.(Juerglusmeyer 1982).

Buddism on the other hand originated in India more them 2500 years ago and became not only the state religion in its early phase but had also acquired international status as it was adopted in many Afro-Asian countries. In India, before conversion of Ambedkar along with nearly five lakhs of his followers (mostly Mahars of Maharashtra) is Buddhism in 1956, this religion was practiced by a couple of thousand of people in South India and also in some parts of north east and north-west of the country (for Buddhism in South India before 1956, see Fiske 1972:113-142). The Buddhist organization formed during the last decades of the previous century in the north-east India was mainly concerned with social reform and there was no explicit account of its activities among the untouchables. Similar was the case of Buddhism in North-West India. But in South India, it was started almost at the same time by some untouchables who converted to Buddhism as degraded position in Hinduism and against their in Christianity in those cases who had earlier converted to it. These, the Buddhism started as a protest movement and had its links with some countries in south-east Asia and Africans mentioned above. Out of the major constraints before Buddhist conversion movement in independent India there has been the fear among the schedule castes of losing their special constitutional benefits as these benefits were initially meant only for the Hindu scheduled castes and the scheduled castes converts to Sikkhism. Inspite of that the conversion movement was going on in the north Indian states like Uttar Pradesh, Gujarat, Rajasthan, Punjab, Himachal Pradesh, etc. (for details see Fiske 1972:113-142; Lynel 1974; Patwardhan 1973). However, the conversion movements at the massscale took place in Maharashtra in 1956 and in Uttar Pradesh. (Agra) in eightees. Side by side, a movement was carried by 'neo-Buddhist' of Maharashtra to extend the special constitutional benefits to their on the ground of their being ex-untouchable and their socio-economic and political backwardness and the untouchability and discriminations practised against them even after their conversion. The results of their long struggle were heeded to and the constitutional benefits meant for the scheduled castes have been extended throughout the country. Since then, some scattered conversions of the Dalits to Buddhism has been going on in different parts of the country but one would have expected more and more mass conversions of Dalits to Buddhism especially of those who are followers of Dr. Ambedkar and who believe in his ideology.

Dalit Literature Movement

Contrary to the conventional connotation of the literature which emphasizes more on sementics, phonetics, metephors, etc., the Dalit literature movement is concerned with the self-realised themes of suffering, expertation and social degradation of the Dalit masses. It originated in a collective form sometimes in late 1960's in Marathi language in Maharashtra. Initially, a couple of Dalit youth graduated from various colleges and universities in Maharashtra found the existing Marathi literature as prejudicial and partisan which not only golorified the socio-cultural and literary hegemonistic supremacy of the upper castes and classes but also legitimized the degraded states and economic peuperisation of lower castes and classes in the godly ordained frame of *karma* (deeds) and rebirth (transmigration of soul). Such state of affairs was all pervading in the psycho of the people at large including even Dalits who remained contended with their fate. Even the educational institutions and government organisation were not free from suck psyche where the local experiences of Dalit students and officials were refreshed by their teachers, peer groups and senior officials.

This made the Dalit educated youth to revolt against the existing Marathi literature and write it a fresh which could represent the actual states of sufferings social degradation and economic exploitation of the *Dalits* and the allied masses. Thus, the *Dalit* Marathi literature originated not only with total rejection of the established Marathi literature but also of the Hindu social system and culture and the resultant social relations among different groups (castes and sub-castes) in Maharashtra. "Today's Dalit literature rejects the degraded Hindu social set-up, Dalit writers neverthlessly, expose the inhumanities and prejudices of caste society and instil a new social and cultural consciousness" (Pantaware 1936:80). Not only that but the Dalit literature as a whole rebels against the assumptions of Hindu ideologies and rejects the attitudes and behaviour of Hinduism which were obstacles in the path of self-respect and freedom of Dalits. It also rejects the concept of God" (ibid:83). One interesting aspects of the Dalit literature is that it is not to establish counter literature per say though it has proved to be , rather it is a part of the wider Dalit protest movement for self-liberation. "It is one of the several movements which go to constitute the wider liberation movement of hte ex-untouchables. The target of their (Dalit writers) protest is mainly the Hindu intellectual tradition . So, to treat this movement purely as a literary movement is to misunderstand the basic character of the movement. It is a social movement with wider social objectives. It is an extension of the general crusade for the complete liberation of the ex-untouchables."(Bhoite and Bhoite 1977:64).

The Dalit literature has been created in almost all the literary forms of poetry, fiction, short stories, drama, satires etc. But their styles have been severely criticised by the upper castes/classes Marathi literators on the ground that these seldom fulfil the requirements of a literary creation. Instead , the Dalit literature is reistic and abusive and, in aone way, can be accepted as a literary creation. Anyway, through such literary forms the Dalit poets and writers have attacked on the Hindu socio-cultural and religious traditions, the treaklerous life of Dalits in the faceless villages and urban slums which they consider a deathcell, and the various kinds of their deprivations. Besides such literary creations of rejection, they have also encouraged and inspired the Dalit consciousness, religious conversion, relationship of Dalit Marathi literature with Buddhism, Marxism, etc. (see for instance, Singh and Bandivadekar 1982, Jog 1985, Gamgarama and Mahajan 1986, Dangle 1992,etc.) The efforts have also been made to analyse the nature, forms, and the philosophy of the Dalit literature(Kurabhojkar 1984, Nirublakar 1986). Some Dalit writers have tried to highlight the sufferings of Dalit masses through their autobiographies (see for instance, Pawar 19. The Dalit literature movement has drawn its positive inspirations from the life struggle, philosophy and mission of Dr.Ambedkar and from his scholarly writings highlighting the miseries of the Dalit masses, besides from the teachings of the Dalit saints of the Bhakti period. It also attacks on the atrocious contents of the Marathi literature written by the upper caste and classed Hindu writers. Thus, the prime objective of creating Dalit literature is to attack on the Hindu social system, on one hand , and on the other, highlight the miseries of the Dalits.

Besides the stated contributions made by the Dalit literature movement in Maharashtra, one very significant part it has played is that it has inspired the Dalits in other states like Karnataka, Gujarat,

Uttar Pradesh, Bihar, Rajasthan, Madhya Pradesh and also in the south-eastern states like Kerala, Tamil Nadu, Andhra Pradesh, Orissa, West Bengal etc., where also the educated Dalit youth have started creating Dalit literature in their respective languages.

Movements for self-respect, social dignity and respectful identity.

It may not be easy to identify those movements of the Dalits launched in modern time except for gaining their self-respect, social dignity and respectful identity in different parts of the country. The reason is that their social respect, dignified social status and distinct identity are tied with their freedom from caste system, traditional bondage, economic exploitation and untouchability; with their free access to public places including Hindu temples, economic resources and political power; with their conversion to and equal social recognition of other religion, and os forth. In other words, whereas there seem to be very few cases of Dalit movements carried for their self-respect identity etc. The issues undertaken in their movements overlap as stated at the very outset. However, the mention may be made of two movements one each of pre and post-independent India. In 1925 a self-respect movement was launched by Periyar E.V Ramaswamy Naiker in the composite province of Madras with seeking basic change in the traditional social system, negating the supremacy of Hinduism and Brahmanism and emphasising on intilling new system of values of self-help and equality and self-respect especially among the Dalits and then offer socially backward communities. Though this movement achieved some success, it turned ultimately into a political movement (for details, see Natrajan 1962).

The movement for self-respect in free India was launched by the Dalits-Jatavas of Agra city (U.P.) in 1978. Though this was short-lived, the unity and valour of the agitators was highly commendable in terms of creating emotional turmoils among the Dalits in the entire country. The movement was preceded by an incident, which took place on April 14, 1978 when the Dalit(Jatavas) procession celebrating the birth centenary of Dr.B.R. Ambedkar was in its way ahead, attacked by some miscreants in a caste Hindu locality. This was taken by the processionists as a disgrace to Dr.Ambedkar and Lord Buddha whose portraits were enthroned on the back of an elephant walking with the procession. This was also accepted by them as a carve on their basic rights , self-respect and a distinctive collective identity. A complaint against this incident was formally registered with the district administration with a demand of punishing the culprits. This was countered by the caste Hindu residents of the locality where the incident had taken place who also had demanded to change the route of the procession in future. After a few days, the Dalits carried out another procession through the same locality to the collective protesting against the incident and inability of district administration for not punishing the culprits. This was strongly condemned and opposed by both caste Hindu residents of the locality and district administration for not punishing the culprits. This was strongly condemned and opposed by both caste Hindu residents of the locality and the district administration. But the Dalits continued for days their protest in the forms of agitating in front of collectorate and getting then court arrested. A third procession was organised marching towards collectorate to appraise the administration to protest their rights and honour. Incidently, a peaceful and non-violent movement was turned into violent through not only attacking on the processionists by the police in collusion with the caste Hindu influentials in the city but the Dalits localities in most part of the city were physically attacked, their houses were smashed and belongings looted and destroyed. Even the Dalit passer-bys were identified by their cast name and were beaten severely. A few Dalits lost their lives. The situation was finally controlled by the Armed Forces and the movement was subsidised after sometimes(for details, see Lynch 1981, Ram 1984).

What is important to mention have is that, unlike the Periyar's Self-Respect Movement of 1920's , the Dalit movement the late 1970's in Agra it was organized by, the local Dalit leaders but the issues pertained to the social dignity and self-respect of the Dalits of all over the country. Hence, it was later supported by the Dalit leaders from other states and even by some national Dalit leaders

. It is also derived emotional and the material from the—— . This provided a lot of emotional strength and pride to the Dalits to assert and agitate for their rights, social dignity and a respectful identity. In the long run, this provided a reference model to the Dalits of other areas to fight for self-respect and dignity.

In the early 1990's , a country-wide movement was organized by the *Dalit Sena* (Dalit army), headed by Ram Vilas Paswan, then Janata Dal M.P and the former central minister, which had its main base in Uttar Pradesh. The movement was started on December 6, 1991 from Tuesday(when 22 Dalits were massacred), on the death anniversary of Dr.ambedkar, in the form of *Ambedkar Nyaya Jyoti* (Ambedkar right for justice) which travelled through out the country and assembled in Delhi where it was welcomed by a grand procession of lakhs of Dalits who marched through main parts of the city. The procession or rally was called *Atma-Samman* Rallu (rally for self-respect). Though the whole movement continued for four-five months, it had whole movement continued for four-five months, it had generated considerable amount of self-awareness and socio-political consciousness among the Dalits in the country.

Movement for socio-economic liberation

Dalits have struggled, since long against their different parts of the country. They had launched movements time and again, for leaving the customary uncleaned practices and caste occupations, traditionally assigned to them under the *Jaimani system*(system of patrox-client relations), which bestowed on them the most down-graded status in the society. They had also carried out society. They had also carried out a few movements opposing their economic exploitation, and for payment of prescribed waus, access to surplus and *benami* (government) land. Since these related together caused various types of atrocities and physical violence against them especially in rural areas.Here we shall briefly mention a few such movements.We shall examine first some agitations and movements which the Dalits had launched for leaving. Their customory caste practicises their assertions. This will follow analysis a few movements carried out in respect of safeguarding their economic interests. Both types of movements largely pursued the overlapping issues but we shall mention here only those movements which had emphasised more either on social or economic issues.

(a) Movemnets against social disabilities

Though some Dalit movements would have been launched in the previous century, a little systematic accounts are available about those movements which had been carried out since the beginning of this century. During the present century a number of reformative Dalit movements had been launched in northern India against the forced continuation of their customary caste practices like removal of dead cattle of caste Hindus , their women's attending caste Hindus women at the time of their former's delivery, beating drums for caste Hindus on festivals and other ceremonial occasions. These movements were also against the practice of collecting cooked food from caste Hindu households during festivals and on other occasions, obeying ban on their women folks net putting on gold and silver ornaments, not weaning reasonably good clothes, similar to the caste Hindus, not carrying their marriage processions and many other social disabilities. These were directed even against forced *befars* (in paid labour) and fulfilling many other obligations of caste Hindus under the *Jajmani system*, and extending unconditional regards to caste Hindus. It may not be possible here to cover all such movements. However, to substantiate the point we shall mention about one or two such Dalit movements.

A movement was carried out during the 1930's by the *Jatavas* (chamars) of central and western parts of Uttar Pradesh, particularly in the districts of Agra, Aligarh, Kanpur, Unnao, Etah, Meerut,etc. The prime issues were to shelve away the traditional customs and practices which supposedly caused to their low and most degraded social status *visa-vis* statuses of the upper and middle level castes, particularly in rural areas. They also asserted for achieving economic self-dependence and sharing the political power traditionally enjoyed by the upper castes and classes. This continued for years/ together during which they had to face a lot of atrocious behaviour physical violence, social tensions and conflicts, social boycott, etc. The Jatavas also adopted the path of recourse and ultimately succeeded in their strives to live a relatively respectful life. Some of them migrated to the nearby towns and cities, but many remained in villages and improved their lot. The most interesting aspect to mention is that the movement (or movements) was (were) organized and carried mainly by the educated and socially conscious local youth and their elders extended full support for the purpose. Later, these educated youth established their links with politicians, entered into active politics and settled in urban areas. They also wrote some books booklets (in Hindi) reminding their fellowmen and women about their glorious past and persuading them to revive the same based on personal conversations with some old and knowledgeable persons of the regions in the mid 1970s. Another movements was carried out by the Bairwas (chamars) during 1943-1950 in adjoining areas of Rajasthan and Madhya Pradesh in which the major issues were their resistence against the age-old social disabilities imposed on them by caste Hindus. Their strikes for achieving occupational mobility and for retaining the peasant status were also inclusive (Vashishtha 1985:717-728).

Similar movements were carried out by the Dalits in the eastern districts of Uttar Pradesh. One of the oldest movements in the region was launched during the 1950's in Alimapur, a village located in Saidpur Tehsil adjoining to Varanasi district pf Gazipur district. This movement also was started by the local chamars under the leadership of a Dalit village school teacher and was later supported and strengthened by the Dalit politicians and educated officials of Varanasi city. The issues undertaken by the movement were again related to leaving the traditional customary occupations and practices assigned to them in the village. This movement continued for years during which the Dalit labourers had to lose their wages, bear various kinds of humiliations, atrocities, violences and social boycotts to face bans on use of civic and physical facilities available locally to the village folk. Ultimately, they succeeded in achieving their goals and today they live a relatively better and respectful life even in their own village.

During the following decades of the 1960s, 1970s and 1980s

,similar movements had been launched the Dalits in other districts of the region in which almost same kinds of violent activities and other courses of action had occurred against them. But in most of the cases they had certainly succeeded in their aims. It is however, interesting to note here another successful movement carried out by the Dalit students and other educated Dalit youth in the same tehsil of Ghazipur district in some villages located a few miles away in the north of Alimapur village in eastern Uttar Pradesh during the early 1970s. As stated above, the leadership was taken by a few Dalit students of the neighbouring villages who were pursuing their graduation and post-graduation studies in colleges and universities in Varanasi, Allahabad and other district towns in the region. The most interesting part of this movement was that its strategy combined both modern and traditional institutions which led the movement to its logical end. More precisely, the initiaters of the movement published a leaflet urging the Dalits (Chamars) of the areas to leave their traditional customary practices of removing dead cattle of caste Hindus, carrying out other uncleaned activities of both upper and lower castes, doing beggar of (work without or even nominal wage) and paying unqualified respects to the upper castes in villages. The leaflet was allegedly to be issued by late Sri Jagjivan Ram (who was then alived), the most powerful chamar politicians from Bihar, playing since long the much effective and crucial political role not only for Dalits but also for the people of the entire country. He was then regarded in absence of Dr. B.R Ambedkar as a symbol of Dalit political institution of caste panchayat, operative at the village level, was used in the manner in which all the *Chaudharies* (heads) of the caste panchayat in each village numbering fifty two which is considered the distant territory of a caste in villages were invited to assemble at a particular place and deliberate on the proposed issues. Interestingly, all agreed to carry out the unanimous decision through exerting the Panchayat's pressure on the caste members and imposing the customary punishments of ex-communication from the caste ——— on the violaters. The decisions to these effects were conveyed, through the *Kotwals* (official messengers) of caste panchayats to all the Dalits in the villages under juridisdiction who faithfully obeyed due to fear fo their ex-communication from the caste, the most severe punishment in a village. They faced all kinds of antagonisms, violences, tortures discontinuation of their sources of livelihood, even limited community services and social boycotts of caste Hindus, but could not dare to disobey the collective decisions of the caste panchayat. The entire movement continued for a year or two and was suspended only after achieving its desired goals (based on the personal observations of the author who comes from the same region and has comprehensive accounts of this and many other similar movements carried in this area during his student days).

(b) Movements for economic liberation

Movements carried in this area during his student days . Looking at the space constraints, it may not be possible to mention about many social economic liberation of Dalits in different parts of the country. It is however, desirable to refer briefly to some movements of Dalits carried for their economic liberation in some parts of the country. Broadly speaking, three types of movements have been carried out by the Dalits for their economic liberation from the landed peasantry of upper and middle level castes. These are movement, i) against ejection and userption of their land. ii) including surplus land allotted to them, iii) for payment of increased wages prescribed by the government. We shall discuss here only three specific Dalit movements which may be accepted as representatives, of movements launched elsewhere against various types of economic exploitation. Since the 1970s a large number of movements have been carried out in Bihar, Andhra Pradesh, Maharashtra, Tamil Nadu etc. Some of these were organized by the leftist political parties and their splinter groups and others by the Dalit labourer themselves. Many of these movements were carried out for the payment of increased wages, especially at the prescribed rate. One such movement was launched by the Dalit labourers in Belchi village of Patna District in Bihar during the late 1970s. The movement was led by Singheshwar Paswan, a Dusadh by caste. He mobilised the labourers and made them socially and politically conscious of their economic exploitation by the local middle caste landlords, especially the Kurmi caste. In the course of their movement , the labour demanded payment of wages at the increased rate, retaining their right of share-cropping, etc. They slowed commendable resistance to their exploitation by the landlords. Since the landlords were not ready to heed to their demands, they lived goons and attacked on the labourers, burnt their houses, beat them and even burnt alive at least a dozen of labourers including their leader in a publically arranged bonefire. Those spared, left the village and sought refuge elsewhere. The incidence took place on May 27, 1977. The movement ended with a growsome form of atrocities on the landless Dalit labourers (for details, see Bose 1985:180-211; Ram 1988: 125-154).

Another movement was carried out in 1970 by the Dalits and poor Muslims some villages in Baste district of eastern Uttar Pradesh. Herem the issue was forceful possession of *benami* or government baren land. The movement organized in a background of relative peace and middle class prosperity in the area , was widely known as land grab several other parts of the country. It was sponsored by the left-oriented political parties (CPI and CPM) and the leaders were mostly from outside the district. The targets were primarily the new landlords of the Kumi (middle level) caste who had illegally occupied the *benami* land and misured it for oppression of the landless labourers. This movement continued for a start time and its slogan was "Muslim- Harjan bhai bhai, Hindu jati Kahan se Aai" (the Muslims and Harijans Dalits were brothers and from where the Hindu castes had come that means the Hindu castes material). On the other side, all the caste Hindus got united and retaliated to crush the Dalits (chamars) and Muslims. As a consequence, the movement got aborted due to emergence of communal forces and government interventions. The movement miserably failed and could not make even a minor dent on the existing caste and class relations in Basti" (Singh 1978:737;for details , see his 1974).

Lastly, the Land Ceiling Act was passed in 1961, but was not uniformly adopted and implemented in all parts of country. Due to numerous types of malpractices adopted by the landlords to save their lands from the land ceiling, there were problems of identification and distribution of surplus lands among the landless people. In some cases where the land was distributed, the allotees were not allowed to have actual poss——————tried to get possession,but their efforts had resulted into severe disputes between them and the landlords, the earlier possessors of the land. Still, in few cases the new proprietors launched movements to get actual possession of the land allotted to them. One such movement was organized in the Bajitpur village in Jelanapad district (earlier Gaya district) of Bihar state. About 160 hectares of land owned by a prosperous landowner was declared surplus under the Bihar Land Ceiling Act. The landlord's appeal to the court was rejected and the land was distributed among 154 landless labourers and small peasants of the village. Whereas the labourers aand the small peasants were carrying out in organized way, their movement with the active support of the cadres and files of the left it political parties like CPI (M.L.) . To get the land distributed among them , the landlord was preparing himself, with his henchmen, to retaliate any more of the former to occupy forcefully this land. Ultimately, there was violent attack by the landlord's musclemen on the organisers of the movement in 1978 and this termed into the atrocities on the Dalit landless labourers and small peasants. This movement also could not succeed in achieving its goal of getting the surplus land smoothly distributed among the landless Dalits (for details, see Sachidanand 1988; 51-52; PUDR report 1989:1693-1695). It is clear from the above accounts that the Dalits have organized, sometimes with the help of others and sometimes on their own, numerous types of movements relating to their self-respect, new identity and to getting their rights prescribed by the constitution and the state. Yet, it is true that in most of the cases their movements have not directly and exclusively addressed to the annihilation of the caste or caste system, especially in the modern time. Also not many of their movements have succeeded in getting their goals achieved. In any case, not going into further details of the Dalit movements, we shall briefly examine here the ways and the extents these movements have contributed to bring about any change or changes in the caste system in India. But the extent to which these changes have been affected by the Dalit movements is to be statistically reassured through the factor analysis which we have neither done for the present purpose not it is possible in the case of the macro-level analysis done in this article. However, in absence of that we shall try to analyse qualitatively the nature and types of changes that have occurred in the caste system due to the Dalit movements carried out in different parts of the country. But before doing this we shall briefly look at the state of caste or caste system in the contemporary Indian society.

Caste in Contemporary India

It is not sufficient merely to say that caste is a unique institution or the caste system is an extreme (closed) form of social stratification in India. Instead, it is necessary to briefly spell out the ways in which this institution is unique and the system is extreme or the closed one. This can be explained through looking at the traditional features of the caste system and also enquiring into whether these are still prevailing in some significant forms in the contemporary period. Bougle (1971) has emphasized on hierarchy, repulsion or separation and interdependence as he three major characteristics or features of the caste system. That is for him each segment (unit or stratum or jati) is structurally arranged in descending order, in the hierarchy which is primarily religious or ritualistic in nature. Each segment(jati) is separated from other through endogamous marriage but all the segments are functionally dependent though in restricted on one another in the form of *Jaimani* system.

Accepting these three as valid propositions Dumont (1980:33-64) adds one more principal feature of purity *qua* impurity. According to him, "The (above) three 'principles' (features) rest on one fundamental conceptive and are reducible to a single true principle namely the opposition of the pure and the impure. This opposition under his hierarchy, which the superiority of the pure to the impure, underlies separation because the pure and the impure must be kept separate, and underlies the division of labour because pure and impure occupations must likewise be kept separate. The whole is founded on the necessary and hierarchical co-existence of the two opposites (of pure and impure)" (Dumont 1980:43). He further argues "it is the whole (founded pure and impure) which governs the parts, and this whole is very rigorously conceived as based on an opposition" (ibid;43-44). But he does not claim that the opposition between pure and impure is the foundation of the Hindu society. Instead, he says, "it is by implicit reference to this rational to those who live in it" (ibid). We shall come to this in the later discussion. It is, however , necessary to mention, here one more principal aspect of ideology which is under the caste system and has been emphasized most forcefully by Dumount. It is the ideas, beliefs and values pertaining to the caste or caste system which constitute its ideology and which encompass it. In the words of Dumount (1980:228), "_ _ _ the politic-economic domain (of social life) is encompassed in an overall religious setting. This remains true even when there is a weakening of the opposition between pure and impure (groups-jatis and their and their statuses occupations), the opposition we have considered as the ideological core of the system. Here resides the secret of the caste system's plasticity, and the ambiguous nature of the undoubted changes. Everything happens as if the system tolerated charge only within one of its secondary spheres." What is implied here is that the politic-economic changes are incapable of bringing any fundamental change in the religious ideology of the caste system contrary to this, the Dalits consider at present both these secular and ritual aspects separately and emphasize on the former. They also insist for change of the caste system. Then for Dumout, some change is possible in but not of the caste system. One may or may not agree with this position of Dumont. But our immediate concern is to look at some more traditional features, if there are any, of the caste system and then examine whether these are still prevalent in the contemporary time in the Indian society. Ghurye (1979:1-30) has listed six major features of the traditional caste system. These are : caste system is a segmental division of Hindu society divided into castes and sub-castes ; it has a hierarchy, primarily religious in its nature, in which all the segments have been ranked in the descending order below the Brahman castes it has restrictions on feeding and social intercourse (commensality); there are civil and religious disabilities of those castes and sub-castes which are at the bottom and privileges of which are at the top; the segments (castes and sub-castes) are strictly endogamous and marriages outside the segments are prohibited; and there is lack of unrestricted choice of occupation- each caste and sub-caste is traditionally assigned separate occupations which carry prestige or stigma in proportion to that of the caste or sub-caste in the hierarchy. About this last characteristics or feature of the caste system. Gould says,; In my opinion, this is the fundamental social 'dilemma' so to speak, of the caste society; it is of necessity resolved by putting certain groups identified with impure occupation in the position of being simultaneously outside the pale ritually yet inside the pale functionally. This is achieved not by *ostracizing* the practioners of such occupations from the community but *circumscribing their range and type of social interaction* in whatever way and to whatever degree the dominant and 'pure' groups in the society believe is necessary to 'protect' themselves from ' contamination" (Gould 1987:79). But how the caste system, with such characteristic, became 'pan Indian' with the variations of the different types of occupational pursuits is a pertinent question to which Gould replies that it is not the aseriptire quality per of the caste system which has made it peculiar. " its distinctiveness arose from the fact that Hinduism integrated the occupationalization of work and the stratification of occupations into a metaphysical model that made no hard and fast distinctions between economic and religious functions. All occupations were 'rural statements; so to speak, and key behavioural components of rituals were 'stated' in occupational terms (here, this point is closer to that of Dumont who believes in disjunction between status- ritual and since economic power (ibid 75-79). The result was a tremendous proliferation of occupational categories, *or jatis* , based on an almost limitless variety of functional criteria" (Gould 1987:50). Such characteristics of the caste system has been endorsed by Max Wober also who adds endogamy rules of commensality and social rank to it. In his words "Rules of endogamy , however, always form the essential basis of a caste. Dietary rules and rules of commensality are always characteristics of the caste___ " (Wober 1967 :32) . He says further, "___ a caste is usually related intimately to special ways of earning a living, on the one hand , and on the other, to social rank" (ibid:33).

Contrary to all these , Ambedkar had criticized both the occupational and racial characteristics of the caste system. According to him, caste system was formed through poision super of endogamy on exogamy which was prevalent among the Hindus before the system got crystallized. The system itself was creation of difficulty in disposal of surplus men and surplus women trough the endogamous marriages. (Ambedkar 1979:9-14), occupational categories no longer remained as divisions of labour in the relatively simple economic system but these also became the divisions of labourers which were identified as castes and sub-castes and were graded one above the other in a hierarchy (Ambedkar 1979:47) based on religions or ritual consideration. He further states that the divisions of labour or labourers were based not on individual choice, aptitudes and efficiency but on the dogma of the predestination' (ibid:48) and thereby these become hereditary.

Whether the above mentioned features of the caste system were strictly adhered to since its inception or were there some variations here and there is a teleological question and requires detailed examinations and probings of the indological literature. But that is not the purpose of this article. Instead, the very purpose of listing these features of the caste system is to compare the caste system of the contemporary period with that of the earlier time and in the process to highlight some changes that have occurred in it. It is clear from the literature that by middle of the nineteenth century, considerable amounts and types of changes had taken place in the caste system, especially in its aspects of commensality (restrictions on feeding and social intercourse), civil and religious disabilities of some and privileges of other castes and sub-castes, and restrictions on marriages. Marriages became possible between the persons of two castes or sub-castes at least between those which were closer in ranks in the hierarchy of castes and sub-castes found at the local levels or which between those which were similar in their socio-economic and to some extent ritual statuses. Though the caste system remained a system of segmental divisions of Hindu population, the earlier emphasis on identification and ranking of each segment in the local caste-hierarchy got shifted from ritual to the socio-economic and power considerations. The hierarchy of caste itself became loose (not only at the middle rungs, as Bailey (1964) said, but also at the two extreme poles- top-Brahman and the bottom-untouchables of the caste system) with accommodation of claims and counter-claims of different caste groups for placing them at the relatively higher status(es) or rank(s) in the caste system. A point is to be noted here that all these happened when the British regime in India introduced means of transport and communication, census enumeration , a number of educational institutions, printing press, etc. The Britishers also enacted a number of legal and social reforms. The people of different castes and sub-castes used the new avenues and in many cases got their claims and counter-claims recorded legally and formally. By this time, the process of modernization and economic development had also started taking place which helped the people of different sections to do better in various walks of their life. The migration of people from one place to the other not only helped them to go for new types of occupations, but they also began to interact with people of the different socio-economic and cultural backgrounds. This enabled them, to become aware of social and cultural life of people of the different people of the different socio-economic strata, and of castes and communities. Consequently, there began a process of interesting and of adaptation. The migration of people to towns, cities and even to the villages of different regions contributed to reading the relation significance of caste. The caste system started getting loosened in terms of undermining the inter-caste ritual and social distances, ignoring sometimes one's caste background, not remaining particular to caste commensality, going for occupational diversification, etc. The British regime in India contributed, sometimes directly and sometimes indirectly, to all these changes. However, the state action during the British rule could not assure the untouchable castes their entry to temples maintained by individuals or public trusts which used to get state grants occasionally. Though the caste group solidarity weakend, the state action could not set aside totally the caste customs unless these were opposed to public policy. Thus, "caste retained its cultural integrity" and these remained more caste rigidity among the higher castes and less among the lower castes.

The labelling and pigeonholding of caste through census led to crystallization of caste system in many parts of the country (Ghurye 1979:81). The new opportunities helped the middle and lower level castes to raise their socio-economic and power position and Hereby caste status in the local caste hierarchy. But it also made the people more caste conscious. According to Srinivas , "A low caste which made money as a result of new opportunities presenting themselves to it, made attempts to raise its status *vis-a-vis* the other castes, and this resulted in opposition from the latter. Even eventual consent ti sycg a claim did not lessen immediate opposition _ _ _ the newly rich castes only pressed for a higher status for themselves –they did not urge that the caste system should be abolished". (Srinivas 1986, 17). He further says "It is true that the economic forces released under British rule resulted in greater mobility within the caste system, but that is quite different from making progress towards an egalitarian society "(ibid) After independence the state policy of ignoring caste importance has lessened the significance of caste in contemporary India. The state actions in the forms of evolving number of welfare and development schemes for the people irrespective of caste and community considerations, exacting several social legislations, decentralizing political power in the form of panchayati raj and empowering the village council have eroded importance of the caste council *vis-a-vis* caste authority both in rural as well as in urban areas. This, however, does not mean that the caste or caste system is fast disappearing. In fact, at the surface of it caste seems to have become weak but in its core it grows stronger with its multiplex functions which it performs in the present time. "It is paradoxical yet true that caste is getting stronger and weaker at the same time(This is more visible in rural areas and less in cities where it appears to be negligible). Caste at the level of endogamy is generally not breaking down. The members feel a strong sense of solidarity when it is a question of mutual benefit. The emergence of caste associations with a political aim and the developing hierarchy of social dominance reflect in the sufficiently relevant attributes of caste. Occupational shifts and changes in the interactional pattern also belong to the same category. Peripheral changes in name and dress patterns are also noticeable in some cases (in villages). The division of labour has generally maintained its traditional pattern with only occasional minor changes, particularly in the mode of payment " (Atal 1979:228). Thus, according to Atal, "The castes and the caste system continue to persist because of their capacity to absorb and assimilate the new functions. It is because of this resistence that vivcissitudes are much tardy and less prominent than the regularities of the system" (ibid:231). People are in two minds on the future of caste in Indian society. A small minority of people in both rural and urban areas "sees caste as a menace to our national likes. For them, caste is a poisonous evils in the Indian society and it, therefore, must go. "But it is still true to say that vast majority of people do not consider caste an exit. It is essential to remember this fact, for nothing effective can be done unless the people themselves are made to realize that caste necessarily means casteism , and that the benefits it offers are bought at a heavy price for the country as a whole" (Srinivas 1986:70). This fact, however, cannot be denied that the ideological or religious aspect of the caste system has weakened in the recent years. Not withstanding the politicization of caste and its extensive use in politics, the multiple forms of changes are visible in the caste system. " Castes are not merely evaporating, however. Instead, they are restructuring and consolidating themselves in order to perform important adaptive functions for their members in the context of the more open forms of social stratification now prevailing" (Gould 1987:64). Gould further says, "castes, in other words, are acting as co-optive instruments in the domain of access to jobs and social mobility. We see them acting in this way in both the productive and political sectors of Indian society. To the extent that given castes succeed in these efforts, their internal milieu takes on more and more of the attributes of a class system. That is, members acquire modern occupations in offices commanding differential wealth and prestige that radically affect life styles, educational standards and mobility patterns in the whole caste. Although this process has not as yet led to any serious abandonment of caste endogamy, it has resulted in more and more interaction between Indians along class time. This is visible at both the top and the bottom (and also in the middle) of the status hierarchy" (ibid:65). But the class system, though at the formative stage, is not a phenomenon. Instead, it changes both in the form and magnitude through the passage of time. Talking about the changes in both the caste system and class structure in the context of a South Indian village Beteille says, " Whereas in the caste system the tendency has been towards a certain convergence of adjacent segments (sub-caste or *jatis*), the class system has shown increasing mobility. Ownership of land (in the rural areas) passed more easily from one set of people to another, and new classes tend to develop. Further, the class system has progressively ditached itself from the caste structure, although there is still a high degree of correspondence between the hierarchies of caste and class" (Beteille 1971:221). More so , the caste system has subsumed within itself the 4 different organizations of production and the distribution of power (ibid:223).

Changes in the caste system have both positive and negative effects on the social life of the people in India. The positive effect can be seen in the forms of socio-economic improvement , better interaction patterns and mobility of status(es) of the people of different castes, including the lower castes- the Dalits. But the negative effects of such changes specially among the Dalits are seen in the forms of growing discontents, tentions and conflicts between them and the upper and the middle level castes. In a not so open system of a village society the relationship between caste and social mobility and economic change leads to social conflict. "Caste is not attacked (even) by spatial mobility (from one region to the other or from a village to the city). The battle is only in the field of social mobility: and even that is fought on the home ground of the caste system. This is the reason why the conflict is carried on in the idiom of caste, not only when the local structure of caste groups can cope successfully with economic change, _ _ _ (but) when the local structure of caste groups reacted to the economic change by extruding these groups and thrusting them into the larger polity, where the Administration rules" (Bailey 1972 :272). To what extent the lower castes the Dalits have been involved in such conflict and bringing out some significant change in the caste system is to be seen in the following section.

III

Dalit movements and changes in the caste system:

It is most difficult yet controversial to analyse role of the Dalit movements in bringing about, some changes in the caste system in the contemporary period. It is difficult in the sense that neither the Dalit movements have directly addressed to the caste system or attacked on it in the recent past as stated earlier not analysis of that has been mad. These controversy around the present argument could be generated due to the fact that the majority of Dalits even today are part of the caste system though they are highly criteal to it and whether the changes discussed above are largely caused by their movements or are part of the on going general process of social change in the country. Anyway, changes that have occurred in the caste system are visible both in its structure and functions along with that in its institutional and organisational aspects. The traditional beliefs, ideas, values and in a word, ideology of the caste system have not obliterated but changed these function at present more at the national rather than at the substantive level. Further, at the level of Dalits themselves changes can be noticed in their socio-political consciousness about their self and society. In other words, there is considerable degree of change in their worldview. This has resulted into both qualitative and quantitative changes in the traditional equation of their socio-personal relations with the superordinate groups, castes or communities. They seek their new identity and social status, or improvement in the earlier ones, not always in the traditional or new frame of caste system but even outside that. We shall discuss these changes below.

Apart from the factors which have contributed to bringing various types of changes in structure and functions of the caste system including its different institutions and organizations as mentioned above, the specific types of changes that have occurred are in the *jagmani* system given by some scholars, it had have both social and religious sanctions of the caste system. It is true that the *jagmani* system provided some security to the functionary castes but in lieu of that they were ever tied with their *jagmans* (patrons-master) and were not free to easily change one to the other. That means, the *jagmani* system which remained an important situational part of the caste system and was the basis of interdependence of the castes. (Reading to homogenity among them) got changed due to specific movements carried out by the Dalits at the local levels. In fact, the system is no move operative. The various types of social and religious disabilities of the Dalits were also attributed to their position (s) both in the *jajman*i system in the caste system. Hence, in spite of less effectiveness of various legal provisions the social and religious disabilities of the Dalits are receding due to absence of the *jajmani* system and also some movements carried out by them. Their movements had addressed to those customary caste practices which were even out of the *jajmani* system. Consequently have disappeared now.

Dalits movements have also questioned legitimacy of the beliefs, ideas, values, ideology etc., of the caste system. It is time that these have changed due to other factors also. But the upper and middle have realised that the practice of their social relations and interaction with the Dalits *in accordance with are no more possible strict rules of the caste system.* The Dalits in such areas enjoy more freedom of occupational choice both in their village and towns or cities .Both the social and ritual distance between Dalits and upper and even middle level castes, which is oneof the basic feautures of the caste system, has also diminished in most of the cases. Those Dalits with better socio-economic standing and power position are now accepted to participate in social and religious ceremonies performed by the upper castes and classes even in the rural areas.

There is considerable degree of change in the socio-political consciousness of the Dalits in the regions where they have successfully or even otherwise carried out their movements on one issue or the other. Such consciousness has not only reduced the superordination and subordination between them and upper and middle level castes but in they have also captured political power at the village level in some cases where they are more in number. This has increased their bargaining power in respect of their wages, working conditions etc. This has also resulted into improvement in their caste status *vis-a-vis* their status in the traditional caste system. Interestingly, both Dalits and the upper and middle level castes adopt various types of soio-economic changes to enhance their social standing not always within the frame of caste or caste system. These changes are adopted by individual and not all members of these castes though other members, get inspired by them. Then, with regard to implications *of such changes to the caste system* "_ _ _there is no reason why the caste system cannot continue to function adequately even when members of a caste engaged in different occupations and vary in degree of individual prosperity. Thus, this attribute of caste has undergone modification, but the system remains" (Kless 1980:133). A sizeable number of Dalits in the country negate the caste or caste system as is evident from their conversions (movements) to other religions and their dissociation from caste customs, and social and religious disabilities due their social movements launched for the same. This is also clear from their social identification with the system other than the caste or caste system(Ram 1988b). But amidst all this they maintain a dual-identity of being within and without the caste. Their association with caste remains intact through the practice of endogamous marriages and their resultant relations with their kith and knis of the same caste. In case of those converted to other regions there remains discrepancy in their not being fully absorbed in the community of their new religious faith. Even there also they are discriminated against. In such situation they continue their relations with their kith and kins who are still members of the caste system. At the cultural level, some of those converted to other religions do practise some of the Hindu calendrical festivals besides observing important events of their new religious faith (Patwardahan 1973). They remain a caste-scheduled caste- for the purpose of getting some constitutional benefits under the protection discrimination policy. Otherwise, they criticize and negate the legitimacy of the caste system which, in their reckoning, is a highly exploitative system and root-cause of their social degradation and economic exploitation (Mencher 1974:469-93). Thus, at the principle level they are very much opposed to the caste system but, at the practice level, they are still an intrinsic part of it. They seem to be highly critical of the caste system due their low status or rank in the caste hierarchy but very often . They strive for elevating their status in the system (Moffatt 1975:111-22). This contradiction has not yet been resolved by carrying out an exclusive movement(s) against the caste system as such.

Conclusion

We have analysed quite at length, in this article, the nature and types of Dalit movements carried out in different parts of the country especially after independence. We have also examined nature of the caste system in the contemporary period and changes in it due to various types of Dalit movements. We have noted that not a single Dalit movement has addressed exclusively the caste or caste system though quite a few movements have attacked on its evils or dysfunctions alities. The Dalits at large face the dilemma of being yet not being part of the caste system. This dilemma or contradiction needs to resolved it they wish to achieve social equality and fraternity in the society in India.For this, they need to go back to Ambedkar, their inspirator, who has strongly advocated for demolishing the religions sanctity of the Hindu sanskritis texts and practising exogamy and endogamy for the purpose of annihilating the caste or caste system. The latter may begin at home where the Dalits have to for eg: the differences of their castes and sub-castes for the purpose of commensality marital alliance, etc. This requires an initiation and rigorous pursuance of specific movement(s) by the Dalits themselves in which the lead is to taken by the socially and politically conscious individuals, groups and their organizations like that taken in their earlier movements.

REFERENCES

Alexander, K.C. 1972, *The Untouhables in contemporary India*, the University of Arizona Press, Arizona, pp. 153-161.

Ambedkar, B.R 1979, *Castes in India The annihilation of Caste and States and minorities* Dr. Babasaheb Ambedkar :writings and speechless vol.1, Government of Maharashtra, Bombay- (all the three were first published in 1917,1936 ,1947 respectively)

Ansari, Ghous 1960 "Muslim Caste in Uttar Pradesh – a study of culture contact" *Eastern Anthropologist* 13:5-80.

Atal, Yogesh 1979, *Changing Frontiers of Caste*, National Publishing House, New Delhi.

Babb, A.Lawrence 1972, "The Satnamis:Political Involvement of a Religious Movement" in J.Michael Mahar (ed.) *The Untouchables in contemporary India,* pp. 143-151

Bailey , F.G 1972, *Caste and Economic Frontier*, The Univesity Press, Manchester.

Bandivadekar, Chandrekant and Maheep Sing (eds) 1982 , *Sahitya avam Dalit Chetna* (Hindi) Abhivyanyana, New Delhi

Berraman, G.D 1963 1971, *The Hindus of Himalayas*, University of California Press, Berkeley.

______"The Brahuanical View of Caste" Contributions to Indian society 1979

________*Caste and Other Inequit*, Folklore Institution Meerut, Beteille , Andre 1971

_______*Caste , Class and Power*, University of Californ9ia Press, Berkaley.

Bhorite, U. And A. Bhoite 1977, "Dalit Sahitya Movement in Maharashtra: A sociological study," *Sociological Bulletin*, 26(1)

Bongle , Cestine 1971, *Essays on the caste system*, Cambridge University Press Cambridge

Caplan, Lionel 1978, "Social Mobility in Metropolitan Centres:Christians in Madras city" in Satish Saberwal (ed.) *Process and Institution in Urban India*, Vikas Publishing House, New Delhi, pp 193-217.

Dangle, Arjun 1992 , *Poisioned Bread* (ed>) ,Orient Longman, Bombay.

Devalle, Susana B.C 1992 , *Discourses of Ethnicity : Culture and Protest in Jharkhandd*, Sage Publications, New Delhi.

Dube, Saurabh 1992, "Myths, Symbols and community : Satnampanth of Chhatisgarh" in Aartha Chatterjee and Gyanemora Pandey (eds.) *Subaltern studies : Writings on South Asian History and Society*, vol vii pp. 121-158.

Dumont, Louis 1980 , *Homo- Hierarchies*, Universitiey of Chicago Press.

Fiske, Adele 1972 "Schemed Caste Buddhist Organizations" in J. Michael Mahar (ed) *The untouchables in contemporary India*, pp 113-142.

Fuchs, Stephen 1965, *Rebellions Prophets – A study of Massiancic Movement in Indian Religions*, Asia Publishing House, Bombay

Gangavane Kamalakar and Mahajan (eds.) , *Dalit Rangmanch* (Hindi) Krishna Brothers, Ajmer

Ghurye, G.S 1979 , *Caste and Race in India*, Popular Prakashan Bombay.

Gough, E. Kathleen 1960 , "Caste in Tangore Village" in E.R Leech (ed.) *Some Aspects of Castes in India , Ceylon and Pakinstan*, Cambridge University Press Cambridge.

References to be added at appropriate phases

Mencher, Joan P.1974, "The caste system Upside Down , or the not-so-mysterious East", *Current Anthropology* 15

Klass, Morton 1980, *Caste:The Emergence of hte South Asian Social system*, Institute for the study of Human Issues, Philadalphia.

Patwardhan, S. 1973 , *Change among India's Harijans*, National, New Delhi.

Ram, N. 1984 1988, *The Mobile Scheduled Castes : Rise of a New Middle Class* , Hindustan Publishing Corporation, Delhi.

Gould, Harold A. 1987 , *The Hindu Caste system* , Chanakya Publications, Delhi.

Jog, V.S 1985 , Marxism and Dalit Sahitya, Sambodhi Prakashan, Bombay.

Jogdand, P.G 1991, Dalit Movement in Maharashtra , Kanak Publications, New Dwlhi.

Juergensmeyer, Mark 1982, Religion as Social vision, University of California Press, Berkeley.

Khare, R.S 1984, The untouchable as himself , Cambridge University Press, Cambridge

Kumbhojkar, lalita 1984, Dalit Kavita : Ek Darshan (hindi) , Pratima Prakashan, Pune

Lynch, O.M 1974, Politics of Untouchablity , National, New Delhi (first published by Columbia University Press in New York in 1969).

______ 1981, "Rioting as Rational Action: An Interpretation of the April 1978 Riots in Agra, "Economic and Political weekly 6(48) , 28 November.

Mandelbawn, D.G 1972, Society in India, Popular Prakashan, Bombay

Miller Rober J. 1966, "Button, button-great tradition, little tradition, whose tradition," Anthropological Quarterly, 39:26-42.

Moffat, Michael 1975 , "Untouchables and the caste system: a Tamil case study", Contributions to Indian sociology 9(1):111-122

Natrajan, S. 1962 , A Century of social reforms in India, Asia Publishing House, Bombay.

Nimbalkar, Vaman 1986 , Dalit Sahitya :Swaroop va Bhoomi ke (Marathi), probodhan Prakashan Nagpur.

Onvelt , Goul and Bharat Patanker 1979, "The Dalit Liberation Movemetn in colonical Period", Economic and Political weekly 16(7-8).

Oommen , T.k 1990, "Sources of Deprivations and styles of Protest: The case of the Dalits in his Protest and Change:studies in social Movemets, Sage Publications New Delhi, 99 254-271.

Pantawarie , G. 1986, "Evolving a New Identity :The Development of a Dalit cuture" in Barbara R.Joshi (ed.) Untouchable voices of the Dalit libertation Movement, Zad Books, London, pp 79-87.

Patwardhan S. 1973 , Change among India's Harijans, Orient Longmen New Delhi.

Pawar, Daya 1985, Balut- autobiography (in Marathi), Eranthali, Bomaby

Pimpley, P.N. and s.k Sharma 1985 , Struggle for status, B.R Publishers, Delhi.

Ram, Nandu 1984 , "Atrocities and segregation in Urban social structure: views from Bottom", Journal of social and economic Studies 1(4) :373-399 (reprinted in Yogesh Atal (ed.) Understanding Indian Society, Har-Anand Publications , New Delhi, 1992 pp 135-158.

__________ 1988 , "From Atrocities to Protest Movement:An urge for social Development" in S.K Srivastava nad A.L. Srivastava (eds.) Social movements for Development, Chugh Publications, Allahbad, pp 125-154.

Rao K, M.S.A 1978, "Conceptual Problems in the study of social Movements in his (ed.) Social Movements in India, vol.1 Manohar, Delhi, pp 1-15.

Repor 1989, "State Terror in Jeharabad" (Report of People Union of Democratic Rights), Economic and Political Week etc, 24(30)

Sachchidanand 1988 , Social Change in Village India, Concept publishing House New Delhi.

Shah, Ghanshyam 1990, Social Movements in India: A Review of the Literature , Safe Publications, New Delhi.

Singh, I.P. 1958, "A Sikh village", Journal of America Folklore.

Singh , Rajendre 1974, "Agrarian Social Structure and Peasant Unrest : A study of land-Grab Movement in District Bast-Bast UP," Sociological Bulletin 23(1).

___1978 , Peasant Movement in Uttar Pradesh " in MSA Rao (ed.) Social Movements in India vol1, Manthar, New Delhi pp 97- 148.

Singh, Yogendra 1973, Modernization of Indian Traditin , Thompse Press, Delhi

Srinivas , M.N. 1966, Social Change in Modern India and Other Essays, Media Promoters and Publishers, Bombay.

Vashishtha, V.K 1985, "Struggle of the chamar Peasants for the Removal of social Disabilities in a Feudal Estate (Union Thikana) in Rajasthan, 1946-47," Proceeding of the Indian History Congress (45th Session), Annamalai Nagar, Tamil Nadu 717-729)

Weber, Max 1967, The Religion of India, The Free Press, New York.

Webster, John C.B 1992 , The Dalit Christians – A History, Indian society for Promoting Christian Knowledge Delhi

8

Migration and social Mobility in India: Some Theoretico-Methodological Issues

The study of migration has attracted attention more of the demographers and social geographers and less of other social scientists including sociologists. Likewise, social mobility as a concomistant of occupational change has extensively been studied by sociologists. However, in their net analysis the migration process occurs because of push and pull factors (objective conditions) operating at the place of origin and destiny respectively. But these factors do not operate in isolations; rather, the magnitudes of their functions are based on the overall situations prevailing at both the places. Besides, migration occurs also due to the psychological traits of persons, and the valuational and normative set-up present at both the places which facilitates or discourage them to migrate or not to migrate from the place of their origin to that of destiny. It may, then, be accepted that all the three objective Psychological and normative factors, which have also been accepted as three levels of analysis of migrations (Germany 1970), determine together or separately the nature and magnitude of migration of a person, a group or community as a whole.

The migrants are, however, not a homogenous social category. Instead, with their differential mental make-up, they are drawn from the divergent social background, As their choices and preferences of the places of destiny vary, so also differ their intentions of migration.

In some cases, they would migrate to join with their family members or friends, whereas in other cases they would simply wish to acquire new experiences, including the educational one. But the dominant pattern in intentions of migration is economic, where the migrants want to improve their socio-economic condition and achieve social mobility through one channel or the other, However, depending upon the choices and preferences of the place of destiny, the degree of social mobility vis-à-vis effort to achieve that would differ from person to person and group to group.

The present paper, therefore, tries to examine how various factors together or separately determine the chances and decision of a person to migrate to a particular place, be it a village, a town, or a city. These factors involve a historicity or historical account where they go on influencing for quite some times, the material conditions and shaping the mental make-up of those who intend to migrate. Since the knowledge about the material condition and mental make-up of the migrants is a bit problematic for the researcher, particularly in terms of time and resources available at his /her disposal, the paper suggests a technique-an inventory of certain items-to enquire about the specific factors and conditions leading the people to migrate. And finally, it seeks to evolve and suggest a method to measure the perception of social mobility and the degree of its achievement by the migrants at both the places of their origin and destiny. Such a method, along with suggested technique for studying migrations, would provide a better and relatively comprehensive theoretico-methodological perspective to analyse causes and consequences of migration, and, so also, the nature and degree of social mobility of people in the developing societies in general and India in particular.

Multi-faceted migration in India

An answer to "why people move" (Balan 1981) unfolds many reasons for and facets of migration from one place to the other. Besides the above mentioned reasons and factors of migrations, the natural and social calamities, 'system avoidance' (Connel et al 1979), social necessity (as in the of marriage migration), etc. also contribute to migration. These and several other factors determine the nature of migration – whether temporary, seasonal and mass migration or permanent, individual and long distance migration. The demographers always attribute more importance to the push and pull factors, which operate at the places of origin and destination and encourage or discourage migration of the people. But it has been observed that the push factors, obviously operating at the place of origin, have played more dominant role, for the last several decades, in migration of people from rural to urban areas than the pull factors operating at the place of destination. Nodoubt, the pull factors draw migrants from rural areas for limited purpose(s), but once the purposes are fulfilled, the migrants who might have got adjusted, by now, in the alien environment of the town or city became unwanted for the earlier city-settlers or their 'system of avoidance', as Connel et al (1979) have stated. Hence, a large majority of them are forced to live in the squatter settlements and hang around in search of employment for their livelihood. These also influence the in and out or return migration from the points of view of both the places of origin and destination.

Without going Further details of the causes of migration when we look at the specific case of India, we find that since early times to date most of the people in the country have spatially been mobile, either on temporary or permanent basis, and their choices and preferences have been determined by the forces operating at both the places of their origin and destination. More precisely, their spatial shift has been directed from rural to rural, rural to urban, urban to urban, and urban to rural areas. But in comparison to westerners in general and America in particular, Indians have been less mobile mainly due to their strong emotional bond with the place of their origin, uncertainty about their acceptance and adjustment at the place of destination, and the requirement of money to be spent on moving from one place to the other. Hence their purposive and selective migration. Depending upon their resources and conveniences, the rural-folks have also been migrating, and in certain cases once or twice during the off-seasons, to the places within the distance ranging from intra-district to inter-state through intra-state. In other cases, people have been forced to move *en masse* from their place of origin to a new place due to one type or the other of natural and social calamities. However, in all these cases, the rural migrants have been regarded as 'marginal', especially when they have migrated permanently from one village to the other village or city (Ram 1990 :233-244). This is so as the social organisation of a village has simply been localised, parochial and 'cohesive', the people other than those living there have largely been considered as outsiders. Even within a particular urban centre in India, people float from one locality to the other in order to have more access to the better opportunities and resources available there. Very rarely, such migrations occurs due to natural or social calamities. Instead it is often, rational and purposive, though it may be frequent also, in many cases, where migrants may move to more than one locality in a short span of time. Because of relatively openness of the social structure and more purposive and secondary type of social relations in urban areas, such migrants are easily accepted in a new urban locality. Their acceptance is also facilitated by their non- encroachment into the private and to some extent social or public domains of the residents in the new locality. However, in certain cases, they do face either latent or manifest resentment by the residents of the locality, depending upon their (floaters) social background, economic standing and position in power and authority.

Again, in regard to the choices and preferences of the places of destiny, it is evident that the larger cities in India have attracted more migrants than the small and medium size towns. This is so due to many-fold reasons like one before actually migrating to the place of their destiny, the migrants get, very often, both the encouraging and discouraging information about the situation prevailing over there. This becomes available through a certain type of information mechanism (Germani 1970:159-78) either in the form of a 'resource person' – the pre-city settler or other media. Of course, informations about the different types of towns and cities are not always factual and vary in terms of both quality and quantity. These informations about the larger cities govern more effectively the decision of the migrants in their favour.

Secondly, their decision to migrate to a new place is determined by their overall socio-economic, cultural (normative) and psychological conditions, as mentioned above. In event of uniformity or near uniformity of all these conditions, they prefer to migrate to larger cities which obviously enjoy higher or highest esteem in the hierarchy of towns and cities. Besides, a tendency has grown in mind of the people that there are more life chances and employment opportunities open in the larger cities than in the smaller ones. Hence, more avenues there for social and economic improvement. These operates decisively in both the cases where the migrants are drawn from a better socio-economic background and they use migration to improve further their lot, and in the case of those who hail from poor families and wish to earn their subsistence through migrating to the larger cities.

Finally, as the larger cities have adopted and internalised, in their social structure, a kind of cosmopolitan culture and a broad world-view, these find it congenial to accommodate and absorb the migrants drawn from the different religious, ethnic and caste and community backgrounds. In the case of some religious groups and ethnic communities, it may be necessary and also easier to retain with their cultural distinctiveness and, thus, contribute to eulogise (generate) primary urbanisation (Redfield and Singer 1956:161-194). At this level of urbanization, the migrants do retain with them their 'little tradition' with which they may have strong emotional attachment and also they may not find, at least initially, the problem of their adjustment in a totally alien culture and social structure in a larger city. But this is more so in the case of those who migrate from 'folk' (village) societies. Those who migrate either from better socio-economic background in rural areas, or from small or medium size town, or from a more developed region may get easily acculturated and adjusted in the new urban set-up. Contrary to this, it is easier for people drawn from the lower castes and classes or socio-economic position to easily forego their earlier background in the larger cities. After migrating to the larger cities, they may find it easy to 'pass' their previous identity, and once they succeed in that, they adopt an all together different identity which, along with their masses (Gould 19). But both 'passing' of the previous identity and adoption and percolation of a new one is frequent and easy at the individual level, and rare and difficult at the corporate group (caste) level, where identity (status) of the entire group is under alteration at a given point of time.

Migration and social mobility

We have mentioned above that migration is very often directed towards improvement in one's socio-economic status. It, however, does not mean that all migrants are successful and equally benefited in their venture. In fact, their success in terms of improvement in their socio-economic status depends on the levels of their personal ability, social manoeuvring, and the degree of their access to the resources available at the place of destiny. This is also related to the type and extent of their linkages with the place of their origin. Hence, the nature and degree of social mobility varies in accordance with the nature and type of migration. It also varies in the case of migrants drawn from the different socio-economic backgrounds. It is also true that keeping the other conditions constant, the individual migration is more successful in achieving upward social mobility than the group or mass migration. This is so as the individual migrants are generally more selective in regard to their own ability and choices of their destiny. Contrary to that, since mass migration takes place more often due to social and natural calamities, as stated earlier, very rarely it results into upward social mobility of the migrants. Instead, it generally terminates in the form of stationary or even downward social mobility and, in most of the cases, it leads to reverse migration.

Looking briefly at the processual substantiation of the points under reference, we find that during the last decades of the nineteenth century the selective individual migration was more fruitful in those cases where the migrants hailed from the better socio-economic background. This was also facilitated by the introduction of new institutions in India which, in turn, inculcated different sets of ideas, values, appreciation and realisation of different meanings of roles, status or social status among the people. Thus, whereas they achieved certain amount of social mobility through migration, they did experience new types of social inequality in urban areas (Saberwal 1979, Kumar 1983). Such a phenomenon continues even today, though it is more uniform in nature yet varying in degree.

Contrarily, both the mass migration and social mobility did not coincide positively in the case of those who hailed from the lower castes and classes or socio-economic statuses. The cases of Jatavas in Agra city (Lynch 1969, 1974), potters and plodders in Bombay-now Mumbai (Lynch 1979), and Tamilians or little Madras in Bombay (Mythili 1974) and several other cases of migration of such people can be cited. In all such cases, the migrants have not been free from their 'stigmatised' ethnic or caste identity (Berreman 1979), which often comes in their way of socio-economic achievement and thereby their upward social mobility as they migrate with their group or corporate group (caste) status, as stated earlier. Even if they succeed in achieving upward social mobility by improving their socio-economic status in urban areas, they invariably encounter with 'status dissonance' (Saberwal 1972) or discrepancy between their achieved status through upward social mobility, in urban areas and the low ascribed status in caste hierarchy in rural areas in case of their reverse migration. However, this is also true in the case of selective individual migrants drawn from the lower caste and socio-economic background. Being facilitated by the protective discrimination policy or the affirmative action, the migration and social mobility of the Scheduled Castes or Dalit do not often result into the positive consequences (Ram 1976;1985; D'Souza 1978), as their low caste status usually comes in their way.

Some theoretico-methodological issues

In the light of the above discussion, certain issues relating to the measurement and analysis of both migration and social mobility can be raised here. As mentioned at the very outset, the purpose of this paper is not to provide a complete inventory of the items to be included in the measurement of migration and social mobility. Rather, it intends to raise certain issues and makes tentative suggestions about some items to be included for developing a theoretico-methodological perspective or framework to measure and analyse the relationship between migration and social mobility. The list of items can be shortened or broadened in terms of inclusion or exclusion of items, keeping in view the focus on the nature and types of migration and social mobility.

First and the foremost issue is related to the nature and type of migration itself. Whether it is permanent or temporary, in or out, individual or group (mass) migration, directed towards short or long distances of place of destiny from that of origin? Whether it is 'purposive' or non-purposive, 'system acceptance' or 'system avoidance'? What are the values and the prestige which the migrants attach with both the places of their origin and destiny? What are the channels of filtering information down to the migrants about the place of destiny? How do they make choice of the place and what is the actual process through which they migrate to their destiny? What is the psychological trait and social background of the migrants and what are their chances of acceptance or rejection in the place of destiny? Likewise, the list can grow larger and larger, with the inclusion of items and sub-items relating to migration.

Secondly, the meaning and the unit of social mobility is to be taken into account. In other words, whether the focus of measurement is on horizontal or vertical (both upward and downward) or a 'complete' social mobility? Whether it is perfect or quasi-perfect or 'total' social mobility (Ram 1986)? Regarding units, whether it is educational, occupational or power domain in which mobility is being measured? Then, the very social structure of the place of destiny is to be looked into where mobility is to occur. Is it based on class- socio-economic and power or authority based social structure or system or caste and other primordial categories of relations? What is the reference or reference group behaviour of the migrants for their social mobility? Whether the reference of mobility is the social hierarchy or individual's socio-economic achievement, along with his/her location in the structure of power or authority found at the place of destiny or of origin?

Methodologically, the relationship between migration and social mobility is to be examined by bringing together a few or more items mentioned above. In this, migration is certainly to be accepted as independent variable, affecting the nature and degree of social mobility being dependent variables, though in some cases there may not be one to one correspondence between the two. Thus, on the basis of some items relating to the migration and social mobility, a perspective could be developed and verified with the data for its theoretical viability to be achieved at the higher level of abstraction.

Conclusion

The study of migration is extensively in the domains of demography and social geography, whereas the analysis and measurement of social mobility, including social changes, fall predominantly within the sociological enquiry. The enquiry of one process does not usually include the enquiry of the other process to arrive at a comprehensive understanding of the relationship between them. Since both the processes often conjoin and converge at one time or the other, it is needed to analysis them together within a certain theoretico-methodological perspective to be developed for the purpose. This is necessary in view of the fact that migration is a predominant process of spatial mobility not only in the developing, but also in the developed societies of the world where both have, by and large, different units and domains of social mobility.

REFERENCES

Balan, Jorge 1981, *Why People Move?* Unesco

Berreman, G.D. 1979, *Caste and Other Inequities*, Meerut.

Connel, John et al 1979, *Migration From Rural Areas*, Delhi.

Germani, Gino 1970, "Migration and Acculturation" in *Hand book For Social Research in Urban Area*, Unesco.

Gould, Harold Kumar, Ravinder 1983 *Essays in Social History of Modern India*, New Delhi.

Lynch, O.M., 1974 *Politics of Untouchability*, New Delhi.

______, 1979 *"Plodders, Plotters and Podders....", Urban Anthropology*, 8(1):1-27

Mythili, K.L., 1974, "Little Madres in Bombay city…." in Urban Sociology in India, M.S.A .Rao (ed.), New Delhi.

Ram, Nandu, 1976, *Social Mobility and Status Identification among* the Scheduled Castes Government Employees in *Kanpur*- Ph.D. thesis, IIT Kanpur.

______1985 *"Social Stratification and Mobility among the Scheduled Caste in Urban India"* K. Seshadri & E.Haq (ed.), in *Problems of Studies in the Third World Countries.*

______ 1986, "Social Stratification and Status-Identification Among the Scheduled Castes: A Synoptic View" in I. Modi(ed.), *Main Trends in Indian Sociology,* Jaipur.

______, 1990, "Marginalization and social mobility in Urban

India "in Girishwar Misra (ed.) *Applied Social Psychology in India*, New Delhi, Safe Publication, pp. 233-244.

Saberwal, Satish, 1979, "Inequality in colonial India", *Contributions to Indian Sociology*, 13(2):241-41.

9

Migration, Social Mobility and Town – Country Nexus in North India

Social mobility in both the senses of occupational changes and shift from one position to the other in a given social space or system of social stratification is said to be smoother and more excelling in urban rather than in rural areas. That is why, most of the rural people migrate or prefer to migrate to towns and cities. For quite some times in India people used to migrate temporarily to the towns and cities leaving their family members at the places of their origin mostly the villages. Through this they used to continue their links with the rural areas. At the same times, they served as links or agents of interaction between rural and urban areas. They also carried with their certain norms, values, customs, traditions, etc., of the places of their origin to that of their destination and vice-versa. These rites de passage have not only helped them in getting adjusted to their new settlements but also have got routinized as a part of their value-orientation or ideology. Moreover, knowledge about rural and urban lives of the people is now easily available through the most developed media of communication, transportation, etc. In this paper, we shall analyse the nature and type of migration taking place and its role in accelerating the process of social mobility in India. We shall also examine how both the cityward migration and social mobility contribute together to generate, retain and enhance the nexus between the rural and urban areas. Since these phenomenon are even existing in Indian society, we have to concentrate on their processional rather than static aspects. To substantiate our arguments we shall rely on the data pertaining mainly to north and eastern India. Before we analyse the specific type or types of among the three processes, it is necessary to explain concepts of migration, mobility and nexus between town and country.

Other migrants in the stream are those who migrate temporarily to other rural areas in search of employment, or to escape from the natural calamities, or in the form of mass plights to get rescued from the dominance exploitation and atrocities of the local dominant persons or their henchmen. Out of the four lifetime migration streams (rural to rural, rural to urban, urban to rural and urban to urban) in India the most dominant one is from rural to rural migration and 55.63% of the total short distance migration.) this trend becomes weak when the migration stretches to the medium (within the state -11.72%) and long (between the states – 3.91%) distances (Bose 1978:193-195). Again, in the case of short-distance rural to rural migration majority of the migrants are females who migrate mostly due to their marriage. Further, the second dominant migration- stream in India is from rural to urban (again, according to 1971 , it was 6.47% in the case of short distance 4.98% in medium distance and 3.55% in long distance). Barring the marriage migration and a thin percentage of those who migrate for certain non-productive purposes, a large majority of migrants are guided by the economic considerations irrespective of the duration, distance and streams of their migration. More precisely, migration is predominantly linked with the process of social mobility. The migrants always intend to acquire certain degree of social mobility by improving their socio-economic conditions through their access to the opportunity structure prevailing at the place of destination. This is so as there are relatively less avenues and more rigid social space present acceleration of social mobility at the place of origin primarily being the rural areas which do not facilitate of migrants.

Urban and urban to rural areas across the physical distance. The two streams of migration rural to urban and urban to rural- unfold certain kinds of nexus between town and country or urban and rural areas. Besides, nexus between the two is maintained through a number of other devices like extraction of raw materials from rural to urban areas and their reverse flow in the forms of finished goods along with the inflow of technological innovations and appliances to the rural areas. It is argued in this chapter how rural to urban and urban to rural migration and the resultant process of social mobility contribute to strengthen or weaken the nexus between rural and urban areas or between town and country. Also keeping in view the rural vantage point, the emphasis here is more on the reverse (urban to rural areas) and temporary migration rather than on the permanent immigration where I exists a greater possibility of acquiring higher degree of social mobility but also shelves the nexus between the rural and urban areas. This happens so as migrants in such cases leave the place of their origin and settle permanently in urban areas. The analysis presented in this chapter is based on the situations prevailing mostly in north India though the same may be found, with some variations, in other parts of the country also . But before we take up this issue it is necessary to have a brief look at the nature of town and country or urban and rural areas in India.

Town and country: the complex typologies

In the discussion on migration and its contribution in acquiring social mobility less attention has been paid on the socio-spatial characteristics of both the places of origin and destination. This is so because migration is regarded as a sub-process of urbanization increase in population of a town or city. In fact, both town and country or urban and rural areas have been accepted as homologous with independent uniformity of their own. The intra variations are ignored and they are considered as imbibing separately to the uniform social structures of their own. But contrary to the general usage of town,. Thus , putting all these together a town has specific connotation where it has population size of not less than 5000 persons with density of 1000 persons per square mile, three-fourths of population engaged in non-agricultural occupations, municipality or municipal corporation as administrative unit local self government, and some pronounced urban characteristics like newly founded industrial areas, large housing settlements places of tourist importance and all civic amenities needed for urban population a there are six or even more types of urban centres from class and cities with their sub-categorization to class VI cities . In concrete sense, these range from a merely tehsil or taluka town to the four largest metropolis or megapolises through the medium size towns and more than hundred million plus metropolitan cities. These different towns and cities vary not only in their demographic features –size density, age and sex ration of population living patterns of social interaction, institutional arrangements and the magnitudes of existing physical and social amenities. Accordingly, they pull migrants in varying numbers and of divergent social and economic backgrounds from both near and far-off places. In the recent years the bigger cities have attracted more migrants than the small and medium size towns and cities. In both the cases extracted benefits of migration to bigger cities are more than the cost incurred in the forms of spending money and time on travelling and staying much away from the place of origin. There are mainly two reasons for this: one, the bigger cities have relatively more employment opportunities and other amenities basic to their life for migrants specially from the lower castes and communities to forgo their primordial identity and claim for a new one if they are shy of their previous identity and of their non-prestigious jobs if employed in any such jobs.

In the similar fashion, the countryside or rural areas is consisted of numerous types of villages which are dissimilar not only in terms of their physical distance from a town or a city but they also vary in their population size, social and economic development, use of technology and other types of innovations, level of social and political awareness, etc. Since the village India is not homogenous entity as mentioned above, the rural areas in different parts of the country also vary in their belief systems, customs, cultures, social moorings and orientations towards modernity. It is said that the villages falling at the fringe or in the vicinity of a town or city have more urban influence than those located at a far-off place. In other words, migration from such places is easier as it involves less cost in the forms of money and distance than otherwise. Since the mechanism of information about urban areas is readily available and easily accessible to the people of these places, the migrants from these villages are more in number who may not find much difficulty in their adjustment in towns and cities. That means, there exists a stronger nexus between such rural areas and towns and cities than those which are governed by their location at a long physical distance. Keeping the two migration streams rural to urban and urban to rural- constant the nature and degree of social mobility of migrants will also vary in accordance with the physical characteristics of both the places of origin and destiny. For instance, if the migrants are drawn from those rural areas which are less developed and have a relatively closed social system and if they migrate to those towns and cities whose social and physical characteristics area completely distinct and which have diversified opportunities and relatively open social system, then they may find their mal-adjustment at the place of destiny at least in the initial stage. This may accordingly affect the nature and degree of their social mobility leaving scope for two possibilities. One, they may be satisfied with little improvement in their socio-economic status and thereby with limited degree of social mobility in the urban areas. Two, they may try to learn the urban techniques and skills and may strife for acquiring a higher degree of social mobility, either in the urban area itself of at the place of their origin being a village, through extracting and planting the acquired skills and benefits there. There is a third possibility also in which the migrants may return home after being unsuccessful in their venture.

This is, however, not to suggest that either a town-both medium and small size-or a city is completely homogeneous and uniform in terms of its physical growth and social and life of people living in the different areas or localities. Invariably in all towns and cities in India certain localities are physically and socially-culturally more developed, others are moderately developed and still others are less developed or not developed at all. It is the third type of localities which have slums of slum like structures. Again, civil lines, cantonment and, to some extent, old part of a city were more developed and the periphery was almost neglected in the past. But now a reverse trend is witnessed where periphery has drawn more attention of the civic administration and has also attracted a relatively affluent section of urban population. In other words, there exist differentials in opportunity structures, roles and statuses, and social and cultural life of people located in the different parts of a city or a town. The places of destiny-specific localities in a given town or city- differ in the cases of migrants drawn from the divergent socio-economic backgrounds particularly in rural areas. The illiterate unskilled and poor migrants are left with no option except to live in the less developed localities in a town or city. So, also, the nature and degree of their social mobility vary in accordance with the nature of both the places of their origin and destiny.

Social Composition of migrants

Besides the divergence in the nature of places origin and destiny or of rural an urban areas, the migrants themselves are not a homogenous social category. Apart from rural to rural migration, in terms of travelling the distance, the dominated trend, is to migrate to the towns or cities located at the medium distance within the state. The same is true in the case of reverse migration also. Nonetheless, people migrate from rural to urban areas either on temporary or semi-permanent or permanent basis. Though it is not easy to trace the dominant trend in migration in regard to duration of stay in the town or city, it can be relied upon that the majority of migrants in India are those who migrate temporarily and do not shelve completely their contract with the rural areas. Their contacts are maintained or renewed through the casual or regular visits to the place of their origin or such visits of kins or members of the family of procreation located in rural areas to the migrants living in a town or city. Since their prime interests are located in the rural areas, they consider migration as a means to extract benefits from town or city and use that as input to improve their socio-economic status and thereby acquire higher degree of social mobility in rural areas. This includes target migration also where the migrants stay at the place of destiny till their targets are fulfilled. Their targets may include the improvements in their social statuses at both the places or education of youngers in the family and so on. Then, there occurs a reverse migration.

Who are the people migrate from rural to urban areas and why? The second part of the question needs our immediate attention here. Theoretically, people migrate due to three specific reasons: these are objective conditions and normative structures prevailing at both the places of origin and destiny, and the subjective or psychological traits of migrants (Germany 1970:159-178). The objective conditions are in fact economic resources present or absent at the places of origin and destiny. For instance, "The predominance of one form of agricultural production or another is an important source of variation in rural-urban relationships and in the characteristics of migration. Areas of capitalist farming, for example, 'expel' more people than do areas of peasant farming. Areas of peasant production may present, however, a more complex set of urban-rural relationships in which family enterprises span rural and urban locations, with town migrants retaining rights to land and aiming to return eventually" (Roberts 1979:90).

The objective conditions actually work in the forms of push and pull factors. In the case of migration in India the push factors are considered to be stronger which work more frequently in villages though these may converge, in the actual process of migration, with the pull factors operating in urban areas. But these factors do not operate uniformly and they vary in accordance with variations in the objective conditions in different villages and towns and cities and in their different localities. Similarly, as the normative structures differ in various parts of both the rural and urban India, they also vary in effecting the nature of migration. The normative structure in rural India was so pervasive that the migrants were looked down upon by the permanent residents of a village in the past. They were not allowed to participate in the decision making on the vital issues pertaining of the entire village. In fact, for such and many other purposes they were considered 'outsider' and were treated accordingly. But this did not apply in those cases were they migrants were economically well-off and had muscle power or were related to some such of persons and village which they had migrated. As a result, people generally did not live to migrate from the place of their origin. Now, some basic changes have occurred in the normative structure of rural society in India but the measurement of its actual effect on migration is not very simple. So is the case with the psychological traits of people who have already migrated or those who intend to migrate but their migration is equally and sometimes even more forcefully governed by the objective and normative factors operating at both the places of origin and destiny.

The question of who are the people who migrate is directly tied up with the social characteristics and intentions of migrants. Generally speaking, majority of the migrants in India are those who have not acquired any specific type of occupational skill or training before their migration. Barring a small number of migrants (whose exact number may not be easily known) who have been engaged in occupation like tailoring, processing of leather goods, hair cutting, cleansing clothes (especially under the earlier existing village jajmani system) and certain other types of handicraft activities in villages and are engaged in the same or similar types of activities after coming to towns or cities, most of the migrants are unskilled or semi-skilled and have remained the landless agricultural labourers in rural areas. Also, being illiterate or semi-literate they migrate to urban areas in search of relatively stable employment with obviously better emoluments. Over and above, they want to embrace some solace from the social and economic bondage in rural areas through migrating to towns or cities. There are quite a few who migrate to pursue education or acquire better skill, join the kins or family members and alike. Others migrate from rural areas where they have relatively good economic base and posses better educational qualifications though they do not enjoy higher prestige in the village social hierarchy. More precisely, they belong to the lower and lowest castes in the villages. Still, there is a third category of migrants who hail from the upper castes and classes in rural areas. They migrate after leaving behind much better economic base in rural areas have more chances of access to the urban resources.

Then the specific intentions and motivation of migration

may vary in the cases of all the three categories of migrants. For instance, in the first case it is a mere existential sustenance and in the second and third cases the prime motive may be their access to better life chances and achievement of relatively higher degree of social mobility. However, behind all these works the distant economic motive to be fulfilled easily in urban areas though this fact cannot be ignores that there has already started a trend of massive erosion in rural values which keeps some people away from active participation in village social life and move to nearby towns and cities. These is every likelihood that since the migrants who come to towns or cities for bare economic subsistence by leaving behind spouse and other family members in villages, their migration may or may not continue their contact with other members of their family because invariably they are joined in the urban areas, by their immediate family unit-spouse and children whose major interests like education, employment etc. get shifted from rural to urban areas.

Migration and social mobility

Generally speaking, social mobility is explained in terms of occupational change. A better occupation not only draws more emolument but also accords higher prestige and improves one's class or socio-economic status. Keeping aside equivalence, certain rural occupations are also pursued with more emoluments, relatively higher prestige and mechanisation in urban areas. The occupations like hair-cutting saloons, cleansing clothes in the laundry, working with leather in or working shoes and other such goods in the mechanised factory, etc. which have been regarded as caste specific occupations and are pursued solely in rural and largely in urban areas by members of the respective castes may be cited here. Since these are pursued with more cash emoluments and mechanisation in urban areas, their pursuant are considered occupationally mobile. For instance, the datavs of Agra who were associated with worse leather-works in villages before they came to Agra city are largely engaged at present in manufacturing of shoes and other leather goods in the city. Yet, they are considered to have acquired occupational mobility (See Lynch 1974:251-275). The occupational mobility is more distinctive in those cases where the migrants are engaged in the blue or white collar jobs which certainly fetch more emoluments and prestige and which involve greater amount of mechanization.

But in India social mobility is to be understood in terms of multiple dimensions of power and authority, prestige and an overall status in the social hierarchy which cannot be deduced only from pursuing certain type of occupation (Ram1988b:48-68). All these are valued either in the caste or class hierarchy or in a hierarchy consisting of both though the meaningful achievement along on e dimension or the other may greatly influence the nature of social mobility achieved by a person. For instance, if a person is highly educated and possesses qualification required for a job, there is every likelihood that his occupational states will be higher along with fetching more emoluments and enjoying higher authority and prestige in the society. Nevertheless, the meaning of social mobility may differ from one context to the other. For instance, for an unskilled or semi-skilled migrant social mobility means getting some 'respectful' employment, stable income, a house and freedom from bondage. But those who are highly qualified and hail from the better socio-economic background they will strife for further improvement and social mobility for them would mean the achievement of higher amount of power, prestige and privileges, and in a word, a superior place in the existing social hierarchy. Thus, the success of migrants "in terms of improvement in their socio-economic status (and thereby achievement of social mobility) depends on the levels of their personal ability, social manoeuvring, and the degree of their access to the resources available at the place of destiny. This is also related to the type and extent of their linkages with the place of their origin. Hence, the nature and degree of social mobility varies in accordance with the nature and type of migration. It also varies in the case of migrants drawn from the different socio-economic backgrounds" (Ram 1986 ms). Social mobility occurs in a given social space which does not exist uniformly. Generally speaking, the social space in urban India is characterized as open in which social mobility means achievement in the various aspects of life. Contrary to this, the social space in villages is considered to be relatively closed in which the reference of social mobility is the enhancement of one's status in the caste hierarchy. But the general and specific types of changes occurred thus far in India have made both the rural and urban spaces more complex where difference between the two is of certain degree of closed-ness or openness. In other words, these are open in some aspects and closed in the other though in relation to rural social space the urban social space is relatively more open.

Since the major stake of the temporary migrant is the place of their origin- the village- where their family members and some inherited and earned property are located, they are more concerned with achieving social mobility- improvement in both the socio-economic and caste status-in rural areas. For this, they sacrifice many times their possible urban comforts and are satisfied even with low degree of social mobility in urban areas. Such migrants fail obviously to make through their presence, any dent, in urban social and cultural life though they do contribute to its material affluence. However, their role in maintaining certain type of nexus between the rural and urban areas cannot be denied but it becomes weak in the generation of their children especially those who are born and grown in the town or city (Majumdar and Majumdar 1978). Opposed to this, the educated migrants who also hail largely from the better socio-economic background in rural areas are able to further improve their socio-economic status and achieve relatively higher degree of social mobility in urban areas. Since they have better access to the power, privileges, prestige and such in the available urban resources, their's is a successful permanent migration. No doubt. They contribute substantially to the sustenance of social and cultural life in urban areas but in the process their earlier possessed rural attributes get completely submerged in the urban ones. In the long-run, their linkages with rural areas in general and with their kins and other family members in particular get shelved. Thus, they ceased to act as an agent of continuing and strengthening the nexus between the rural and urban areas.

To substantiate the arguments three specific ones studies can be cited here. First is the study of a few small and medium size towns in Bihar and West Bengal conducted by Ramkrishna Mukherjee (Mukherjee 1965:15-58). Based on the dates extracted from both skilled and unskilled rural migrants to these towns, Mukherjee has found the rural-urban dichotomy in those cases where the migrants are permanently settled in an urban neighbourhood and "have cut off their connections with the places of emigration" (the rural-urban nexus is completely missing). Contrary to where the migrants are able to maintain "contact with their previous settlements" – the rural areas- through keeping intact both the rural-urban interaction and rural-urban relationship (the rural urban nexus is relatively stronger.)

The other two studies pertain to Delhi (Ram 1988a: 322-330) and Kanpur (Ram 1988b). Our Delhi data are related to the unskilled industrial labourers who have temporarily migrated from the villages in the eastern Uttar Pradesh. Living in slums they send regularly a major portion of their earnings to their villagers and use that as input to enhance their social prestige and achieve certain degree of social mobility in rural areas. Their occasional presence in the village not only demonstrates their urban adaptation exhibited through their speech, clothings, etc. but also reinforces their assertion for more freedom, equality and prestige to be accorded to them. On the other hand, while living in Delhi city they well maintain their rural-identity through retaining with them the rural social and cultural attributes, affinal and kinship ties etc. Thus, in one way or the other they act as an agent in maintaining the rural-urban interaction or rural-urban relationship.

Contrary to this, our our data from Kanpur city are obtained from those semi-permanent and a few permanent rural migrants who are skilled and educated and are employed in the white-collar government jobs. They live in the city with their spouse, children and in some cases, with a few relatives or members of the family of procreation. They have certainly been able to improve their socio-economic status and achieve relatively higher degree of social mobility in urban areas. But their such achievement is, by and large, incongruent with their overall social status in rural areas where they visit very rarely. As a result , their rural bond is growing weak with the greater possibility of its complete erosion in the generation of their children. Thus, it can be conveniently said that a balanced nexus between the rural and urban areas is well maintained through the temporary migration, where the migrants visit frequently the place of their origin the village due to one reason or the other. Through such visits not only they instill certain urban-industrial values, norms, etc among the people living in rural areas but they alos bring with them varieties of customs, traditions, behavior patterns, styles of life, etc. in urban areas and exhibit them at least in their neighbourhoods where they are not shy at all with their culture amidst the cultures of others.

The town-country nexus: some missing links

Our common sense knowledge of town and country in India is grappled by the rural-urban contrast or rural-urban differences. The rural is not urban and vice-versa. But contrarily, "The distant villages, even if located in the proximity of the growth centres, remain relatively immune from the "adaptative" constraints of urban/industrial culture, and, as such, accept only those changes which do not necessarily endanger tribal or peasant identity. Attachment to such identity does not necessarily entail reaction or resistance to the cultural influence of industrialization" (Akinchan 1979:22). The influence of urban, or industrial culture is extended to the rural areas through a general awareness of the rural people but more so through a general awareness of the rural people but more so through rural-urban migration. A more dominant trend of rural – urban relationship is around the view that "the traditional elements of caste and kinship are as strongly entrenched in the structure of urban community as it is in that of the rural community. This has strengthened the view that the borderline between 'rural' and 'urban' has been blurred so far as the Indian society is concerned" (Chandrasekhariah 1982:186). Not only that but the rural-urban relationship has been regarded as balanced in terms of their mutual inter-dependence of material and non-material aspects of life.

Contrary to this view, it is said that " The city is a 'service station' and amusement centre for the country, and the country is a 'food basket' for the city. But while the diversity of cultural groups (in the city) and the absence of a common culture makes the basis of the integration primarily technical, even this kind of integration requires a kind of cultural consciousness to keep it going. We refer to consciousness of cultural differences and the felling that certain forms of inter-cultural association are of great enough benefit to override the repugnance of dealing with 'foreigners'(Redfield and Singer 1956 :187-188) – the rural migrants. The realization of presence and relative autonomy of other cultures (of migrants) in one's own society (a city here) is a more balanced explanation of rural-urban nexus.

A more recent development in rural-urban relationships envisages a certain degree of rural dependency and urban exploitation. "Villagers, being at the receiving end of the "diffusion", (and villages being treated as the 'food market') and planning and development, lack capacity to act independently. They are mostly caught up in a socio-political statism: they are in a dependency loop" (Sharma 1988:43). This is also supported by the influx of rural migrants to urban areas where they are mostly under-privileged and are compelled to live a substandard life. The rural poverty and low level of living standard amidst the preponderance of raw-material and man-power suggest the rural- exploitation by the growing urban affluence where again the urban poor are the less beneficiaries. However, "The central policy issue is not merely that of rural-urban inequality but the question of balance between the metropolitan centre on the one hand and the small towns and the country-side on the other" (Das Gupta 1981:56). Besides the material aspects wherein the rural migrants are guided primarily by their economic interests, the balanced link between the rural and urban areas is to be traced through their behavior patterns. How they behave in urban areas and there is any qualitative change in their behaviour patterns when they return back to their village. However, the "Explanations of behavioral patterns among migrants of rural origin can no longer be based on simplistic assumptions about traditional values. Whether (their) links with a peasant economy are sustained or not, the kind of links and the degree of dynamism of that economy are important sources of variation in behavioral patterns, which the urban social organization to rural origins. Cityward migration may thus be seen as the kind of link between urban and rural organization, with an impact upon both (Balam 1981:11) .

In sum, the rural-urban nexus appears to be missing in terms of unsuccessful migration where the migrants return to their villages after getting rejected or thrown out by the city. That means, they do not get proper employment, accommodation, emotional support etc. and are unable to achieve social mobility in the urban areas. When they return to their villages, they carry a negative image of urban life. Their attachment with village life gets reinforced by their rural-urban experiences and cross-cultural comparison irrespective of their partisan world-view. Thus, they act as a passive agent in the growing complexity of the town-country or rural-urban nexus.

Migration, Social Mobility and Town-Country Nexus in North India

Social mobility in both the serves of occupational changes and shift from one position to the other in a given social space or system of social stratification is said to be smoother and more excelling in urban rather than in rural areas. That is why, most of the rural people migrate or prefer to migrate to towns and cities. For quite some times in India people mostly used to migrate temporarily to the towns and cities leaving their family members at the places of their origin mostly the villages. Through this they used to continue their links with the rural areas. At the same time, they also served as links or agents of interaction between urban and rural areas. They also carried with them certain norms, values, customs, traditions, etc. of the places of their origin to that of their destination (towns and cities) and vice-versa. These rites of passage not only helped them in getting adjusted to their new surroundings bit also got routinized as a part of their value-orientation or ideology.

In the most recent years there has been qualitative change in intention and the resultant streams of migration. Now, the migrants mostly accompany other members of their family especially their wife and children and get settled permanently in towns and cities. Moreover, knowledge about rural and urban lives of the people is now easily available through the most developed media of communication modes of transportation, etc. which have strengthened the nexus between rural and urban areas.

It is argued in this chapter how rural to urban and urban to rural streams of migration and the resultant process of social mobility contribute to strengthen or weaken the nexus between rural and urban areas or between town and country. Also, keeping in view the rural vantage point, the emphasis here is more the reverse (urban to rural areas) and temporary migration rather than on permanent in-migration (city ward) where exists a greater possibility of acquiring higher degree of social mobility but shelving the nexus between the rural and urban areas. This happens so as the migrants in the latter case leave the place of their origin in rural areas and settle permanently in urban areas. Since these phenomenon are ever existing in Indian society, we shall concentrate on their processual rather than static aspects. The analysis presented here is based on the situations prevailing mostly in north and eastern parts of India though the same may be found, with some variations, in other parts of the country also. But before doing this we shall analyse briefly the nature and types of migration, social mobility and town-country nexus.

Migration, mobility and nexus : Some explanations

Out of the four life-time migration streams (rural to rural, rural to urban, urban to rural and urban to urban) in India the most dominant one is from rural to rural migration and that too within a short distance or within the district itself. According to 1971 census, it is considered 55.63 percent of the total short distance migration. In 1981 it increased to ____percent. This trend becomes weak when the migration stretches to the medium and long distances as it were 11.72 percent and 3.91 percent respectively according to 1971 census (Bose 1978:193-95) am dot decreased further in 1981. Again, in the case of short-distance rural to rural migration majority of the migrants are females who migrate mostly due to their marriage.

Hence, marriage migration in rural areas. The second dominant migration-stream in India is from urban to urban and urban to rural areas. Again, from the point of distance the rural to urban migration according to 1971 census was 6.47 per cent in the case of short distance, 4.98 per cent in the case of long distance. The two streams of migration- rural to urban and urban to rural in which the latter one being the reverse migration –unfold certain kinds of nexus between town and country or urban and rural areas. Besides, nexus between the two is maintained through a number of other devices like extraction of raw materials from rural to urban areas and their reverse-flow in the forms of finished goods along with the in-flow of technological innovations and appliances to the rural areas.

Migration in the case of either streams or distances is spatial or geographical mobility. Here, we are partly interested to know why people more but more to enquire into what happens at both the places of their origin and destination when they move. In other words, the issue of relationship between geographical and social mobility is more pertinent for us at the moment. Answers to why people move have been termed, in the literature migration, as causes or factors which have been classified into push and pull. Instead of going into the detailed analysis of these causes or factors of migration we wish to mention here that these determine the nature and type of migration,whether temporary or permanent and short or long-distance. These types of migration, in turn, influence the nature and degree of social mobility.

Such relationship between the spatial and social mobility existed even during the colonial period and was more evident in the cases of manual workers and the skilled and educated persons. For instance, towards end of the nineteenth century the stream of manual works specially from Bihar and eastern United Provinces (preset Uttar Pradesh) migrated temporarily to the tea gardens , Jute mills in Calcutta, cotton mills in Bombay, Kanpur, etc. Another groups of skilled and educated persons who were employed in bureaucracy or were professional or even merchants migrated to different urban centres through the passage of their transfer in or search for jobs. "With their capital, or skills, or both these groups enjoyed considerable mobility between the various city states (especially in the Saurashtra peninsula). With this mobility would go a certain breadth of experiences and of networks: these resources could be used to advantage in the eighteenth century, for physical mobility would often cover occupational and therefore economic and political mobility too"(Saberwal 1978:3).

In the present century they process of both spatial and social mobility have accelerated and divided the migrants into two categories of temporary or permanent migrants to urban areas. In few cases the purpose is to earn subsistence or get protection from the natural and man-made calamities in the rural areas but in most of the cases it is to receive higher education , get urban employment and substantiate their earning to improve their socio-economic condition and thereby achieve either horizontal or vertical social mobility. Such mobility is directed both within the caste (or community) and class frameworks either at the lace of origin in the case of temporary or even seasonal migrants or at the place of destination in the case of permanent migrants. In the more recent years a distinctive trend of migration has emerged at least in some parts of the country in which more and more people of the upper castes and classes in rural areas have migrated by and large on permanent basis, to towns and cities to receive higher and technical education and take bureaucratic jobs and professional employment. There they have successfully acquired the status of the urban middle classes. Their parental land in villages has either been leased out or sold to the dominant middle level backward castes and in some cases to the lower castes also. This trend is perhaps unwittingly in the earlier order of the upper caste people keeping social distance with the members of backward and lower castes. The main purpose of the backward and lower caste people migrating migrating to towns and cities is mostly to remit their urban earning back to their family in village and invest that in consolidating their socio-economic condition and power position.

A number of phrases and hypotheses have been used in regard to characterizing the rural and urban areas and their inter-relationship. These are: rural-urban dichotomy or differences or contrasts rural-urban continuance; and rural-urban contact, interaction networks linkages and relations; and rural-urban nexus. We shall briefly explain here what these phrases and hypothesis mean. Such explanation are important for understanding the relationships among and the interdependence of process of migration, social mobility and town-country nexus. These are also helpful in analyzing the nature and desirable viability of the nexus between the rural and urban areas. Without going into the conceptual explanations of the terms rural and urban when we look at the hypotheses of rural-urban dichotomy and rural-urban continuum, we find that these primarily analyse the differences and relationships between the rural and urban areas. The rural-urban dichotomy is based on the ideal type characterization of a village and a city. It presupposes that a village is the smallest unit of human habitation. Consequently, it occupies a small geographical territory and is economically and politically self-sufficient with an absolute degree of social and cultural homogeneity or homogeneous social and cultural relations among its members. Such characterization of a rural community derives its strength from three specific sources of the village republic supposedly existed in the ancient Indian society, its characteristics opposed to "urbanism as a way of life" an urban area and its empirical referent systematically analysed for the first time in 1952 by Robert Redfield, in his sturdy of Tepozlan, a small village in Mexico, Latin America. The other phrases like rural-urban differences or contrasts also subscribe to this view of distinctiveness of both the communities or areas.

Contrary to this, the rural-urban continuum hypothesis states that there is a continuum between a folk or rural community and an urban community. In the continuous evolutionary process there exists the transition from a 'purely' rural community to a 'purely' urban one and this transition suggests a continuum moving in the unilinear direction. In other words, the rural society or community advances imbibing the characteristics of an urban community or a village advancing towards becoming a town and the city. Along the continuum, then a village community has to become from a rural farm to rural no farm and finally urban one. Besides, the rural-urban continuum hypothesis also envisages that there is 'continuous gradation' of socio-cultural attribute from rural to urban areas there are ' consistent variations' from one point or stage to another. Our intension here is not to support or refute the arguments put around this hypothesis; rather, we wish to mention here that the phrases like rural-urban contact, linkages, interaction, relations and networks partly reflect this continuum and partly accept the rural and urban communities as they exist and then cannot certain types of relation between the two. The rural-urban or town-country nexus also explains this relationship in some specific ways or contexts. We shall take up this issue in detail later when we specifically analyse this town-country nexus and some missing links therein.

REFERENCES:

Akinchan, S., 1979, "Urban growth and political socialization: a study of rural-urban differentials in value-preferences and leadership behavior in Bihar". ICSSR Research Abstracts Quarterly'

Balan, Jorge 1981 "Introduction n his (ed.) Why People Move, The Unesco Press

Bose, Ashish 1978 India's Urbanization-1901-2001, Tata McGraw-Hill, New Delhi.

Chandrasekhariah K." 1982 "Urban Sociology of India: perspective and research needs" in P.K.B. Nayara (ed.), Sociology in India: Retrospect and Prospect, B.R Publishing Corpn., Delhi, pp.185-196.

Dasguta, Biplab 1981 "Rural-urban migration and rural development" in Jorge Balan (ed.) Why People Move, op.cit. pp.43-56.

Germani, Gino 1970 "Migration and Acculturation" in P.M. Hauser (ed.), A Handbook for social Research in Urban Areas, UNESCO.

Lynch, O.M. 1974 "Rural Cities in India: continuities and discontinuities" in M.S.A. Rao (ed.), Urban Sociology in India, orient Longman, New Delhi.

Majumdar, P.S. and Ila Majumdar 1978 Rural Migrants in Urban Setting, Hindustan Publishing Corporation, Delhi.

Mukherjee, R. 1965 The Sociologist and Social Change in India Today, I notice Hall of India, New Delhi.

Ram, Nandu 1986ms "Migration and Social Mobility in India: some theoretico-methodological issues"-paper presented to the XIth World Congress of Sociology, New Delhi, Aug. 19-22

________ 1988a "Housing and the Urban Poor in India: A Hypothetical Refinement" in R.C. Sharma (ed.), South Asian Urban Experience, Criterion Publications, New Delhi.

__________ 1988b The Mobile Scheduled Castes, Hindustan Publishing Corporation, Delhi.

Redfied, R.and M.B Singer 1956 " the Cultural Role of Cities", Man in India 36 (3):161-194.

Roberts, Bryan 1979 Cities of Peasants: Explorations in Urban Analysis, Arnold-Heimann, New Delhi.

Sharma, A.K. 1988 "Social Implications of Urbanization in India", The Journal of Sociological Studies :35-46.

Saberwal,S 1978 "Indian urbanism: a socio historical perspective" in his (ed.) Process and Institution in Urban India: Sociological Studies, Vikas Publishing House, New Delhi; pp 1-17.

10

Values and Changes in an Industrial Metropolis: The Case of a Slum in Kanpur

Slums or blighted areas are inherent part of an urban centre, though these may not be desired either by the slum dwellers themselves, or city administration, or the urban population as a whole. Slums have been defined in many ways. Some consider a slum as an undeveloped settlement surrounded by the developed localities. It lacks most of the civic amenities like sanitation, water, electricity, etc. Others define it as a centre of poverty and of deviant behaviour where the slum dwellers are engaged in various kinds of criminal activities such as theft, pick-pocketing, vandalism, murder, etc. This they do in the absence of a permanent and 'dignified' source of livelihood. Still, others may accept it as a centre of ignorance and helplessness resulting from repulsion and neglect of the administration and better-off section of population in the city. Housing condition may be another indicator for defining a slum. However, one may not accept merely housing condition but a feeling and social and cultural values associated with that as necessary conditions for delineating a slum (Piettie 1969: 21-22, Ram 1988a: 322-330). One may also analyse the structure and culture or value system of a slum along any of the above considerations. But one may not accept slum as a homogeneous structure, instead, one may find different gradations within it by accepting the most developed and the most underdeveloped structures, in a city, as the positive and negative references respectively. That means, an underdeveloped structure may be the most underdeveloped (*Juggis-Jhoparies*), less underdeveloped (*Chawls*, *Katras),* etc. Accordingly, there may be various types of slums characterised by a variety of social structures and cultures lived with there. We shall analyse briefly the structure and change prevalent in a locality in Kanpur city and show how the latter is influenced by the change in value-orientations of the population living there.

A general profile of Kanpur city

Before analysing the structure and change in the locality under study, we shall briefly look at the larger spatial and social structures of the city of which it is a part. Kanpur city is the sixth largest city in India and the only industrial metropolis in Uttar Pradesh. The population of the city is over 14 lakhs, according to 1981 census, out of which about 70 per cent are Hindus, 20 per cent are Muslims and the rest are Jains, Sikhs, Christians, Buddhists, etc. Kanpur like many cities in India represents a masculine character as males have always outnumbered the female population. The industrial metropolis of Kanpur is famous for its woollen, cotton and leather industries and for numerous factories producing rayon, jutes and other goods. As a result, about 30 per cent of the working population in the city is employed in the different types of industrial activities.

The old city is divided into three main parts : the main city including Old Kanpur, the Civil I dues and the Cantonment. In comparison to the Civil Lines and the Cantonment which emerged and developed during the British period to serve the needs of the civil servants and the military personnel respectively, the main city grew indigenously over a long period of time. It is overpopulated and heavily congested due to location of the numerous types of trade and commercial enterprise, residential structures and presence of the large number of people trans-acting their social and economic activities. These transactions are both traditional and modern in nature though the former too, like the latter, are reinforced by the market economy of the city. That means, both social structure and various types of relations among the people located in this part of the city are nationally modern and purposive or instrumental. Also, the spatial structure of this part of the city is such as there are narrow lanes, congested and ill-maintained roads, improper drainage and sewerage, and old type of clustered houses which generally give a dirty and unhygienic look. Even the Civil Lines and the Cantonment give tormented look as there are ample unutilized and ill-maintained spaces which present the one time's British taste and discriminate utilization of space. The old type of huge bungalows constructed during the British period are used now as godowns and offices, and a number of parts located in between give the unaesthetic sense.

We have mentioned elsewhere (Ram, 1988b : 28-32) that the city has grown fastly, in the recent years, towards its hinterland (only in the south, east and west sides as the river Ganga flows from west to east in the northern side) where it has expanded upto Kidwai Nagar and Nirala Nagar (at the Kanpur-Hamirpur Road) in the south-east side. In the north-east side it has expanded upto New Harjinder Nagar near the Chakerj Military Aerodrome along the Kanpur-Unnao Road. Similarly, in the north-west side the city has grown more recently upto Kalyanpur railway station near the Indian Institute of Technology along the G.T. Road, Kalyanpur-Bithoor Road and Kanpur-Bithoor Road. The expansion is mostly in the forms of private residential accommodations and the government colonies to house the employees.

There are, however, a large number of localities falling in different parts of the city where old type of residential apartments are erected without proper sanitation, drainage, health and hygienic conditions, etc. That is why, Majumdar (1960) in his survey of Kanpur city covering the period 1954-56 has called it a city of slums. This may be true when we compare the spatial and social structures of Kanpur with other metropolitan cities like Bombay, Delhi, Bangalore, Chandigarh, etc. Also, when we compare the better developed localities (including the more recently developed ones) with the old 'Purvas' (urban villages) and other less developed localities which are certainly more in number in the city, we find Majumdar's observation fully justified.

It may also be kept in mind that the physical appearance of slums in Kanpur is totally different from those in Bombay, Calcutta, Delhi, Madras, etc. Unlike *Jhopad-Pattis* and *Chawls* in Bombay, *Bastis- Cheris* and huts in Madras and *Jhuggi-Jhoparis, Katras,* etc. in Delhi, most of the slums in Kanpur are old fashioned constructions built with bricks and, in many cases, with bricks and cement with minimum civic amenities as stated earlier. The *Jhuggi-Jhoparis* are very recent growth especially since mid-1970's and are mostly located near Kanpur Central railway yards, Rawatpur railway station, Parmat, Barafakhana and in a few other areas. The *Ahatas* (tenements) which can easily by com-pared with the *Katras* of Delhi and Agra and the *Chawls* of Bombay arc also part of the slums in Kanpur. The *Ahatas* are generally multi-storeyed buildings erected either in rows or quadrangles with minimum civic amenities like drinking water, electricity, latrines and bathrooms. The incumbents are mostly the working class people who hire a room on the nominal rent. They usually hail from the owners' geographical and linguistic regions.

From the point of view of culture and social life, the Kanpur slums are also different from those found in the other metropolitan cities. Unlike many slums of the different cities in India, the slums in Kanpur do not necessarily possess a 'culture of poverty' (Lewis 1968:4-21) or a 'slum culture' (Clinard 1966:11-14) as such. Rather, there exists a 'dual-structure' of both the culture of poverty and the middle class culture in which the latter may not be mistaken as a culture of affluence. Similarly, social life and activities of the residents are different from those living in slums in other cities. We shall analyse it below in the case of a particular slum in the city.

Spatio-social composition of Colonelganj

Going by the general understanding of slums of Indian cities Colonelganj, which is an underdeveloped locality in Kanpur city, may not strictly be called a slum though a number of sub-localities or neighbourhoods [such a Colonelganj] proper-Dhani Ram *Ka Ahata,* Chunniganj - Maheshganj (studied in this paper), Lakarmandi, Bajaria, and the locality of Colonelganj Police

Station) within its territorial jurisdiction may coincide with certain physical and socio-cultural aspects of a slum. Since the locality of Colonelgang is relatively an older habitation, less developed and lacks most of the civic amenities, we have accepted it as a slum-like structure. However, before analysing its social structure and culture or value-system it will be proper to have a brief look at the physical location and social composition of this locality in the morphology of Kanpur city. Such a description may help us understand its spatial and social structures in comparison to that existing in other localities in the city. It may also facilitate to record itf similarly or dissimilarity with others and view it as a slum or semi-slum structure at the definitional level.

Colonelganj is located in the old part of the city. It lies at the left side of the extreme western end of the Mahatma Gandhi Road. More precisely, it falls triangularly between the Mahatma Gandhi Road and the Dr. Ambedkar Road behind the B.N.S.D. College and Kanpur Electricity Supply Agency (KESA) station-opposite the Lai Imli Woollen Mills. It also covers a part of Chamanganj, a Muslim dominated locality and Idgah Colony to its west which are bifurcated by the Ambedkar Road at the Bakarmandi *Chauraha* (crossing). Near this are two cremation grounds, one for the Muslims and the other for the Christians, on both sides of the Ambedkar Road. There is a small ill- managed animal hospital also behind the Colonelganj Police Station. In the east of it are located both the Colonelganj (proper) and Chunniganj-Maheshganj along the road connecting Chamanganj to the Bakarmandi *Chauraha.* The basis of its territorial bifurcation is the demarcation made by the Municipal Corporation and the administrative jurisdiction of the Colonelganj Police Station which also covers the McRoberts Ganj towards west and some other nearby localities. In the north-west side, opposite the Colonelganj Police Station, a Roadways Station and the Lai Imli Woollen Mills are situated. Outer part of the locality in the north is covered by a small shopping complex, B.N.S.D. College and the KESA as mentioned above. Nevertheless, its cultural and social relational boundaries extend much beyond its spatial boundary and in many respects these are similar to that found in several other localities situated in different parts of the city.

We have stated earlier that the main or central city is most congested and is supplemented with the ecological hazards. Similarly, there are certain parts in the Civil Lines and the Cantonment which are equally ill-maintained and hazardous. The social structure in these areas is also not well developed as it contains partly traditional and partly urban-industrial elements of social and cultural life (Ram 1986: 221). The Colonelganj consisting of the above mentioned sub-localities and neighbourhoods is not different from that. In fact, this may easily be compared with *semi-urban pockets* "which are based on somewhat lower levels of organizational relationships, and continue to lag behind in diversity and sophistication of roles and functions as performed by the individuals and groups in highly urbanized communities" (Trivedi 1975: 28). Yet, in certain aspects Colonelganj contains a more specific structure which we shall discuss in the following section.

Table 1: Population and sex-ratio in Colonelganj

Year	Population ** (persons)	Sex-ratio ** (Females per 1,000 males)
1961	40,068	795
1971 *	52,617	819
1981 *	67,628	862
Total	1,60,313	826

* Estimates based on average for the city.
** Including sub-localities of Colonelganj proper (Dhani Ram ***Ka hata),*** Chuniganj-Maheshganj, Lakarmandi, Bajaria, and locality of Colonelganj Police Station.
Source: Computed from the Censuses of India (U.P.), 1961-81.

The total population of Colonelganj - Chunniganj-Maheshganj area in the recent years is not authentically known. However, at a rough estimate it may be somewhere around twenty thousand persons. Since the area is less developed as stated earlier, a majority of the residents hail from the lower and the middle level castes like Chamar, Kori, Balmiki, Khatik, Dhobi, Ahir,Rajbhar, Kanhar (watercareers), etc. The residents belonging to the Chamar, Khatik and the middle level (backward) castes have migrated mostly from the eastern U.P. and western Bihar. They are, however, settled exclusively in the different sub-localities or neighbourhoods. For instance, a majority of the Chamars are located in the Chunniganj-Maheshganj and Colonelganj (proper) and the Balmikis behind the Chunniganj at the Ambedkar Road. While the Koris are settled in the Chamanganj Korian, the majority of the residents in Chamanganj are the lower class Muslims (Ram 1986: 223).

With regard to literacy and educational level, the residents of the locality are not well educated though there are few who have achieved education upto graduation and post-graduation levels. The average literacy rate is not very high and is much below (around 40%) to that in the city as a whole (50.8%). One of the important reasons may be that most of the male residents are employed in one or the other type of economic activities. This is evident from the fact that, according to one estimate, around 60 per cent male residents in Maheshganj are employed in various mills and factories obviously located at far-off places. A very small percentage is employed in the next door Lal Imli Woollen Mills and the Victoria Mills. Some are also employed as mechanics and labourers in the KESA.

Table 2: Percentage of literates and workers in Colonelganj

Years	Literates **	Workers **
1961	33.3	28.0
1971 *	36.2	25.4
1981 *	39.2	22.8
Average	36.2	25.4

* Estimates based on average for the city.

** Including sub-localities of Colonelganj proper (Dhani Ram ***Ka hata)***, Chuniganj-Maheshganj, Lakarmandi, Bajaria, and locality of Colonelganj Police Station.

Source: Computed from the Censuses in India (U.P.), 1961-81.

Further, some of the residents are employed as white collar workers in the different central and state government offices. While some of the Balmikis are also employed in the government offices, most persons of the Balmiki caste work as sweeper mainly in the

Municipal Corporation in which their families and even children are engaged. Others work as vendors, hawkers, etc. In the Chamanganj area the majority of the Muslim residents are engaged in the cottage and household industries like looms and related works in which their women folk and children also extend their helping hands. A few manage with small merchandise shops and various types of economically productive household activities within the locality itself. As a whole, the residents in Colonelganj are not well educated and are employed in various types of economic activities without much attractive remunerations.

Social Structure in Colonelganj

Social structure is generally defined on the basis of a number of attributes or elements in vogue in a society. Societies which are achievement-oriented and are relatively open lay greater emphasis on class (socio-economic status) type structure than those which are relatively closed, less achievement-oriented and which adhere to traditional norms and values. But in all such societies certain elements or attributes like institutional functioning, structure of roles and statuses and their grading arrangements, perception and attitudes of people towards such structure are commonly acknowleged though the emphasis on them varies from one society to the other in the different time span. By extension, it can also be argued that a less developed urban locality imbibes in it certain elements of a closed and traditional social structure where social interaction and relations are also 'instrumental' or purposive rather than merely 'expressive'. In other words, these are based on mutually, though the nature of expressiveness and mutuality may not be the same as found in a traditional society or a remote village or a tribal community.

In absence of proper civic amenities and resources a less developed urban locality, like a slum, is often prone to be construed as an over emphasized 'deviant structure' which is considered as an unwanted appendage to the structure of a city. Such structure is generally not liked by a vast majority of the city people including even those who live in the locality, as staged at the outset. The latter consider it as a 'slum of despair' instead of a 'slum of hope' (Clinard 1966: 43-44,Piettie 1969: 19). In the slum of hope the residents especially the late settlers live, in the beginning, with the hope of improving their lot. But after some times they visualise no improvement in their social and economic conditions particularly in event of paucity of resources and amenities available at their disposal. This is also caused by the crystallization of a certain type of perception and attitudes of their own and of others towards them and the locality in which they live. In the long-run this results into a slum of despair where they become totally disillusioned about the idealised urban social reality in general and of the slum in particular. In the net result, they get convinced about no improvement in their life chances. This may be true in some sense but it is also true that in majority of the cases the slum-dwellers do not have any option except to live in slum as they do not have an easy access to the resources and opportunities available in the other parts of urban areas. Besides, in those cases where the slum-dwellers have retained link with their places of origin especially in rural areas and their major interests are located there, they may compromise with the *status-quo* and, while living in a slum, they may not have a perception of slum of hope or despair as such.

With such perspective when we look at Colonelganj, we find that in most of the cases structure of the families of orientation is nuclear though functionally they are related with family of their procreation living either in the same locality or elsewhere in the city or in their places of origin—the villages. In other words, though the formal structure of families in Colonelganj is nuclear it functionally operates as a sub-set of a larger or joint families whose roots lie out of the locality. In some cases even kinsmen live under the same roof. On certain ceremonial occasions, all the members of the joint family and kins living elsewhere in the city come together, sometimes even the neighbourers and friends especially from the same caste/community background and linguistic region are invited. Since in most of the cases the composition of neighbourhoods is a primordial collectivity and is based, to some extent, on economic or at least occupational consideration, the social relation among the neighbours is confined largely to these aspects. But in certain cases it easily cuts across such boundaries. That means, social relations in the neighourhood are not always harmonious, rather these become sometimes tense also depending upon the issues involved there. This is so as "The identity of an Indian urbanite is not only found with the urban space, but his caste-status, kin group, language, neighbourhood, religion and region" (Gandhi 1983: 12) and all these do not function at present in the harmonious manner both in urban and rural areas in the country.

However, social relations in the neighbourhoods in the entire locality are, by and large, superscribed by the institutional functioning. For instance, recitation of *Katha-Kirtan* (mythological stories sung musically) or celebrations of calendrical festivals like *Raksha- Bandhan* (tying thread by sisters on the wrists of their brothers by reminding the latters' obligation to protect their sisters' honour), Id, Dusehara, Independence or Republic Day bring not only the neighboured but also the residents of the locality together. So is the case with celebrations of birth or death anniversaries of some important saints and leaders like Prophet Mohammad, Saint Balmiki and Saint Raidas or Ravidas, Dr. B.R. Ambedkar, etc. The neighbourhood relations are also strengthened by the functioning of some voluntary organizations found in the locality. These organizations are initiated and managed mostly by the youngesters in the locality but these also serve as an instrument; for the older people, to change their values and perception about themselves and others in their neighbourhoods, locality, in the city and elsewhere.

This brings us to look briefly at the structure of roles and statuses of and also at the system of social stratification among the residents in Colonelganj. Besides their employment in various types of economic activities as mentioned above, they also play a variety of other roles relating to their life in family, neighbourhood and locality. Their such roles are largely governed by the overall social norms and values and, to some extent, the in-built expectations prevailing in the neigh-bourhood which we shall discuss in the following section. However, various types of roles which they play in different contexts are to be seen in relation to social status acquired by them in their neighbourhood and even in the locality. The reverse is equally true in which their social status is also determined on the basis of their social, cultural and economic roles which they play in their everyday life.

Social stratification in urban areas is an anomaly of both the primordial structures (caste or religion) and class system (Ram 1984: 373-99). But such anomaly is, to some extent, a departure from the traditionality of the primordial structures and the ideal typical class system. In fact, the social stratification is based on certain elements drawn from both the primordial structures and class system. This is more clearly visible in those parts of the city which are spatially and socially less developed and where both the primordial structures and class system are present in overlapping manner. In Colonelganj, social stratification is definitely based on both types of structures. We have stated earlier that the neighbourhoods are composed of the residents drawn largely from a single caste or religious community. Yet, at the stratification level there is no unanimity in the grading of the different castes and religious communities on a single unified scale. Social gradations among the resident s are, however, easily identifiable in terms of different positions acquired by them on the basis of their variety of social, cultural and economic roles. In other words, there are poor and better-off, illiterates and educated persons, government officials, mill-workers and manual labourers and so on. The better- off and educated government officials, petty-shopkeepers and mill- workers are obviously graded superior to the poor, illiterates and manual labourers irrespective of their caste or religious background. It is also true that the residents of a single caste or religious community in a neighbourhood or locality are graded as superior or inferior along these considerations.

In any case, the residents of Colonelganj share a larger social reality persisting in the city. That means, social stratification found among them is, by and large, identical to that practised in other localities in the city. At the structural level, there appears to the similarly of social structure in Colonelganj with that persisting at least in those areas or localities which are equally less developed. It is also linked, to some extent, with a larger social structure existing in the city through one or the other type of relations of its residents with those living elsewhere in the city. Such relations are operative generally through the institutional channels like employment, extension of their familial and kinship relations, adoption of some social and cultural values and practices and so on.

Value-orientations in Colonelganj

Values are socially sanctioned practices, standardised behaviour patterns, customs and norms, ideal traditions, etc. In other words, there are different types of social and cultural values prevailing in a society. It is generally found that the people living in urban areas have both traditional and modern urban-industrial values though the latter have stronger root in the their daily social life. This is so as the very character of Indian cities including even the metropolitan ones is a combination of both types of values. This also goes along with the fact that a city in India has indigenously grown and the spatial and social structures of its different areas are not equally developed. Finally, such structure is reinforced by the continuous flow of migrants especially from rural areas who carry some traditional values which they retain with them provided they are not totally uprooted from their places of origin.

The value-orientations in terms of value-retention and value-adoption of the urban dwellers including the new urbanites (semi-permanent migrants) are dependent on their social characteristics like family tradition, educational level, occupational and income positions, etc. These are based on their location in various types of spatial and social structures found in the different parts of an urban area. Besides, their value-orientations may also be governed by that of their reference groups or individuals, if they have any, drawn from the same or other neighbourhoods/localities in the same or other cities or even in their places of origin. Not going into the details of this type of relationship between the value-orientation and social structure we are interested here to enquire into a reverse type of relationship between them. In other words, we wish to know how value-orientation of the residents in Colonelganj contributes to change in its social structure. In this regard, it is necessary to mention that the spatial a'nd social structures of a city, or for that matter of a locality, are largely inter-related where change in one type of structure (be it spatial structure) determines the nature and magnitude of change in the other structure (such as social structure). More specifically, change in social structure of an urban locality is based on change in social composition of its population, change in economic and other activities and also in its various social and cultural characteristics including value-orientations besides the change in its spatial structure. This obviously takes place over a span of time.

Colonelganj and its neighbouring localities and sub-localities came into the vicinity of the walled city in the 1950's (Chandra 1977:40). Being one of the oldest areas in the city it was developed in I960'sand 1970's though it is still underdeveloped locality as compared to the neighbouring ones. The locality is inhabited by both the earlier settlers (upto 1950's) and those who migrated, during the I960'sand the 1970's, mostly from the eastern U.P. as stated earlier. Like many cases, a substantial percentage of the migrant residents still retain their links with their places of origin. Thus, such residents and even those amongst earlier settlers who are either illiterate or semi-literate and are employed in various mills and factories and other unorganized sector of employment retain greater amount of traditionally in their culture and behaviour patterns than those who are educated and employed as government officials. In fact, the latter have adopted certain items of urban industrial culture and are socially aware and politically conscious not only about the different problems of their locality but also about its spatial and social deprivations in comparison to other localities in the city, They also influence the attitudes of interaction of 'traditional' people in the locality. Today the situation is different although some people still have a fairly strong attachment to the older order. Such people, popularly referred as *Purana type ke log,* 'old type people', are presumably found in all the groups, and in one or two of the groups they even dominate. Among the Ahirwars (a sub-caste of Koris), however, the more progressive have the upper hand, and this is also the case among the Jatavs, one of the Camar (Chamar) subcaste groups, residing in several of the local *ahatas,* ... as well as elsewhere in the neighbourhood" (Molund 1988: 129-130).

The most commonly practised social and cultural values in Colonelganj as well as in other localities in the city in earlier times have been celebrations of a number of religious and ritual rites and festivals like *Katha-Kirtan,* birth and death ceremonies, offering caste/community feasts; beliefs in religious priests and their performances. Besides, some social and cultural values have also been associated with staying voluntarily in the neighbourhoods/ sub-localities of the same caste or community and obligatory participation in its activities; continuing the caste/community affinity through marital alliance; administering authoritarian relations with youngers in the family; and secluding the women-folk from undertaking public activities. The political attitudes and behaviours of the residents have often been stimulated by their primordial linkages with the polity and a number of extra-political consideration. Of course, some changes have been witnessed in Colonelganj in regard to practising some of these values in the recent years though these have gone along the levels of educational and economic development of the residents and also along their orientations towards modern urban-industrial culture and values. Changes have also been dependent on increase in the levels of their social awareness and consciousness. Now, the residents do perform some religious and ritual rites but not with the same faith and devolution as they used to do in the past. Interestingly, they show more inclination towards celebrating secular festivals and occasions

There is a considerable degree of liberalization in the relationship among the family members. Now, women are not only allowed access to education but also to work outside especially in the primary (public) and tertiary sectors of employment. In the changed circumstances, in Colonelganj and also in the entire city the residents do not live, by choice, in the neighbourhoods of the people drawn from their own castes and communities. Instead, in the given paucity of space and tremendous hike in land price and house rent in the city the residents of Colonelganj stay in the locality though they do not derive the same emotional supports from their

Table 3:Social Structure and Value-orientations in Colonelganj till 1960

Socio-economic status of residents	Types of Social structures in the locality	Value-orientations of the people
Lower	Traditional-allegiance to primordial collectivities of caste and religious community through living in neighbourhoods of such collectivities, social stratification based on caste and community consideration, expressive social relations; links with kinship and joint family.	Retention of traditional values in terms of celebrations of all religious and ritual rites and calendrical festivals; political participation based on primordial linkages.
Medium or Moderate	Transitory-partly primordial collectivities and partly social classes (socio-economic status and social and cultural similarities) type; both expressive and instrumental social relations with relatively greater emphasis on the former; social stratification on both ascriptive and achievement criteria.	Combination of both traditional and modern urban-industrial values; celebrations of both sacred and secular occasions; political values directed to community welfare.
Relatively Higher	More inclination towards social class type; social status based on achievements; instrumental social relations; allegiance to persons of similar achievement level.	Emphasis on modern urban-industrial values; celebrations of secular occasions; efforts for self-development; political participation based on ideology and individual commitment.

caste/community as they used to do in the past. There also exists an increasing tendency among them to extend their relations only with those members of their castes and communities who are of the similar social and economic standing. Their political views are governed by the levels of their mobilization which has shifted greatly, in the recent years, from the primordial collectivity to the 'politics of commitment'. They are not belied by the political parties, working actively in the city, through exploiting their caste and community sentiments though this is not equally true among Muslim residents of the adjoining locality of Chamanganj. On the whole, political values of the residents of Colonelganj are rooted in their concerns for the locality as well as in their self-interests rather than in the welfare of the caste and community people only.

Values and Change in Social Structure

A certain type of change has definitely occurred in the social structure of the locality as there has also been change in value-orientations of the residents since its inception and physical growth. To what extent the change in its social structure has been contributed by value-orientations of the residents as compared to other factors required factorial analysis and other statistical measurements. Since we have not done that exercise for the purpose of present analysis, we can surmise that value-orientations of the residents have contributed much to the change in social structure of the locality. This is evident from the fact that unlike the residents of a typical slum who live with the culture of poverty (Lewis 1968:4-21) as stated earlier, most of the residents in Colonelganj have improved their socio-economic conditions and gone for higher education, bureaucratic jobs, a better style of life, etc. They have also adopted certain amount of urban-industrial culture though in all these they clearly lag behind the residents of more developed localities in the city.

Changes in their religious values have enabled them not only to possess secular outlook but have also brought them closer to live as a 'community' with the obvious material and social variations in the locality. Their community life is regulated by their overall concern for the locality and collective observance of a number of secular festivals and occasions as mentioned above. It, however, does not mean that the allegiance of the residents to their primordial collectivities is completely wiped out. In fact, they are very much conscious of their such collectivities but these are confined mostly to their personal affairs like marital alliance, worshipping the family and caste or community deities, etc. and these do not obsessedly alter the secular and neighbourly relations among them. This is clear from the fact that not even a single incident of caste or communal tension and conflict has occurred in the recent years in colonelganj. Caste and community associations do not exist in the locality. The liberalization in family relations have resulted into more happiness and better social and economic positions of family accruing to the differentials of the urban- industrial types in the neighbourhoods and in the locality.

All these together have contributed to the changes in social structure of Colonelganj. Though it is difficult to trace the exact period since when changes started to occur in the locality, yet it can be said that in the mid-1960's a number of improvement schemes were introduced in the adjoining localities including even some sub-localities of Colonelganj. The city administration enacted several welfare and developmental measures like providing the financial and banking loans to start cottage industries, construct houses, caring for health and sanitation, etc. in the locality. In the process the common infrastructural facilities like a community centre and a *Barat Ghar* (a hall of performing marriage ceremonies) have also been provided in the locality. This has improved not only the spatial and social structures in Colonelganj but has also changed the value-orientations of its residents. A synoptic view of changes both in value-orientations and social structure in Colonelganj can be obtained from Table 4.

Table 4: Value-orientations and changing social structure in Colonelganj since 196C's

Socio-economic status of residents	Shifts in value-orientations of people	Change in social structure in the locality
Lower	Retention of traditional values and adoption of selected urban values; limited liberalization in family relations; political participation based on primordial link-ages and community welfare.	Social stratification consists partly of primordial collectivity and partly socio-economic achievement; both expressive and instrumental social relations; social status based on caste and community considerations and partly on achievement.
Medium or Moderate	Celebrations of selected religious- ritual rites and secular occasions; adoption of relatively more urban values; political values directed to ideology of commitment and community welfare.	Less emphasis on primordial collectivity and more on socio-economic achievement, more emphasis on instrumental social relations, structurally nuclear but functionally joint family.
Relatively Higher	Adoption of modern urban-industrial values; celebrations of secular occasions; emphasis on self-development; political participation based on ideology and individual commitment.	Social status based on achievement; class type social stratification; instrumental social relations; allegiance to persons of similar socio-economic achievement.

Their value-orientation in terms of retention of certain traditional values is also reinforced by their continuing link with their places in origin, as stated earlier. Due to this and also due to their relatively less access to the existing resources and opportunities, they cannot freely go for the adoption of an urban-industrial culture and value- system. As a result, they have partly retained with the traditional values and have partly adopted some urban-industrial values. Both have enabled them to continue their link with their places of origin and their normal residence in the locality of Colonelganj. At the same time the social structure of Colonelganj, though it has undergone considerable change since its inception, has been influenced by value- orientations of the residents to the extent that it is partly traditional and partly modern. The modernity of the social structure is visualised in terms of the resident's practising some aspects of urban-industrial culture persisting in the city with its reflective influence on their social interaction and behaviour patterns. Likewise, traditionality of social structure in Colonelganj is demonstrated through the persistence of primordial collectivities, segregated neighbourhoods, celebrations of certain festivals, rituals and religious rites and so on.

Conclusions

We have mentioned above that Kanpur city, though an industrial metropolis, has failed to evolve an exclusively modern social structure and instill the urban-industrial culture and values among its population. However, such structure does not exist uniformly in all parts of the city. Rather, the localities which are physically more developed accommodate people drawn from the middle and upper-middle classes than those localities like Colonelganj, Chamanganj, etc. which are less developed and are inhabited by people belonging to lower and working classes. In the case of value-orientations also, the former have adopted more urban industrial culture and values than the latter. In both the cases social backgrounds of the residents and the spatio-social structure of the localities have contributed much to the degree and nature of their value- orientations.

The social structure of Colonelganj and value-orientations of its residents are, however, to be seen as largely related to that found in other parts of the city. In other words, Colonelganj is not an isolated structure; it is connected with the surroundings and other localities in the city through the physical interaction and various types of social and economic transactions of its residents. Moreover, the locality is not regarded as a slum by the surrounding neighbourhoods though its residents perceive it as a physically underdveloped area. Thus, neither the 'culture of poverty' nor the 'poverty of culture' (not in the Marxian phrase) is found strictly persisting in Colonelganj though in relative sense both can easily be located there.

REFERENCES

Chandra, Subhash (1977), Social Participation in Urban Neighbourhood, National, Delhi.

Clinard, M.B. (1966), *Slums and Community Development,* The Free Press, New York.

Gandhi, Raj, (1983), "Social Structure of Urban India: continuities and change" in G.R. Gupta (ed.), *Urban India,* Vikas Publishing House, New Delhi.

Lewis, Oscar (1968), *Study of Slum Culture,* Random House, New York. Majumdar, D.N. (1960), *Social Contours of an Industrial City*, Asia Publishing House, Bombay.

Molund, Stefan (1988), *First We Are People—The Koris of Kanpur between Caste and Class,* University of Stockholm, Stockholm.

Pieltr, Lisa R. (1969), "Social Issues in Housing" in B.J. Frieden and W W Nash (eds.), *Shaping an Urban Future,* MIT Press, Cambridge.

Pain, Nandu (1984), "Atrocities and Segregation in an Urban Social Nti ni t urc: Views from the Bottom", *Journal of Social and Economic Studies* 1(4).

Ram, Nandu (1986), "Scheduled Castes: Social Stratification and Sources and Mobility in Urban India" in K.L. Sharma (ed.), *Social Stratification in India,* Manohar, Delhi, pp. 213-239.

Ram, Nandu (1988a), "Housing and the Urban Poor: A Hypothetical Re-finement" in R.C. Sharma (ed.), *South Asian Urban Experience,* Criterion Publications, New Delhi.

Ram, Nandu (1988b), *The Mobile Scheduled Castes: Rise of a New Middle Class,* Hindustan Publishing Corporation, Delhi.

Trivedi, H.R. (1975), *Urbanization and Macrosocial Change,* Chug Publications, Allahabad.

11

Housing and the Urban Poor in India: A Hypothetical Refinement

Through the process of diffusion and growth dynamics, the settlement pattern of population in urban India has witnessed a radical and fundamental change in the recent times. Now, an altogether different pattern of growth of the urban centre has emerged in which there is a shift in the location of power and privileges from the core or main part of a city to the fringe or periphery. In spite of this, main city still serves the major interests of the urban dwellers. It provides them a social and community life, religious and cultural ethos, values and specific ways of life which are, in a way, missing in the most developed fringe area or places located in between the two. Not only that, but a relatively major portion of resources and opportunities, and their management and regulation, are still located in this part of the city.

The housing rather social housing is a rare commodity in cities. The city managers (administrators) try to diffuse the situation by constructing houses out of the public resources and also with the help of the private developers. In many cases, the administration and several agencies provide subsidy loans and land at the cheap rate, and encourage the people to build their own houses obviously in the localities which are late starter in the socio-ecological development. All such endeavours go invariably in favour of a few privileged groups of people who know the art of social manoeuvring and have relatively easy access to the city managers (Bose, 1978). Consequently, due to over-population and socio-ecological congestion lying in the main part of the city, the people of a certain socio-economic background and definite bent of mind have moved out and settled in the fringe area or spaces available in between the fringe and the main part of the city. There, they have constructed houses mostly out of their resources. In other cases, especially in the case of the government employees, they have constructed houses in such localities out of the credit loans obtained on easy terms from the semi-government financial agencies and organizations. The city administration, on its own, has developed the required infrastructural facilities and made available the desired civic amenities there. It has also provided, in many cases, the housing accommodation, exclusively on the rental bases, and has constructed and sold multi-storied houses to the people, including the government employees, who have relatively stable source of income against which the loans are easily available.

However, the people of the lower socio-economic background do not and cannot have easy access to the resources and opportunities located in both the fringe area and the main part of the city. Instead, they have to remain 'satisfied' with their poor socio-economic condition and 'scarcity' of resources and opportunities of which housing is the most crucial one. ". . . . the cause of housing shortage is found not only in the equal distribution of incomes and wealth, but also in legal ignorance. For the great mass of any national population 'law' and custom are hopelessly confused; illiterate people may migrate from ancient village settlements where each individual obtains shelter by well established social usage to modern urban settlements in which custom no longer holds sway and the acquisition of legal forms of tenure are beyond their reach, not only because of poverty but also through illiteracy and general ignorance. The populations of shanty towns and squatters enclaves in developing Third World Countries are examples of the great social problems which arise when property ownership and occupation rights are not available to a large substratum of a society "(Nevitt, 1978, 186-7). Although the legal aspect is important in regard to housing, but we have emphasized here on extra-legal considerations in the case of housing for urban poor in India.

In fact, a large majority of the urban poor are forced to remain as houseless or live in squalor houses. Even the very purpose of developing hinter land or land available in between the main city and the hinterland either by the city administration or the private developers gets self-defeated in the event of rising land prices, cost of construction, and cost and benefits of commuting, especially for the poor. So is the case of the 'social housing also as the potential occupants of this type of houses are to be Government employees or persons with a relatively stable economic position, as mentioned above.

In such situation, the urban poor are doubly-disadvantaged as, within the main city, they are unable to build a house (even a small roof on their heads) due to an already socio-ecological congestion present there and a multiplied hike in land price which is absolutely beyond their reach. Nor can they build house in the fringe area or in localities available in between the fringe and the main part of the city due to the aforesaid reason. Even if they have one which is usually located at the far-off place in the underdeveloped area, the cost (both social and economic) of daily commuting from residence to the place of work is more than the benefits they derive from owning a house in the urban area. The present paper attempts to verify and refine the above-mentioned hypothesis that the urban poor are the most disadvantaged ones, especially in the context of housing.

The Data

The housing rather social housing has remained in its infancy in the sociological inquiry. However, some major areas have been suggested to include in the sociology of housing. These are: "***(a)*** historical and socio-cultural perspectives (relating mainly to the methods of analysis in urban housing); ***(b)*** sociological insights into patterns of current housing); ***(c)***housing and social change; and (***d***) analysis of social processes related to housing policy and administration" (cf D'Souza, 1974, 127-8). The present paper, in a way, covers (b) and ***(d)***areas of sociology of housing. .

The chances of people to have an access to the resources and opportunities including housing, are both spatially and socially constrained in urban areas (Paul, 1975). Such constraints operate more effectively in the case of the urban poor who, with bleak chances in housing, are forced to live in the squalor settlement. That is why, the verification and refinement of the hypothesis has been made with the help of data pertaining to a squalor settlement—Azadpur-Shadi-Nagar—located in Old Delhi. The location of the settlement and socio-economic pursuits of its residents are relevant with regard to verification of the above-mentioned hypothesis.

Azadpur-Shadi Nagar : Its Spatio-Social Structure

The settlement had emerged as a satellite of a cotton textile mill—The Ajudhya Textile Mill—located in the factory area in North Delhi. Initially, Azadpur was a village and still preserves its reminiscences. It is bifurcated now into Azadpur village and Azadpur market—on the left side of the Ring Road (coming from the Inter-State Bus Terminal - ISBT). Shadi Nagar is a squalor settlement behind the Azadpur market and stretches between a broad gauze railway line and the Ajudhya Textile Mill. In the extreme southern end are located the Wazirpur industrial area and Ashok Vihar—a posh colony of the upper-middle class residents. In the west of it are the areas of Sarai Pipal Thala and Shalimar Bagh, and the Rana Pratap Bagh is located in the east. Beyond the railway line, a large number of factories are located which employ thousands of workers, including a few from the Shadi Nagar Squalor settlement. Thus, both the Shadi Nagar and Azadpur village and market constitute one locality known as Azadpur and lie under the Wazirpur Industrial Area.

Side by side a road, which connects the Azadpur market to the railway station across the settlement, there is a nallah of dirty water thrown away from the different factories, including the Ajudhya Textile Mill, which in absence of proper sanitation, spreads bad smell and produces countless mosquitoes and diseases. Consequently, the entire settlement is full of filth and unhygienic atmosphere, and is below the condition of human living. According to the latest Industrial Act, the workers are to be habitated or rehabilitated within a radius of 16 kms., and the their housing responsibility is entirely of the factory management. The basic spirit of the Act about the distance of the residential location of the workers is their health and safety, which the management has to keep in mind while making arrangement of housing for them. But from the production point of view, the nearby residential location of the workers is desirable though their health and hygienic condition are to be given top priority. The location of Azadpur Shadi Nagar squalor settlement, accommodating mostly industrial workers, is a complete violation of the Industrial Act, especially in regard to housing, health and hygiene.

Social Composition

There are about 3000 ***jhuggis***—squalor houses—which have grown like mushrooms without any proper planning of lanes, lights and water facilities. Amidst these***jhuggis,*** there are about 150 one-room apartments constructed, in low lying area, by the Ajudhya Textile Mill to accommodate its workers. In between, there are a handful single and double-storied rooms built of mud and bricks. In any case, the jhuggis accommodate around 8,000 persons—males, females and children migrated from the different States like U.P., Bihar, Haryana, Punjab and Rajasthan. Nearly 50 per cent of the population is drawn from U.P., particularly eastern U.P. and 25 per cent of that are employed in the Ajudhya Textile Mill. The rest are employed in factories located in far and nearby areas. Yet, some are casually engaged in loading and unloading works in the Azadpur Subzi Mandi — Vegetable Complex — biggest in Asia — and in some other works. Interestingly, a very few females do some casual works in the Azadpur market, while majority of the children go to the Municipality school.

A large majority of the residents hail from the lower castes, especially the different Scheduled Castes and a number of backward castes like Yadav, Nonia (Chauhan), Bhar or Rajbhara, etc. There are a few families belonging to the Brahmin, Rajput (Kshatriya) castes. It has also been found that till recently, a sizeable number of the

Scheduled Caste residents had not disclosed their real caste identity perhaps out of fear of getting discriminated against by others in the neighbourhood or locality. A large majority of the residents in the settlement belong to the lower economic background. Since they are employed mostly in the unskilled and semi-skilled works in factories and elsewhere, as mentioned above, their monthly average income is about Rs. 500 out of which a major portion is sent to their villages. This shows, in a way, their uprootedness in urban life.

The residents are divided according to their caste and regional (States) background which are demonstrated from their separate neighbourhoods. Their social interaction and social relations are usually confined to their neighbourers and do not cross both the physical and social boundaries within the locality. However, the neighbourhoods are intact and homogeneous, and transactions of goods and services are hardly made across them.

The Unintended Residential Shift

Since its inception in about 30-35 years ago, the settlement has not been disturbed, except once during the emergency period when there was a move to demolish the huts and clean the locality under the slum clearance campaign, A few hundred families from the locality were offered, as compensation, the alternative accommodations in the Jahangirpuri resettlement colony located at about 20 kms. away from the Azadpur Shadi Nagar settlement but in a relatively low level area. These accommodations were single room apartments, with a small kitchen but no latrine and bath rooms. There were provisions of public latrines and bath rooms. On the whole, they lacked proper amenities like roads, street lights, dispensary, schools, recreation and community centres, etc. Being located in the low level area, the locality was flooded with water during the rainy season. Not only that, but the resettlement colony was lacking a proper civic sense and urban culture with specific urban values and life styles. Thus, the resettlement colony, being located in the then fringe area, drew less or almost no attention of the city administration. And it continues to do so even today, though some more facilities have been made available there in the recent times. The resettlement colony enjoys low social prestige in the hierarchy of different types of moderately developed residential localities, particularly in north Delhi.

Many of those who had gone there either have rented out or sold their apartments and shifted elsewhere, including their earlier locality, due to the fact that the new resettlement colony was located at a relatively far off distance from their work place, it also carried a low social prestige and very little physical facilities and civic amenities, as mentioned above. However, this fact also cannot be denied that these owners fell in the trap of an ongoing phenomenon of disposing of the compensated plots or apartments and putting up another jhuggis elsewhere in the city and consequently claiming for ransom once more. We actually do not have information in this regard rather; we are of the view that the urban poor are brought out of one sub-standard housing situation and placed in the other one, which may be a little better but with less physical facilities and civic amenities in comparison to many other housing localities found in the neighbouring areas, as is clear from the situations present in both the Azadpur-Shadi Nagar squalor settlement and Jahangirpuri resettlement colony.

Those left behind, in the Azadpur-Shadi Nagar squalor settlement, are persistently disadvantaged in regard to the prestige and privileges underlying there, though they do not pay the cost of commuting a long distance between their 'home' and the place of work. In other words, since long there has not been any increase in the physical and social amenities *vis- a-vis* prestige present in the settlement and, contrary to that, there is always a danger from the Municipal Corporation to demolish these jhuggis and cleanse the entire area. It is an altogether different matter that, amidst a mushroom growth of squalor settlements in the city, Azadpur-Shadi Nagar may live a long life.

The Cost and Benefit Analysis

When we make a cost-benefit analysis of an untended shift of population from one area or locality to the other in the city or from one city to another, we find the imbalanced situation as is clear from the facts about ***the*** two settlements under reference here. At the face of it, the benefits should be more in the case of such shift because the new resettlement colony has certainly been better equipped with both the social and physical amenities than the earlier one. Similarly, there is a little enhancement in the social prestige of the resettlement colony simply because of its authorized status, whereas the Azadpur-Shadi Nager settlement stands as an unauthorized encroachment on the Corporation land. Hence, low social prestige for both the residents of the settlement and the corporation-administration. Then, the costs (in both the material and non-material senses), including the cost of daily commuting from home to work place, paid by the owners of apartments in the new resettlement colony are certainly less than the benefits they derive from having a house—a shelter or an asset in the city. But as in comparison to civic amenities and social prestige available in other localities, the resettlement colony is much more backward, the residents have to pay, and in fact they pay, more cost in terms of enjoying low prestige of the colony and spending more on commuting than the benefits they derive from having a house in Delhi.

In the same fashion, the residents of the Azadpur-Shadi Nagar squalor settlement, due to its further low or lowest social prestige, pay more cost than the benefits they derive from owning a shelter —a hut. This may also be seen in the context that the settlement is actually a slum where the jhugis are completely unauthorized with no proper lanes, sanitation, drinking water facilities, etc., as mentioned above. There is always a naked sword of Corporation hanging on the heads of the residents regarding demolition of their huts and being thrown away. Yet, they are a little fortunate in having at least a shelter, though a temporary one, unlike thousands in Delhi or millions in several cities in India. Then, the benefits they derive may be accepted as more than the cost they pay for such a shelter. The benefits are also more as they do not have to pay house rent or meet the cost of commuting from residence to the work place.

However, the state of affairs in the cases of both the settlements are not very simple but complex one, and cannot be explained in proper fashion simply through cost and benefit analysis. Instead, these are to be seen in totality wherein the uprootedness of the residents from the place of their origin, their different linkages in the city, the residential status and type of accommodation, etc., influence greatly their life in the city. Not only that, but this is also to be understood in the sense where in urban areas "Housing, over and above its general scarcity, is a differentiated commodity, presenting a whole gamut of characteristics, in terms of its quality (amenities, comfort, type of construction, life-span, etc.), its form (individual, collective, as architectural object, integration in the housing context as a whole and in the region) and its ***institutional status*** (without title-deeds, rented, owned, owned in common, etc.), which determine the ***roles the levels*** and the ***symbolic loyalties*** of its occupants" (Castells, 1979: 146-48). Thus, the hypothesis - that the urban poor are doubly- disadvantaged is to be verified in the totality of the housing and the related contexts in urban areas, and not in the isolated sectoral contexts of either housing or the employment and income position of the urban dwellers.

In sum, the urban poor with their bare subsistence wage or earning cannot afford to have a house in the main part of the city. Also, in localities where land is developed and plots are available for constructing houses, they do not have access due to high land price and cost of construction. Even if they get an accommodation in the rehabilitation colonies which are invariably located in areas far from their work place, they pay more cost in terms of low prestige and less privileges underlying in these localities. They also pay more cost in terms of time and money spent in daily commuting than the benefits they derive from having a house in the city. Those who live in squalor settlement are doubly-disadvantaged in terms of housing and poor employment, and in economic position.

REFERENCES

Bose, Ashish, 1978, India's Urbanization (1901-2001), New Delhi.

Castells, Manuel, 1979, The Urban Question : A Marxist Approach, London.

D'Souza, V.S., 1974, "Urban Studies" in A Survey of Research in Sociology and Social Anthropology, Vol. I, ICSSR, New Delhi.

Nevitt, A.A., 1978, "Issues in Housing" in Issues in Urban Society— Rose Devies and Peter Hall (eds.), Penguin Books.

Pahl, R.E., 1975, Whose City?, Penguin Books.

12

The Growth of National Capital Region (Delhi): Some Critical Issues

The metropolitan cities in the Third World Countries have been attracting a large number of migrants not only from the country-side but also from small and medium size towns. This is also visible in the case of urban development in India where metropolitan cities like Bombay, Calcutta, Delhi, Madras, etc. have grown larger in the recent years with million plus population. Such pattern of growth of these cities has resulted into multiple problems of congestion of population concentration, social adjustment, equitable distribution of available resources including employment opportunities, social justice to be accorded to all the segments of population especially the urban poor, stagnation of spatial growth of the city, etc.These cities have also been charged with exploiting the fringe villages, small and medium size towns located in their region.

Certain alternative strategies have been adopted to overcome some of the problems experienced by the larger cities in India. But the growth and development of a twin or satellite city has not very successfully serve the purpose of easing dependency on the metropolitan cities. More recently, the Government of India has adopted a very novel strategy of growing and developing a National

Capital Region (NCR) around Delhi to overcome, more effectively, the urban problems found not only in the capital city, but also in the neighbouring small and medium towns located in the region.

More precisely, the NCR consists of the entire Delhi Union Territory, part of the western Uttar Pradesh, and parts of Haryana and Rajasthan. With the view to make proper use of land, manpower and other infrastructural facilities, and develop the small and medium size towns located in the region. These, in turn, would ease the problem of excess in migration to Delhi metropolis and get the migrants confined to other towns and cities in the region so that cost of their migration to the place of destination could be minimized and the necessary linkages between the places of their origin and destiny be retained. It also envisages that the growth and development of the NCR Would facilitate to overcome the problems of unemployment, housing, etc. faced within the Delhi Metropolis. Distantly, the NCR is expected to help develop rural areas lying both within and outside the region. It would also facilitate the equitable distribution of resources and provide greater justice to the people living in Delhi, in the NCR and beyond that.

The present chapter attempts to examine the feasibility of the growth and development of the NCR and its viability in restraining the in-migration to the Delhi metropolis. It also intends to enquire into the expected: growth and development of the entire region in the connected ones, the emergence of new social and cultural ethos, and the social adjustment of the population living in it.

The N.C.R.: its objectives and administration

The very idea of having the NCR was conceived in 1961 with an objective of developing the rural and urban areas by using property land, manpower and other infra-structural resources available in the region, as mentioned above. The idea was based on a true assumption that the region has an unlimited physical and human potential for its dynamic growth. Through a long deliberation for about two decades idea of the N.C.R. has almost reached to acquire a concrete shape, though there still exist one or the other reservations on the part of the concerned states. Some of the reservations are about the administrative jurisdiction of the NCR, proportion of its benefits to be shared, and the consent and nature of use of the agricultural land, especially the land which lies in the green belt and the extensive farming. There are several major differences in regard to in-migration, unemployment, housing, sanitation, etc. among the Delhi Metropolis and other medium and small size towns in the region.

Yet, the NCR "is regarded as a fairly homogeneous and contiguous region having common problems of flood and drainage, water supply, power and transportation" and several others. Hence, the idea of growth and development of the NRC is being pursued to fulfill the following objectives:

(a) To acquire a rational and orderly growth of Delhi as the beautiful National Capital, symbolising the life and aspirations of the Nation.

(b) To organise and develop fully the urban places in the National Capital Region in a physically efficient pattern and socially desirable environment, with effective participation of the local would units that would sustain dynamic growth in accordance with National goals;

(c) to achieve an "Integrated and coordinated development of the transport system, drainage and power supply of the region, within a broad regional framework";

(d) to have a "Healthy rural-urban relationship and protection of the freshness of air and water In the region";

(e) and, Finally, to evolve a "sustainable development planning of the region and effective implementation of Plan in close integration with economic development of the country with a suitable organisational machinery." In other Words, ".... This scheme, details of which are under review, is expected

> to develop growth centers well away from Delhi so that they act as a barrier to the influx of population in to Delhi and encourage migration away from Delhi to these centers."

With such objectives of growth and development of both the rural and urban areas in the NCR, a comprehensive regional plan has been formulated (though modified recently with regard to the resource allocation) and the collaboration of the concerned state governments is sought for its effective implementation. The Draft Regional plan for the NCR "envisages rational development of Delhi and balance development of the region. For this purpose, it proposes dispersal of economic activities on self-contained regional towns, restructuring of the regional transport network and integrated development of land and infrastructure." Initially, the plan proposed a sum of Rs.20 crores as 'Seed Capital' to begin with and, at present, it proposes for a sum of Rs.400 crores or more to concentrate on development of the priority towns in the First instance. In the subsequent years, the resources are to be allocated and specific policies within the frame of already stipulated major policy are to be evolved to develop the rest of the towns in the region. However, all this has to depend on continuous and sustained co-operation of the concerned state governments and the people in the region.

Spatio-social structure

Between 1959 and 1974, Delhi has witnessed a continuous physical expansion and an intense population growth. Over all these years, the city of Delhi had acquired about 70,000 acres of agricultural land for its planned physical growth and it may acquire another 70, 000 or more acres of land by the year 2001 A.D. (Rabeiro 1485:46). However, this may not solve the city's multiple problems of population growth including population of migrants), housing, water, sanitation, electricity, etc. "By far the most important issues for immediate attention pertains to employment policies that call for a drastic reduction in the rate of growth in the Delhi Metropolitan area which is just emerging a frightening and contiguous megalopolis of nearly 20million in habitants by the year 2001. There is no known institutional capability to provide urban services for a population of this size... It is imperative therefore that policies towards induced growth be kept away from the Delhi Metropolitan Area and transferred instead to other levels of towns within the NCR and to counter-magnate outside the NCR" (ibid:49).

The Delhi Metropolitan Region (and the NCR is obviously extended beyond that) constitutes tentatively an area within a radius of 25 miles around main city of Delhi out of 1290 settlements in the region,12 are towns like Shahdara, Narela, Dwarka Najafgarh and Mehrauli (Delhi Union Territory); Faridabad, Gurgaon, Ballabgarh, Sonipat (Haryana state); and Ghaziabad, Baghpat and Dadri (Uttar Pradesh). More than hundred (111) villages in the region fall within the urbanizable limit, according to 1981 census, and may be called as urban villages, besides 25 villages having more than 5000 population each (Nangia 1971) Further, "...towns within a radius of 25 miles around Delhi are under a strong and intense influence of the metropolis in terms of their population growth, population structure, retail and wholesale trade and also in terms of their daily interaction (transactions of goods and services) with the city" (idbi.3). However, the Metropolitan area has not significantly contributed to ease many problems, which the city of Delhi faces at present.

Besides, the NCR consists of the Union Territory of Delhi, part of western Uttar Pradesh, and some partitions of Haryana and Rajasthan, as mentioned above. More precisely, It includes Delhi-New Delhi urban areas (440 sq. kms.), rural areas inUnion of Territory Delhi (1036 sq. kms.); both rural urban areas of Rohtak, Sonipat and Gurgaon, Rewari, Jhajjar, Ballabhgarh of Rohtak district, Mahendragarh tehsil of Mahendragarh district, as well as Panipat tehsil of Karnal District in Haryana; the entire districts of Meerut and Gaziabad, Bulandshahr, Khurja and Hapur of Bulandshahr in Uttar Pradesh; and five tehsils of Behror, Mandwar,

Kishanganj, Tijara and alvar of Alwar district in Rajasthan. Thus, the NCR covers more than 30,000 sq. kms. and extends beyond the Delhi Metropolitan Region (see Map).

Most of the areas in the region are rural and, with the alluvial type of soil, fall under the intensive cultivation. With a moderate rainfall (60-100 cms.), the entire area is irrigation through canals, wells and tubewells. The food crops are wheat, paddy, cereals, barley, maize, etc. supplemented by cash crops like sugar and cotton. Beside the agro-based industries like sugar, vegetable oils, etc., there are other types of Industries such as chemicals and automobiles, cotton textiles and synthetics. In any case, the entire area in the region is agriculturally productive and has tremendous potentials for development of small and medium size Industries also with the easily available manpower. Besides, the area has a better transport system and different towns in the region are easily connected with either through railways or roads. Yet, looking at the traffic load both in the rural areas and in the township in the region, the NCR requires a much better system of transport and communication. This is also necessary for making the maximum use of potentials lying in the region.

Table Migration to Delhi it up to 1961

S.No.	State*	From rural areas	From urban areas	Total	Percentage
1	Uttar Pradesh	30,994	390,226	421,220	44.65
2	Punjab	40,757	299,847	340,604	36.10
3	Rajasthan	7,195	84,437	91,632	9.72
4	Tamil Nadu	41	19,094	91,135	2.02
5	West Bengal	69	15,462	15,351	1.65
6	Madhya Pradesh	97	11,556	11,653	1.23
7	Jammu and Kashmir	166	10,900	11,066	1.17
8	Kerala	26	10,207	10,233	1.08
9	Maharashtra	46	12,568	12,614	1.34
10	Bihar	133	9,590	9,723	1.03
Total		79,427 (8.43)	863,887 (91.57)	943,411	100.00

*Only those states are included from where roughly 10,000 or more people had migrated to Delhi city.

Source: Census of India, 1961.

Total population of the NCR (both in rural and urban areas) had been projected to be more than 30 million (322 lakhs) by the year 2001 A.D., against that of 13 million according to 1981 census. If this turns out to be true, then it may be so due to "...over-enthusiastic employment generating locations within the NCR and to cater to limited objectives that would create a 'bulge' for subsequent corrective servicing. The distribution of 322 lakhs population within the NCR by the year 2001 A.D. is envisaged in a 2 tier hierarchy, (1) an employment disincentive policy for the Delhi Metropolitan

Area comprising of Delhi-urban and Rural and the Ring Towns and intervening areas, and (11) an employment incentive policy for the rest of the NCR where nearly 85 other urban settlements are ripe for induced growth in varying degrees". (Rebiro 1985). But this is to be coupled with a well-planned migration policy, which may discourage in-migration to Delhi or Delhi Metropolitan Region and facilitate the migrants to concentrate on the other towns in the NCR. For migration to the main city of Delhi, see the Following table.

It is evident from the table that Uttar Pradesh, Punjab (combined with Haryana) and Rajasthan have sent major bulk of migrants to Delhi city. During the last two decades, there has been rapid increase in the number of migrants from different states to Delhi city, but this has not disturbed substantially the State-wise pattern of migration to the city. Hence, the NCR, with its present composition, policies and strategies of its development has the consideration of over-population in Delhi city and Delhi Metropolitan Area and, to put a curb on inmigration through the development of the Capital Region. Besides, the policy also envisages the growth and development of the areas within the NCR, as stated above. Yet, the proposed growth and development of the region depends on the balanced focus of the policy rather than its tilt either to the intentional check of migration to Delhi or the growth of the NCR. Such balanced focus would also determine the extent of support of the concerned states, local administrations, private entrepreneurs and the people inhibiting both in and outside the region.

Sociology of the NCR

When we look at the density of population in Delhi city, Delhi Metropolitan Region and beyond, we find that the mean density of population is over 2050 persons per square mile within a radius of 1-2 miles (in Delhi city) and around 700 persons per sq. mile within a radius of 15 miles, and even less in a radius beyond that. Than Likewise, there are more than 1300 males per thousand females within a radius of 2-3 miles and about 1100 miles per thousand females within a radius of 15-16 miles, and even less when we go beyond that (Nangia 1976:51). With the growth of the NCR, a relatively even distribution of population and a balanced sex ratio would perhaps be achieved which, in turn, would provide a congenial social and familial environment in the region.

We have already mentioned that the area falling within the NCR has a lot potentials for economic and industrial growth and social development. It has also capability of generating employment opportunities to meet job-requirements of the local people. Once such potentials are geared and utilized in the desired manner, the employment level and literacy rate will increase not only in urban but also in rural areas. This will also facilitate the people of the weaker sections, including women, to participate, in greater proportion, in the social and economic activities in the region. This will accelerate better interaction not only among them, but with others and ensure their overall social and economic progress.

Urbanization in the sense of increase in population is, at present, more in the metropolitan cities than in small and medium size towns. This is true in the case of Delhi metropolis also since it pulls more migrants from outside than other urban centers in the region, as stated earlier. But the same is true in the case of sociological meaning of urbanization where people living in the metropolitan cities have conformed more to modernity, egalitarianism, secularism, scientific world-view, etc. They have also adopted more urban values, culture, style of life, behaviour pattern and so on in comparison to those people living in small and medium size towns or in urban villages. In the larger cities, various institutions like educational, economic, political, religious, etc. have modified their functions to cater to the urban needs of the people, whereas the same in small and medium size towns and urban villages have not witnessed the substantial change.

The growth of the NCR would, therefore, not only balance urbanization in demographic sense, but it would also encourage and facilitate people to inculcate the urban values within the region and not to look towards the metropolitan centre like Delhi for the purpose. In other words, a proper growth of the NCR would take care of both the economic and social and cultural needs of the people living within and outside the region where in the case of the latter the urban influence would extend further towards the periphery of the NCR.

Conclusion

The strategy of the NCR envisages an integrated and coordinated growth and development of both the rural and urban areas within the region through the maximum utilization of the infra-structural facilities available locally, and investment and application of innovation and technical know how's drawn, if necessary, from outside the region. It also visualises an extended outflow of the NCR to the growth and development in other parts of the country. The purpose goals of the NCR are expected to be achieved through a proper co-operation and co- ordination of the Delhi administration, the concerned state governments, local self-governments, and the industrial entrepreneurs from both within and outside the region, as mentioned above. More specifically, the NCR plans an even distribution of population, especially the migrant population, and insurance it to contribute in meaningful manner to the spatial growth and socioeconomic development in the region.

However, in the light of the feasibility and viability of the NCR, a number of issues are raised which are to be sorted out for extracting proper and more useful gains of the envisaged growth and development in the region. The issues are as follows: one, which development strategy - either decentralisation or centralisation - would be appropriate for the NCR? It appears that the aim of the NCR is to develop the national capital within a manageable limit of its spatial and demographic growth. In other words, the national capital is the focus of growth and development rather than the region as a whole, and in this the decentralisation strategy may not be of much help. Secondly, what would be the cost and benefit analysis of the NCR, whether the NCR would flourish on the cost of the resources located outside the region? If yes, then what benefits rest of the country would derive from it? Or, if it is to depend on the local resources, then whether the proportionate benefit would go to the local people? If so, what proportion would the NCR contribute to the national development? Thirdly, what kind of spatial organisation is contemplated for the NCR? Whether it would converge on or diverge from Delhi? What effect would it have on the agricultural land and economy of the region? And, finally, whether the NCR would provide better opportunities and thereby distributive justice to the people of the weaker sections in general in the county those in the regional in patients.

These and many other related important issues may be kept in mind while making any modifications, in future, in the policy and proposals of the NCR. With these, an effective implementation mechanism is to be evolved to develop the region and to provide better ease to Delhi city, Delhi Metropolitan Area, the NCR and the country as a whole, though the benefits of growth and development of the NCR may not uniformly be apportioned.

REFERENCES

1. Ribeiro, E.F.N., "Urban Land Policy - The Delhi Experience and possible corrective Thereof" in Urban Development Planning Strategies and Techniques - N.S. Sain and Mahabir (eds.), New Delhi: School of Planning and Architecture, 1985, p.46.
2. Nangia, Sudesh, Delhi Metropolitan Region, New Delhi: K.B. Publications, 1976, p.1.
3. Ribeiro, E.F.N. "The National Capital Region: The Framework for Co-ordinated Growth" - paper presented to the Seminar on Delhi Master Plan in the Context of the National Capital Region, held at Jawaharlal Nehru University, New Delhi, Sept. 20-21, 1985.
4. Krishan, Gopal "Some Question Marks on the National Capital Region"- paper presented to the Seminar on Delhi Master Plan in the Context of the National Capital Region, held at Jawaharlal Nehru University, New Delhi, Sept. 20-21- 1985.